6 Mar

1602

WITCH HUNTER ANGELA

1602
WITCH HUNTER ANGELA

Marguerite Bennett
Writer

Stephanie Hans
Artist

With Further Entertainments by...

Kieron Gillen & Marguerite Bennett
Writers

Marguerite Sauvage (#1), Irene Koh & Jordie Bellaire (#2), Frazer Irving (#3) and Kody Chamberlain & Lee Loughridge (#4)
Artists

VC's Clayton Cowles
Letterer

Stephanie Hans
Cover Artist

Jon Moisan
Assistant Editor

Wil Moss
Editor

Tom Brevoort
Executive Editor

ANGELA CO-CREATED BY TODD MCFARLANE & NEIL GAIMAN

COLLECTION EDITOR: **JENNIFER GRÜNWALD**
ASSISTANT EDITOR: **SARAH BRUNSTAD**
ASSOCIATE MANAGING EDITOR: **ALEX STARBUCK**
EDITOR, SPECIAL PROJECTS: **MARK D. BEAZLEY**
SENIOR EDITOR, SPECIAL PROJECTS: **JEFF YOUNGQUIST**
SVP PRINT, SALES & MARKETING: **DAVID GABRIEL**
BOOK DESIGNER: **JAY BOWEN**
EDITOR IN CHIEF: **AXEL ALONSO**
CHIEF CREATIVE OFFICER: **JOE QUESADA**
PUBLISHER: **DAN BUCKLEY**
EXECUTIVE PRODUCER: **ALAN FINE**

1602 WITCH HUNTER ANGELA. Contains material originally published in magazine form as 1602 WITCH HUNTER ANGELA #1-4 and MARVEL 1602 #1. First printing 2016. ISBN# 978-0-7851-9860-4. Published by MARVEL WORLDWIDE, INC., a subsidiary of MARVEL ENTERTAINMENT, LLC. OFFICE OF PUBLICATION: 135 West 50th Street, New York, NY 10020.

ALAN FINE, President, Marvel Entertainment; DAN BUCKLEY, President, TV, Publishing and Brand Management; JOE QUESADA, Chief Creative Officer; TOM BREVOORT, SVP of Publishing; DAVID BOGART, SVP of Operations & Procurement, Publishing; C.B. CEBULSKI, VP of International Development & Brand Management; DAVID GABRIEL, SVP Print, Sales & Marketing; JIM O'KEEFE, VP of Operations & Logistics; DAN CARR, Executive Director of Publishing Technology; SUSAN CRESPI, Editorial Operations Manager; ALEX MORALES, Publishing Operations Manager; STAN LEE, Chairman Emeritus. For information regarding advertising in Marvel Comics or on Marvel.com, please contact Jonathan Rheingold, VP of Custom Solutions & Ad Sales, at jrheingold@marvel.com. For Marvel subscription inquiries, please call 800-217-9158. **Manufactured between 12/18/2015 and 1/25/2016 by SOLISCO PRINTERS, SCOTT, QC, CANADA.**

10 9 8 7 6 5 4 3 2 1

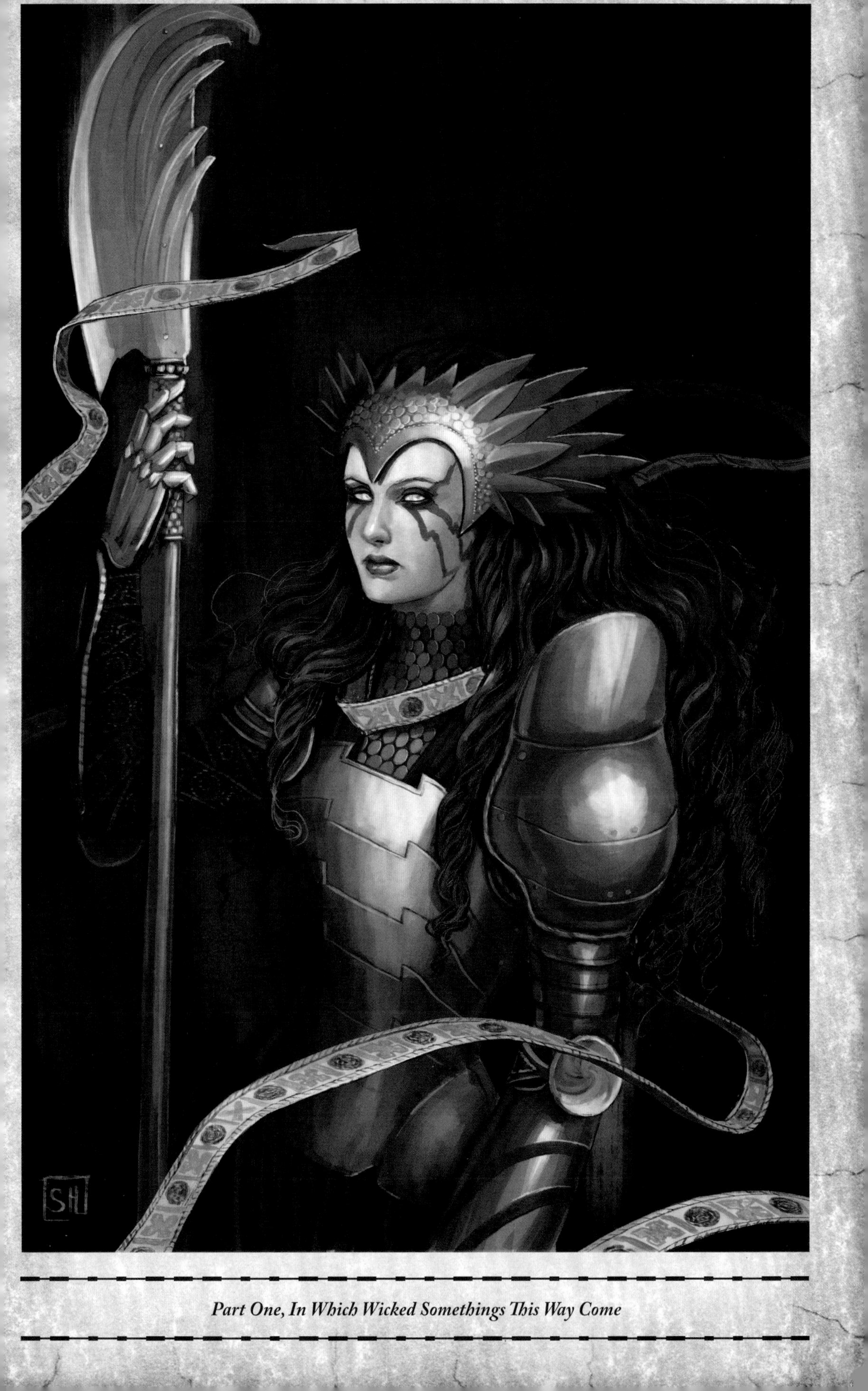
SH

Part One, In Which Wicked Somethings This Way Come

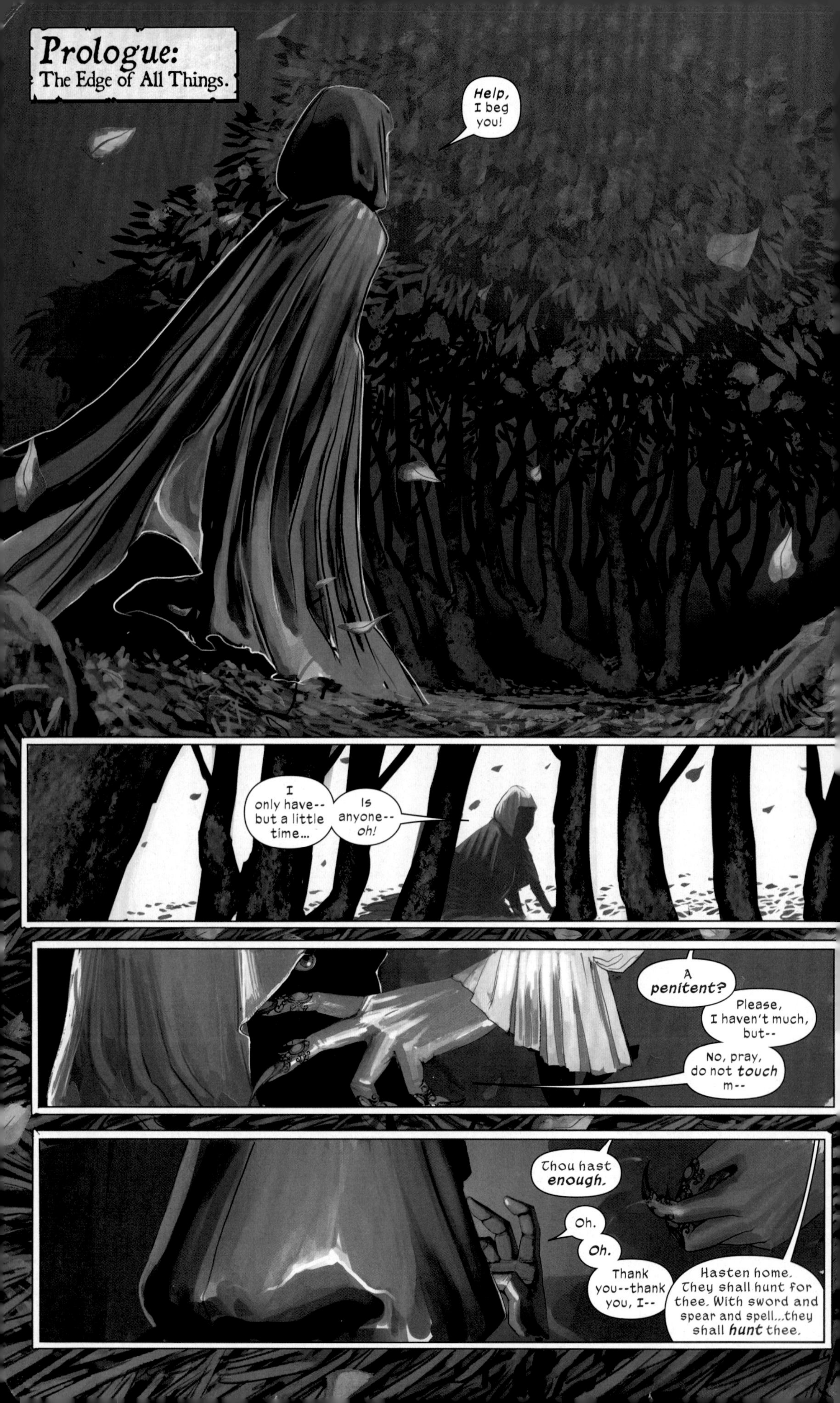
Prologue:
The Edge of All Things.
Help, I beg you!
I only have-- but a little time...
Is anyone-- oh!
A penitent?
Please, I haven't much, but--
No, pray, do not touch m--
Thou hast enough.
Oh.
Oh.
Thank you--thank you, I--
Hasten home. They shall hunt for thee. With sword and spear and spell...they shall hunt thee.

Secret Wars

-------- • --------

The Multiverse was undone!

•

The heroes of Earth-616 and Earth-1610 'twere powerless to save it!

•

Now, all that remains is...Battleworld:

A massive, patchwork planet compos'd of the fragments of the worlds that have left this mortal plane, maintain'd by the iron will of its god and master, Victor Von Doom!

•

Each climature is a domain unto itself!

-------- • --------

1602

WITCH HUNTER ANGELA

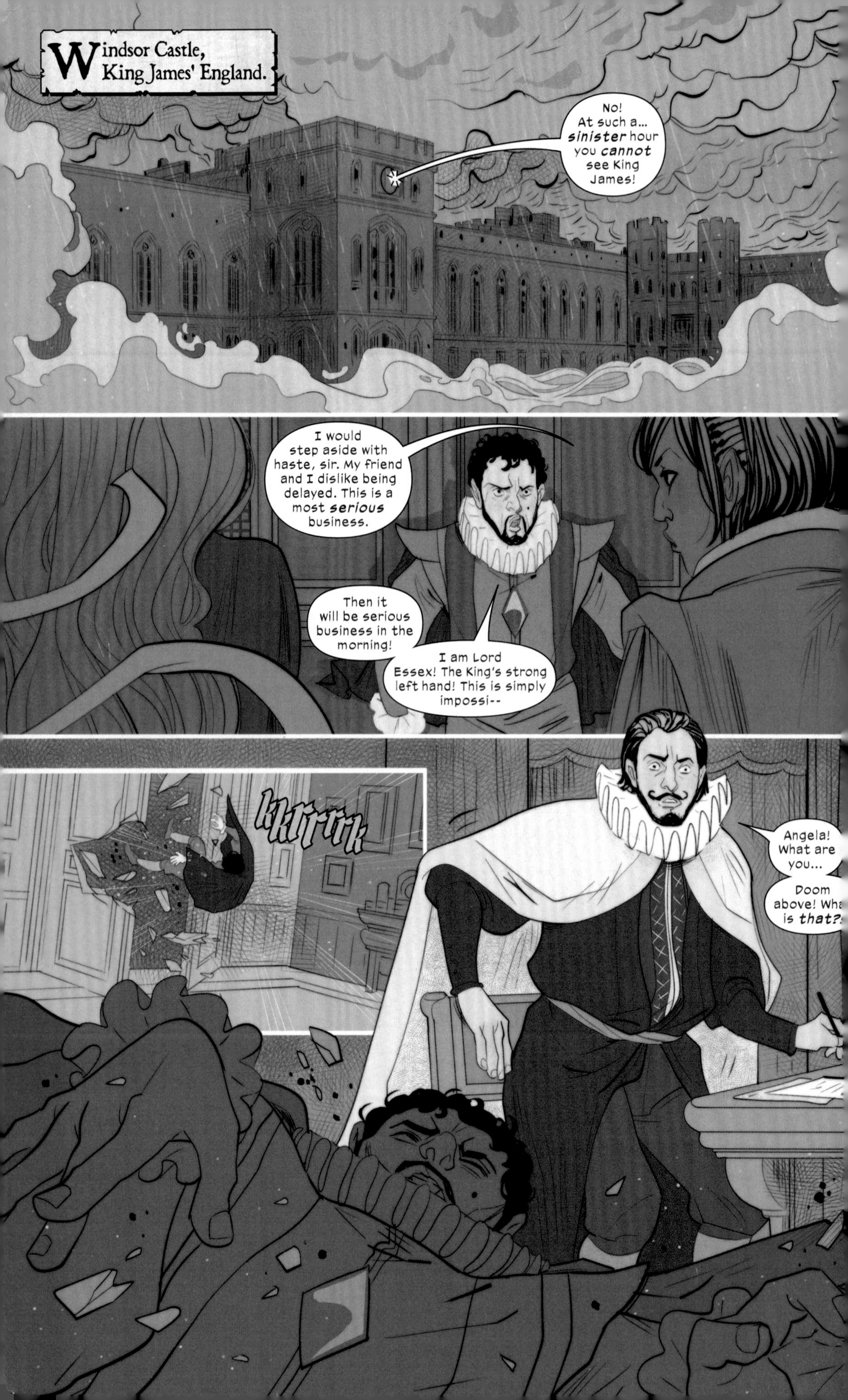
Windsor Castle, King James' England.
No! At such a... *sinister* hour you *cannot* see King James!
I would step aside with haste, sir. My friend and I dislike being delayed. This is a most *serious* business.
Then it will be serious business in the morning!
I am Lord Essex! The King's strong left hand! This is simply impossi--
kkrrrrk
Angela! What are you...
Doom above! Wha is *that?*

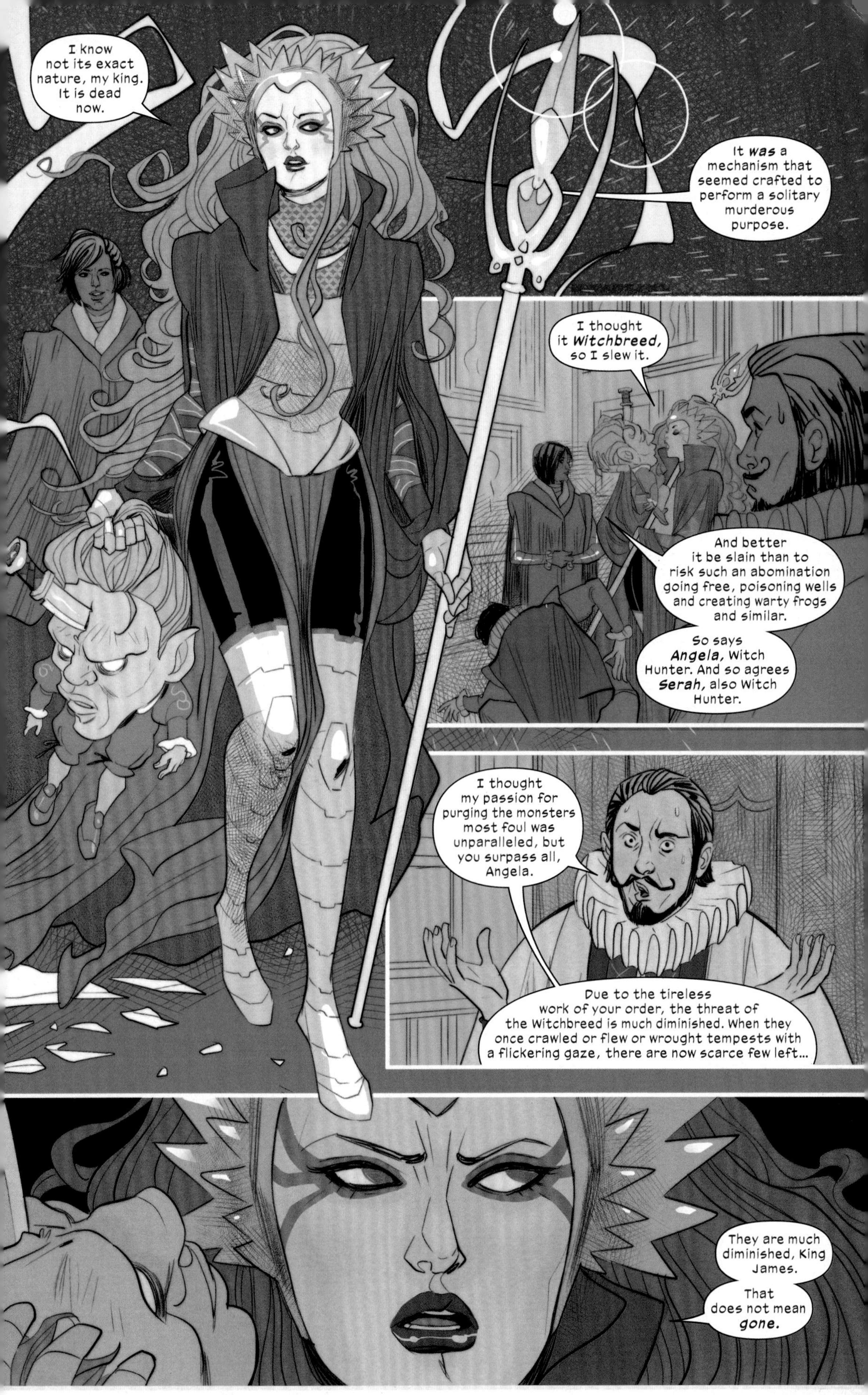

I know not its exact nature, my king. It is dead now.
It *was* a mechanism that seemed crafted to perform a solitary murderous purpose.
I thought it *Witchbreed,* so I slew it.
And better it be slain than to risk such an abomination going free, poisoning wells and creating warty frogs and similar.
So says *Angela,* Witch Hunter. And so agrees *Serah,* also Witch Hunter.
I thought my passion for purging the monsters most foul was unparalleled, but you surpass all, Angela.
Due to the tireless work of your order, the threat of the Witchbreed is much diminished. When they once crawled or flew or wrought tempests with a flickering gaze, there are now scarce few left...
They are much diminished, King James.
That does not mean *gone.*

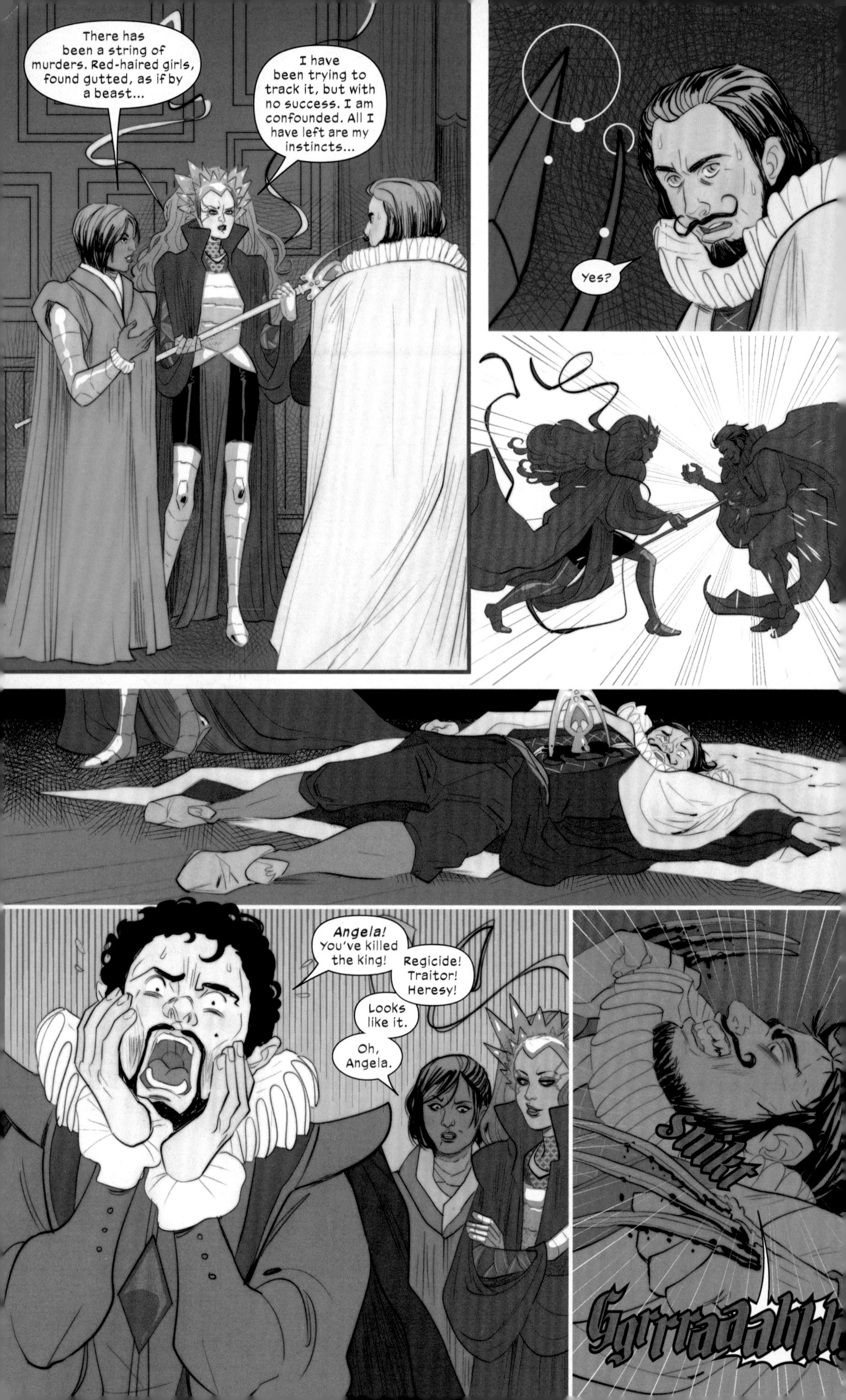
There has been a string of murders. Red-haired girls, found gutted, as if by a beast...
I have been trying to track it, but with no success. I am confounded. All I have left are my instincts...
Yes?
Angela! You've killed the king!
Regicide! Traitor! Heresy!
Looks like it.
Oh, Angela.
Gyrraaahhh

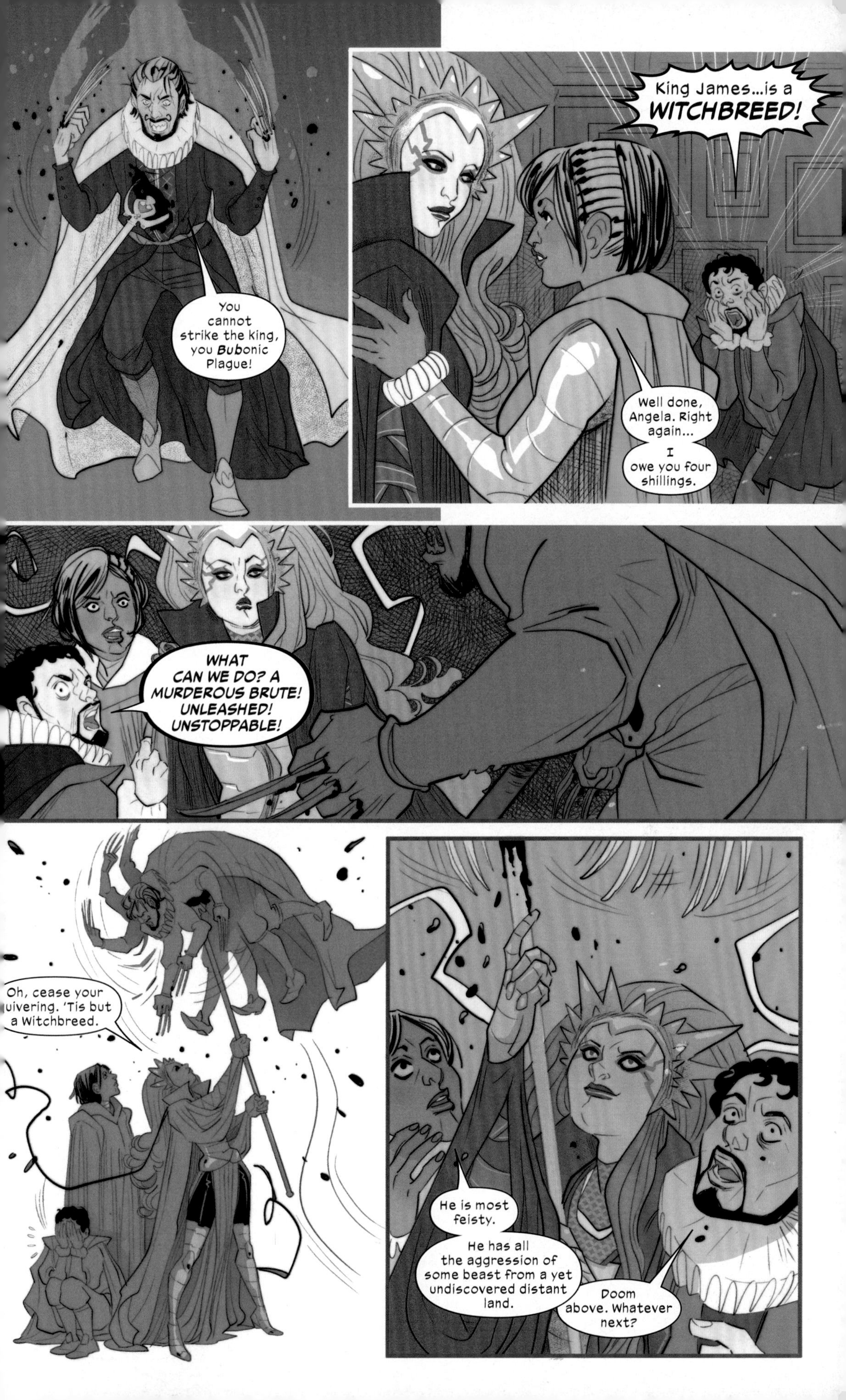
You cannot strike the king, you Bubonic Plague!
King James...is a WITCHBREED!
Well done, Angela. Right again...
I owe you four shillings.
WHAT CAN WE DO? A MURDEROUS BRUTE! UNLEASHED! UNSTOPPABLE!
Oh, cease your uivering. 'Tis but a Witchbreed.
He is most feisty.
He has all the aggression of some beast from a yet undiscovered distant land.
Doom above. Whatever next?

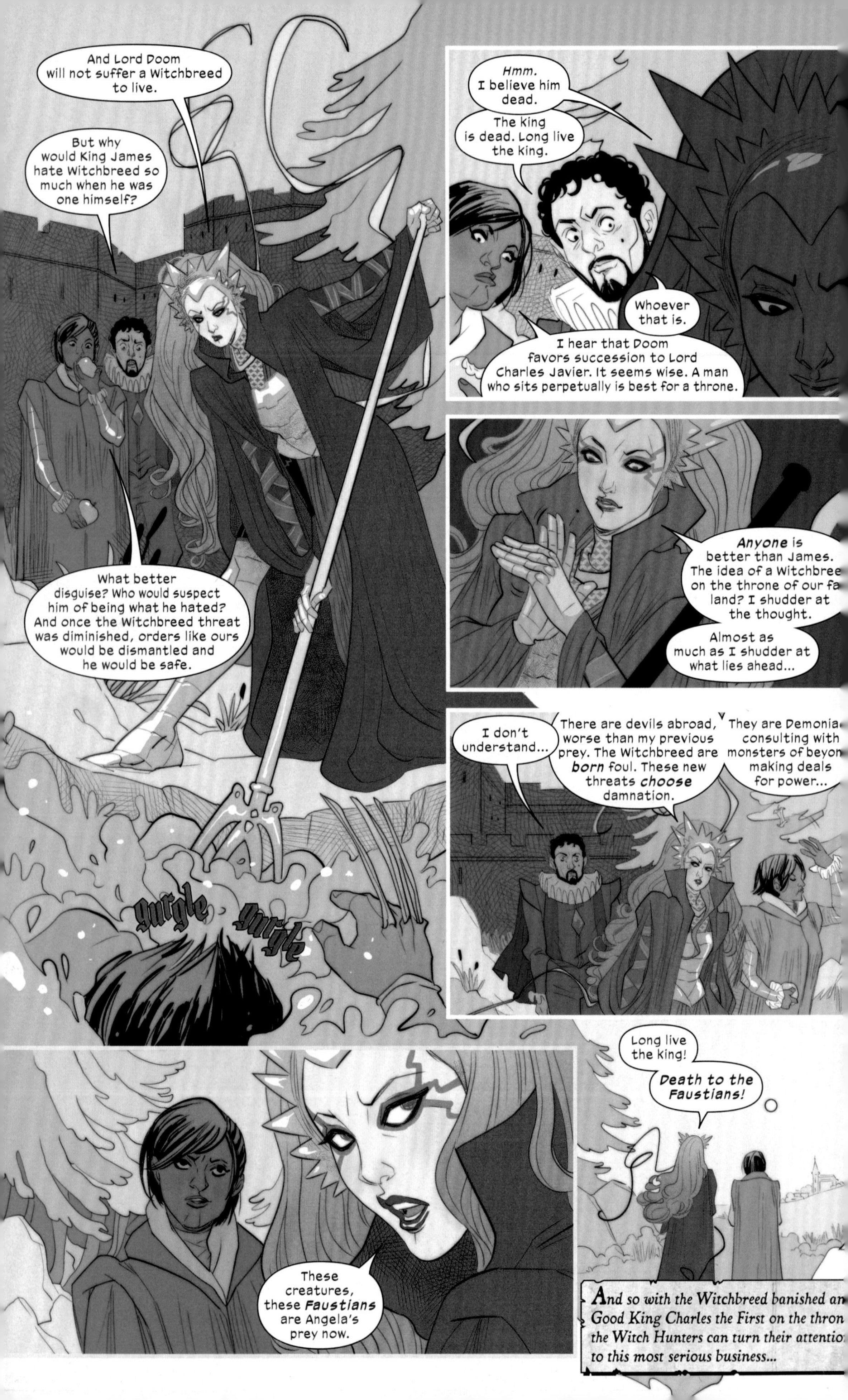
And Lord Doom will not suffer a Witchbreed to live.
But why would King James hate Witchbreed so much when he was one himself?
What better disguise? Who would suspect him of being what he hated? And once the Witchbreed threat was diminished, orders like ours would be dismantled and he would be safe.
gurgle
gurgle
Hmm. I believe him dead.
The king is dead. Long live the king.
Whoever that is.
I hear that Doom favors succession to Lord Charles Javier. It seems wise. A man who sits perpetually is best for a throne.
Anyone is better than James. The idea of a Witchbree on the throne of our fa land? I shudder at the thought.
Almost as much as I shudder at what lies ahead...
I don't understand...
There are devils abroad, worse than my previous prey. The Witchbreed are born foul. These new threats choose damnation.
They are Demonia consulting with monsters of beyon making deals for power...
These creatures, these Faustians are Angela's prey now.
Long live the king!
Death to the Faustians!
And so with the Witchbreed banished an Good King Charles the First on the thron the Witch Hunters can turn their attentio to this most serious business...

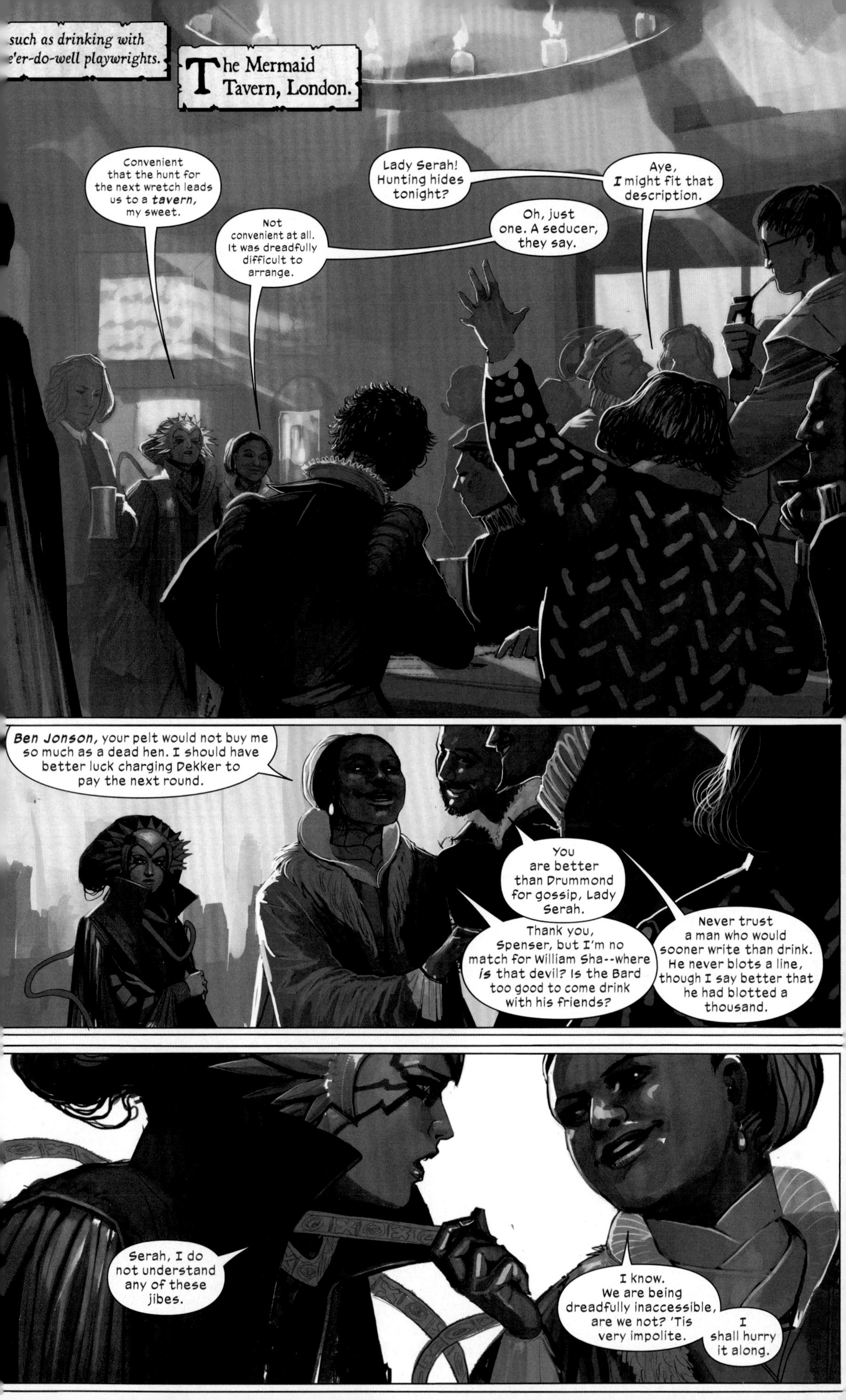
such as drinking with e'er-do-well playwrights.
The Mermaid Tavern, London.
Convenient that the hunt for the next wretch leads us to a *tavern*, my sweet.
Not convenient at all. It was dreadfully difficult to arrange.
Lady Serah! Hunting hides tonight?
Oh, just one. A seducer, they say.
Aye, *I* might fit that description.
Ben Jonson, your pelt would not buy me so much as a dead hen. I should have better luck charging Dekker to pay the next round.
You are better than Drummond for gossip, Lady Serah.
Thank you, Spenser, but I'm no match for William Sha--where *is* that devil? Is the Bard too good to come drink with his friends?
Never trust a man who would sooner write than drink. He never blots a line, though I say better that he had blotted a thousand.
Serah, I do not understand any of these jibes.
I know. We are being dreadfully inaccessible, are we not? 'Tis very impolite.
I shall hurry it along.

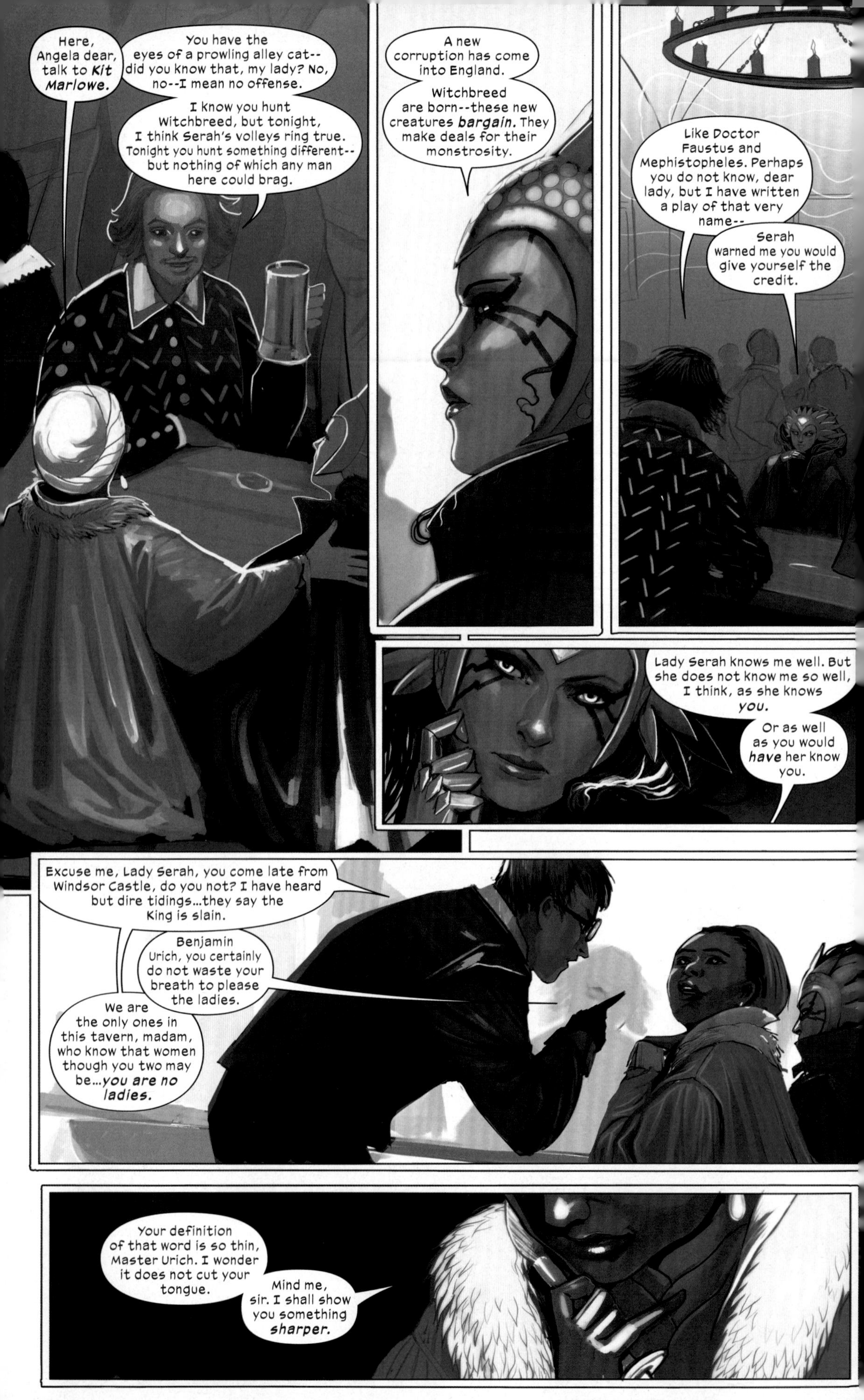

Here, Angela dear, talk to *Kit Marlowe.*
You have the eyes of a prowling alley cat--did you know that, my lady? No, no--I mean no offense.
I know you hunt Witchbreed, but tonight, I think Serah's volleys ring true. Tonight you hunt something different--but nothing of which any man here could brag.
A new corruption has come into England.
Witchbreed are born--these new creatures *bargain.* They make deals for their monstrosity.
Like Doctor Faustus and Mephistopheles. Perhaps you do not know, dear lady, but I have written a play of that very name--
Serah warned me you would give yourself the credit.
Lady Serah knows me well. But she does not know me so well, I think, as she knows *you.*
Or as well as you would *have* her know you.
Excuse me, Lady Serah, you come late from Windsor Castle, do you not? I have heard but dire tidings...they say the King is slain.
Benjamin Urich, you certainly do not waste your breath to please the ladies.
We are the only ones in this tavern, madam, who know that women though you two may be...*you are no ladies.*
Your definition of that word is so thin, Master Urich. I wonder it does not cut your tongue.
Mind me, sir. I shall show you something *sharper.*

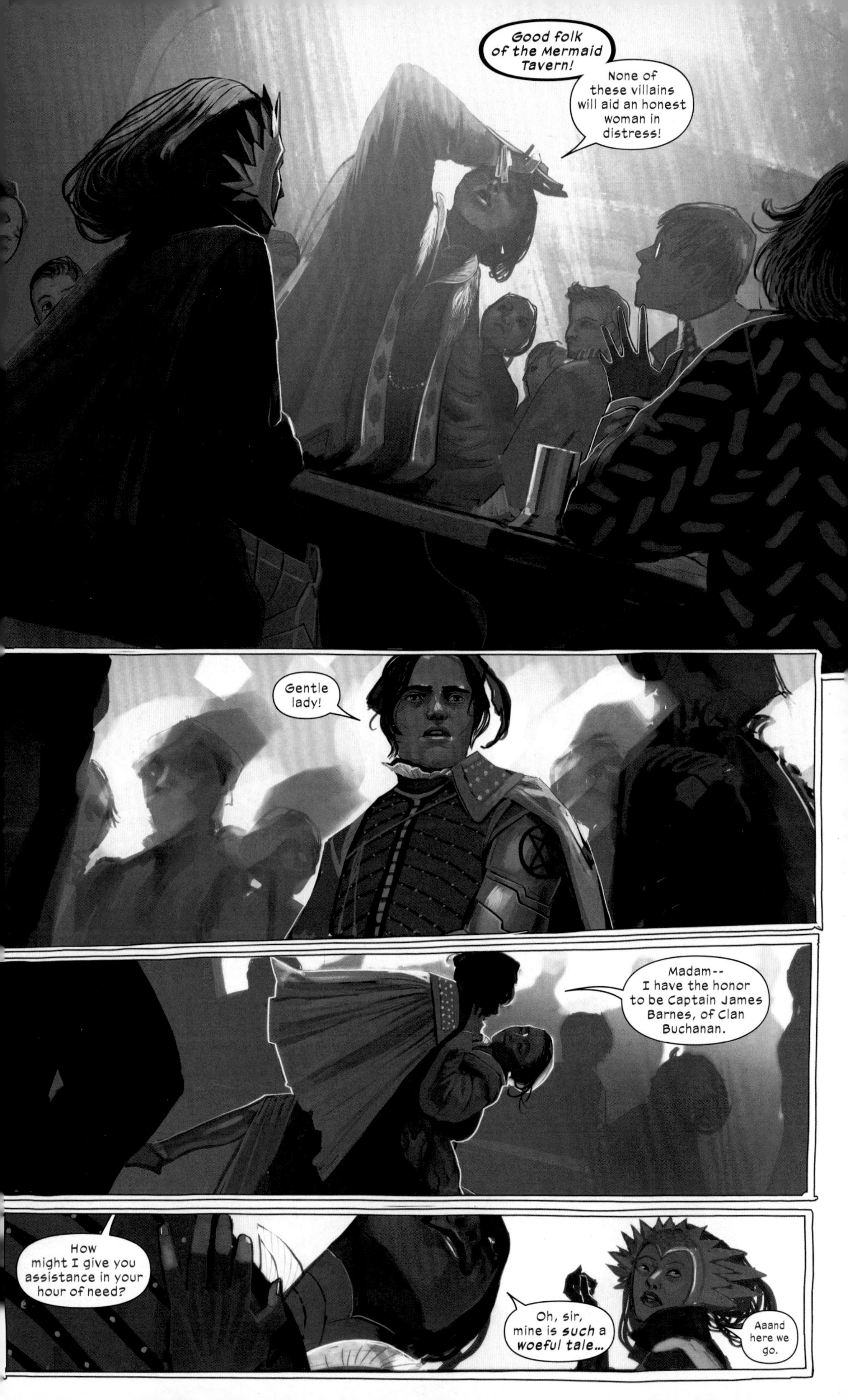
Good folk of the Mermaid Tavern!
None of these villains will aid an honest woman in distress!
Gentle lady!
Madam-- I have the honor to be Captain James Barnes, of Clan Buchanan.
How might I give you assistance in your hour of need?
Oh, sir, mine is *such* a *woeful tale...*
Aaand here we go.

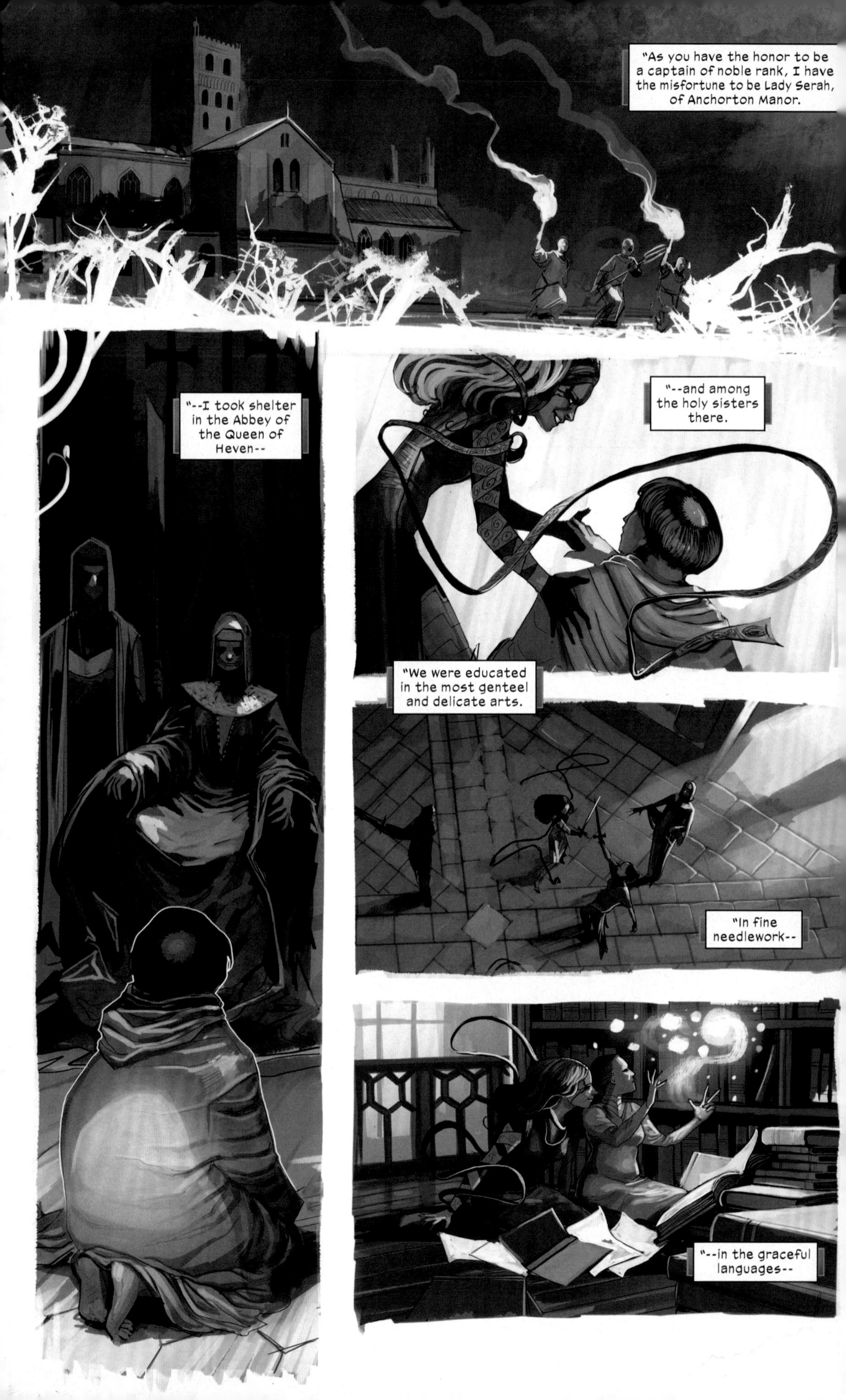
"As you have the honor to be a captain of noble rank, I have the misfortune to be Lady Serah, of Anchorton Manor.
"--I took shelter in the Abbey of the Queen of Heven--
"--and among the holy sisters there.
"We were educated in the most genteel and delicate arts.
"In fine needlework--
"--in the graceful languages--

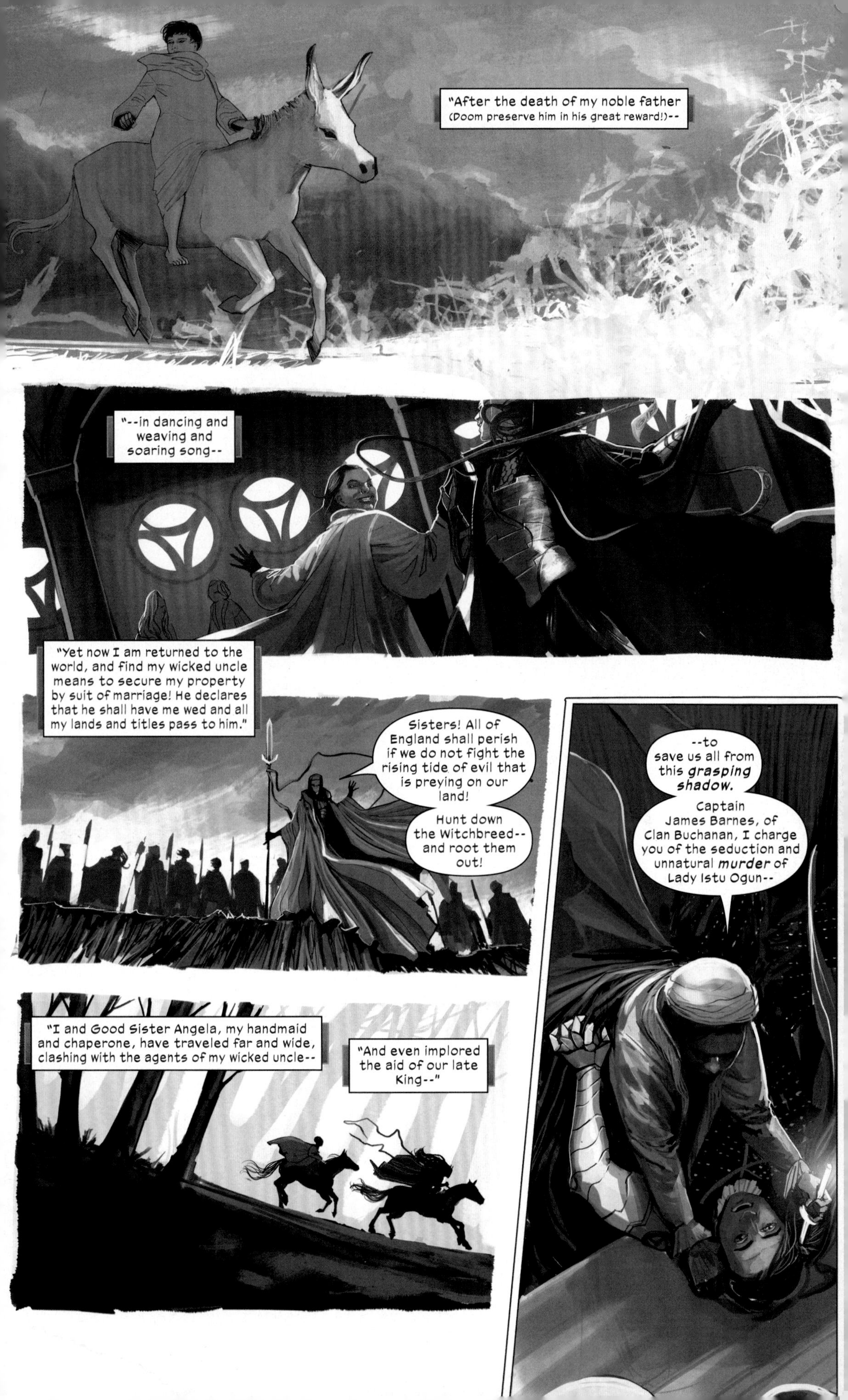
"After the death of my noble father (Doom preserve him in his great reward!)--
"--in dancing and weaving and soaring song--
"Yet now I am returned to the world, and find my wicked uncle means to secure my property by suit of marriage! He declares that he shall have me wed and all my lands and titles pass to him."
Sisters! All of England shall perish if we do not fight the rising tide of evil that is preying on our land!
Hunt down the Witchbreed-- and root them out!
--to save us all from this *grasping shadow.*
Captain James Barnes, of Clan Buchanan, I charge you of the seduction and unnatural *murder* of Lady Istu Ogun--
"I and Good Sister Angela, my handmaid and chaperone, have traveled far and wide, clashing with the agents of my wicked uncle--
"And even implored the aid of our late King--"

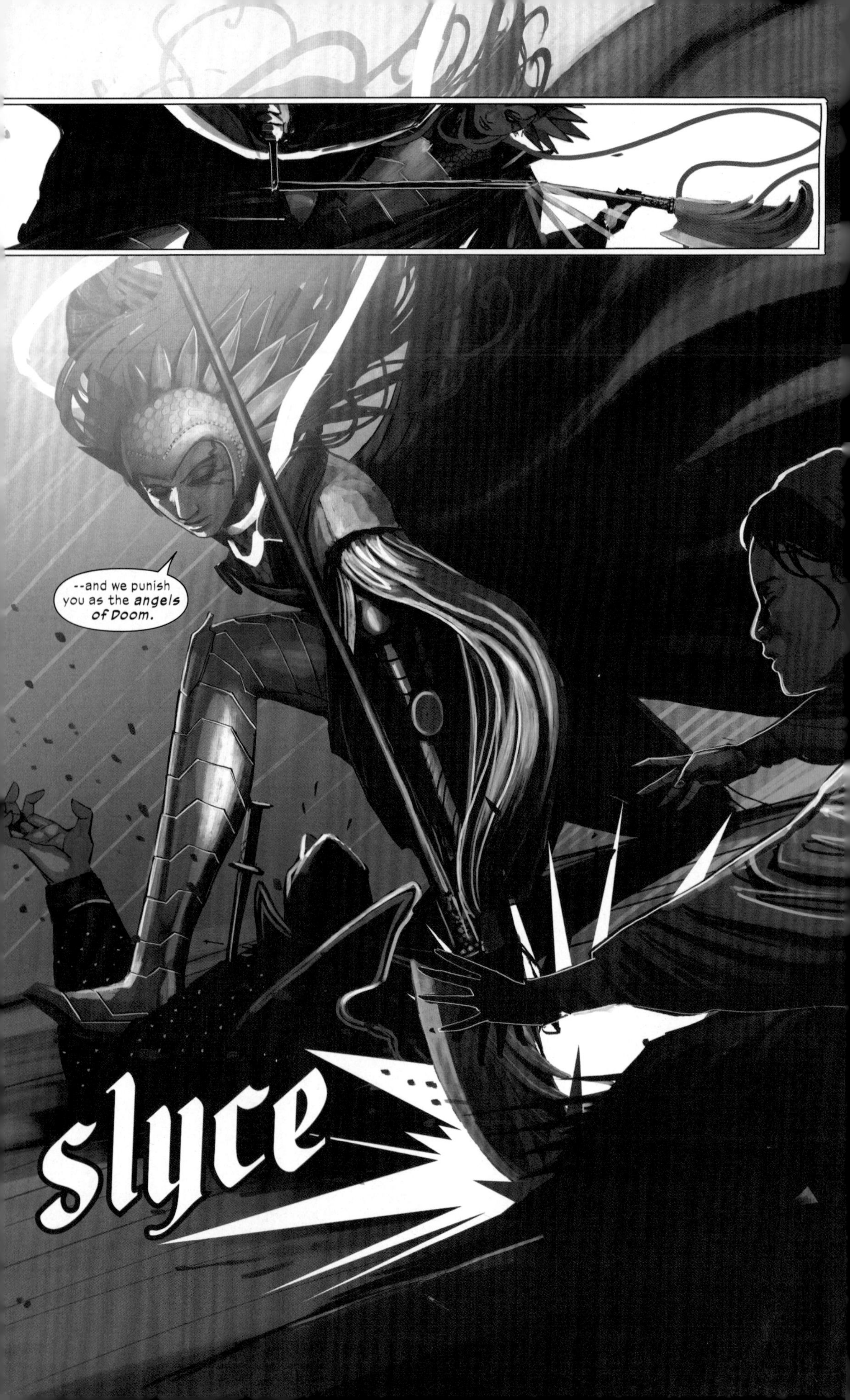
--and we punish you as the *angels of Doom.*
slyce

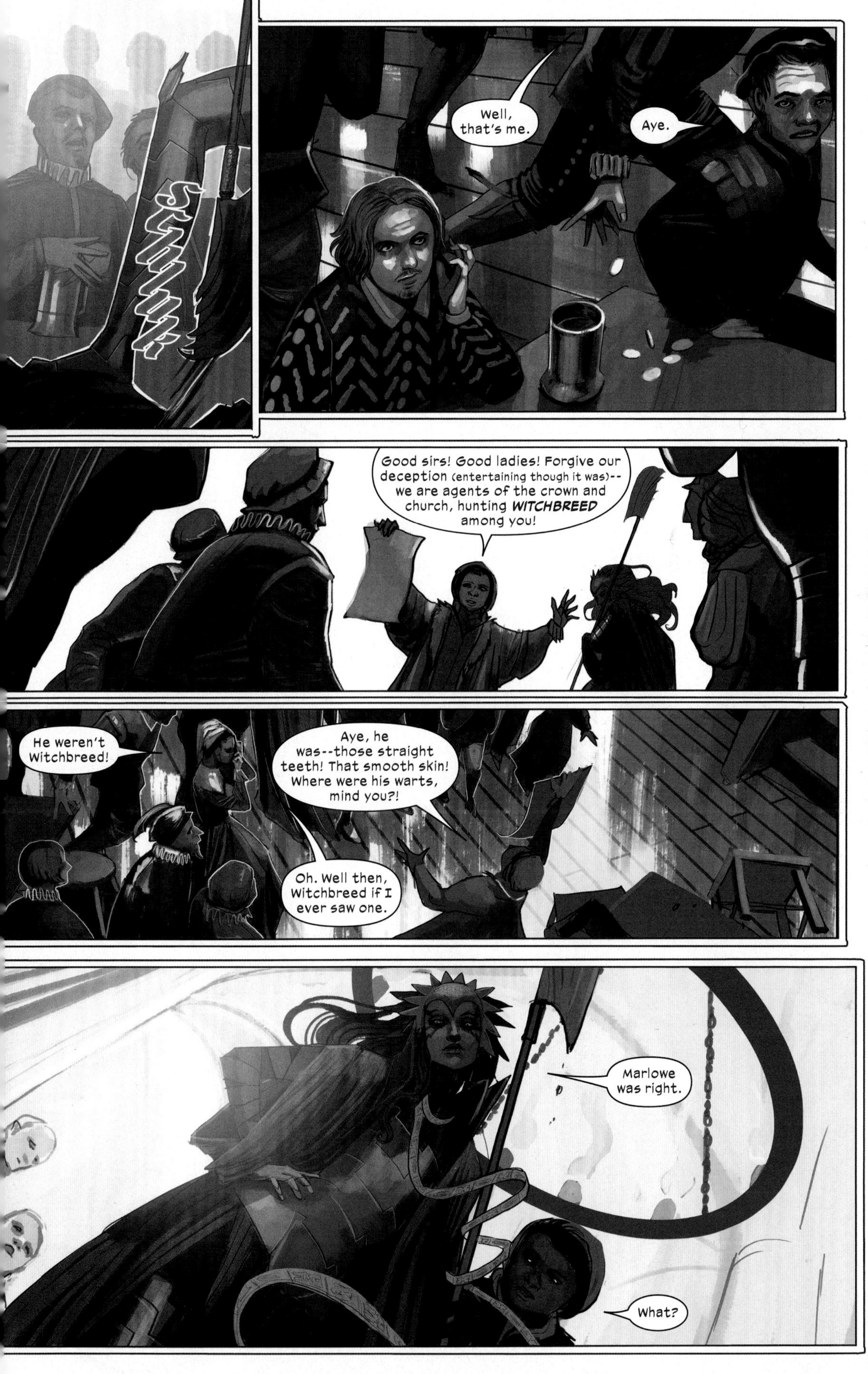
SCHLUK
Well, that's me.
Aye.
Good sirs! Good ladies! Forgive our deception (entertaining though it was)--we are agents of the crown and church, hunting WITCHBREED among you!
He weren't Witchbreed!
Aye, he was--those straight teeth! That smooth skin! Where were his warts, mind you?!
Oh. Well then, Witchbreed if I ever saw one.
Marlowe was right.
What?

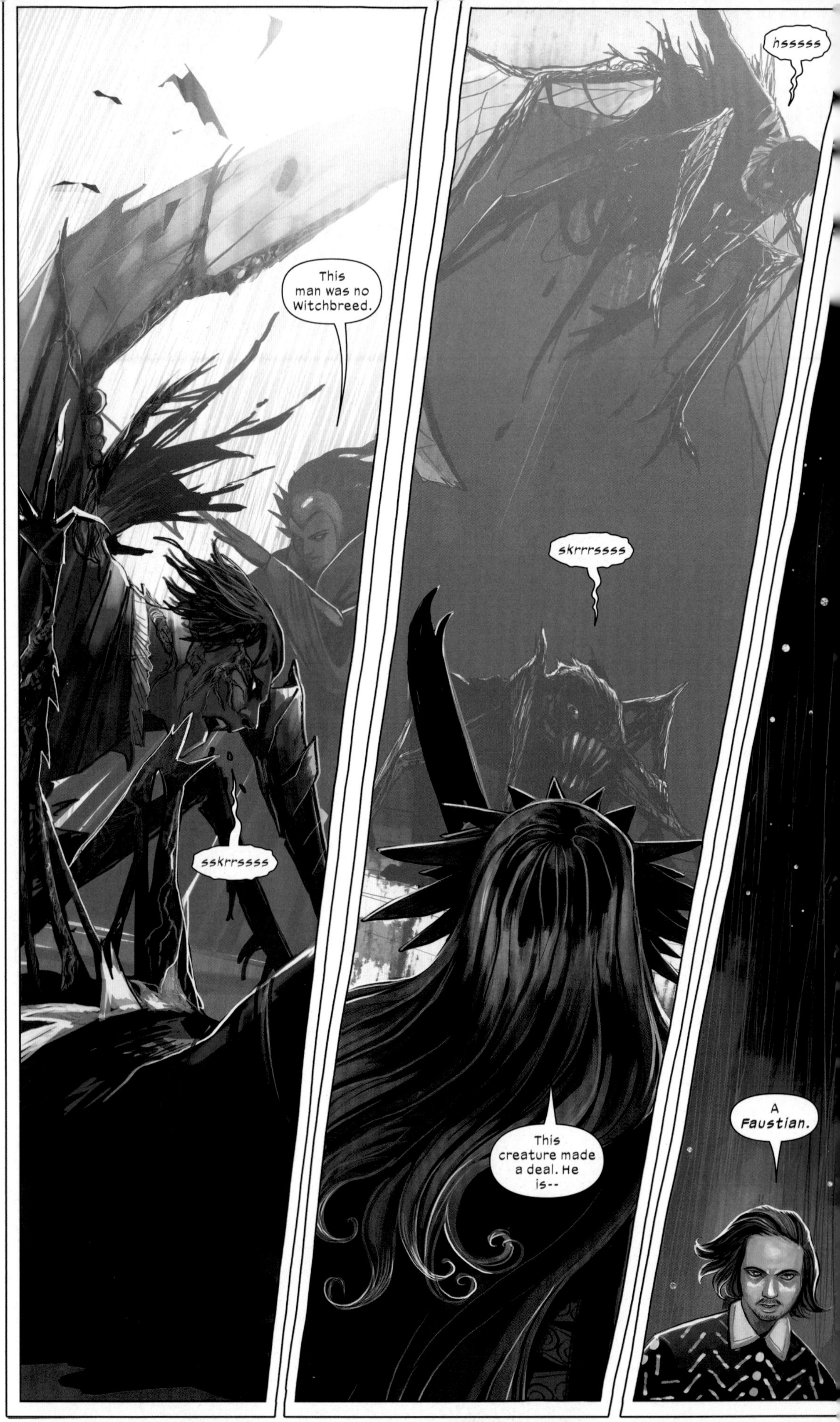
This man was no Witchbreed.
sskrrssss
hsssss
skrrrssss
This creature made a deal. He is--
A Faustian.

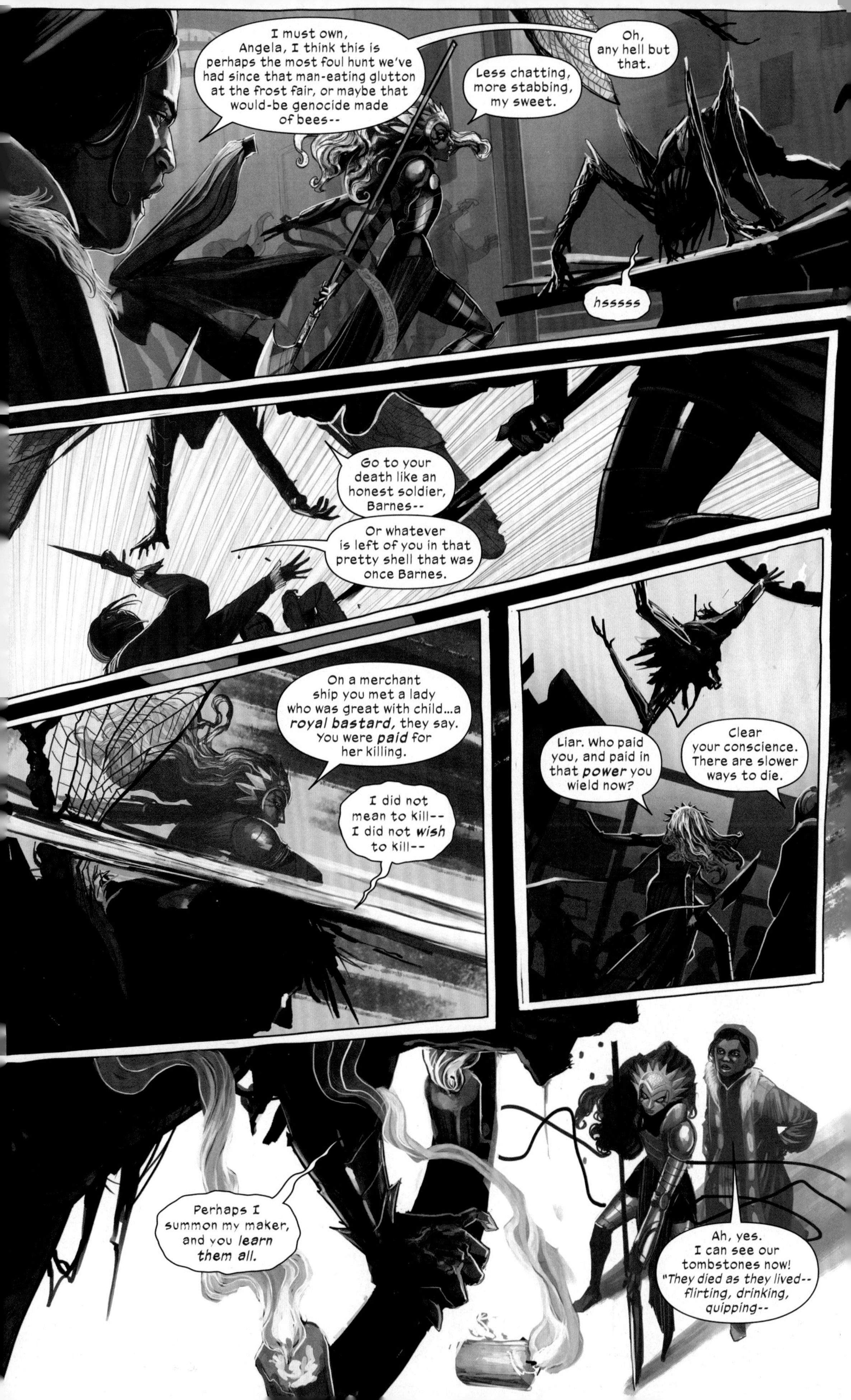
I must own, Angela, I think this is perhaps the most foul hunt we've had since that man-eating glutton at the frost fair, or maybe that would-be genocide made of bees--
Less chatting, more stabbing, my sweet.
Oh, any hell but that.
hsssss
Go to your death like an honest soldier, Barnes--
Or whatever is left of you in that pretty shell that was once Barnes.
On a merchant ship you met a lady who was great with child...a *royal bastard,* they say. You were *paid* for her killing.
I did not mean to kill-- I did not *wish* to kill--
Liar. Who paid you, and paid in that *power* you wield now?
Clear your conscience. There are slower ways to die.
Perhaps I summon my maker, and you *learn them all.*
Ah, yes. I can see our tombstones now! *"They died as they lived-- flirting, drinking, quipping--*

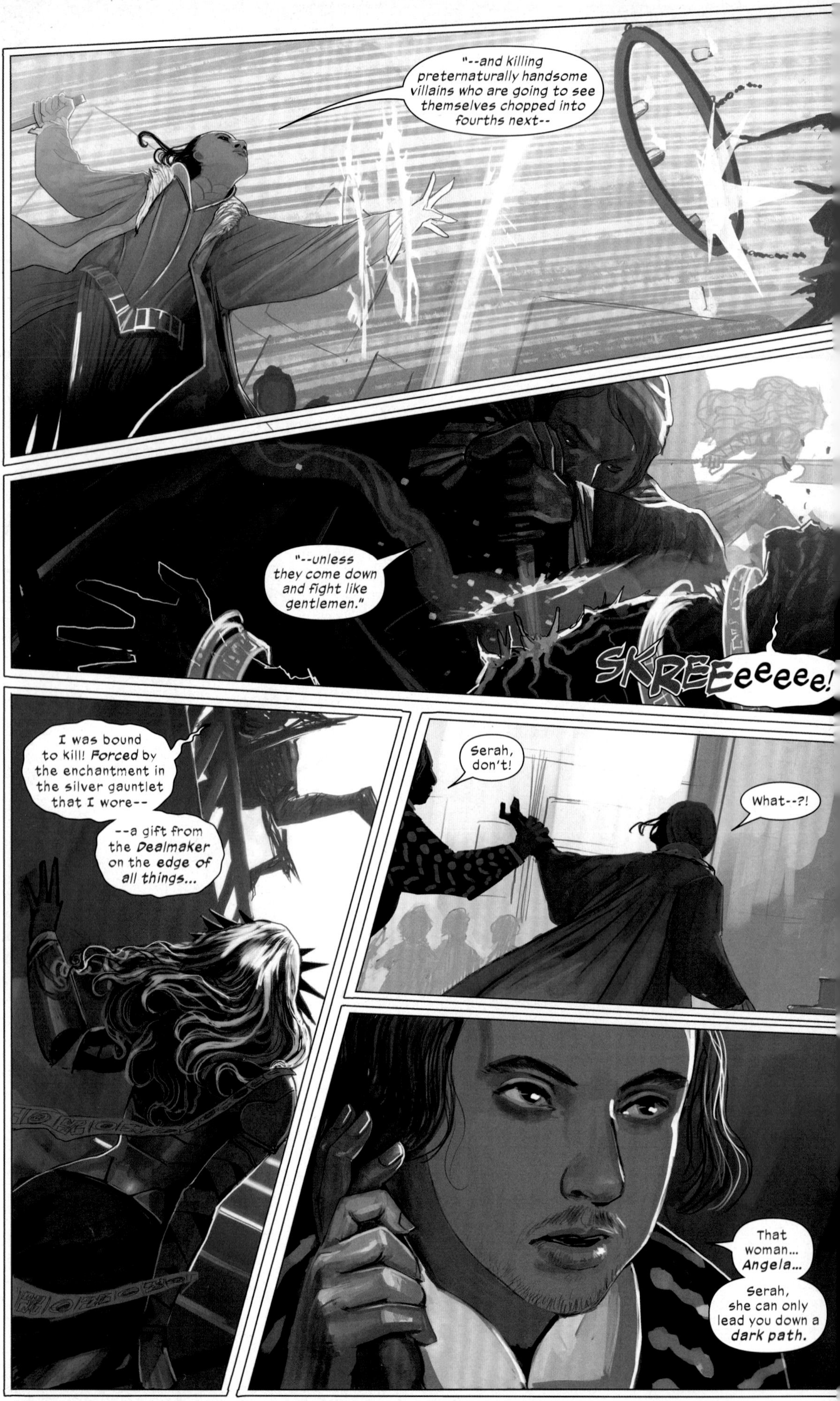
"--and killing preternaturally handsome villains who are going to see themselves chopped into fourths next--
"--unless they come down and fight like gentlemen."
SKREEEeeeee!
I was bound to kill! *Forced* by the enchantment in the silver gauntlet that I wore--
--a gift from the *Dealmaker* on the *edge* of *all things*...
Serah, don't!
What--?!
That woman... *Angela*...
Serah, she can only lead you down a *dark path*.

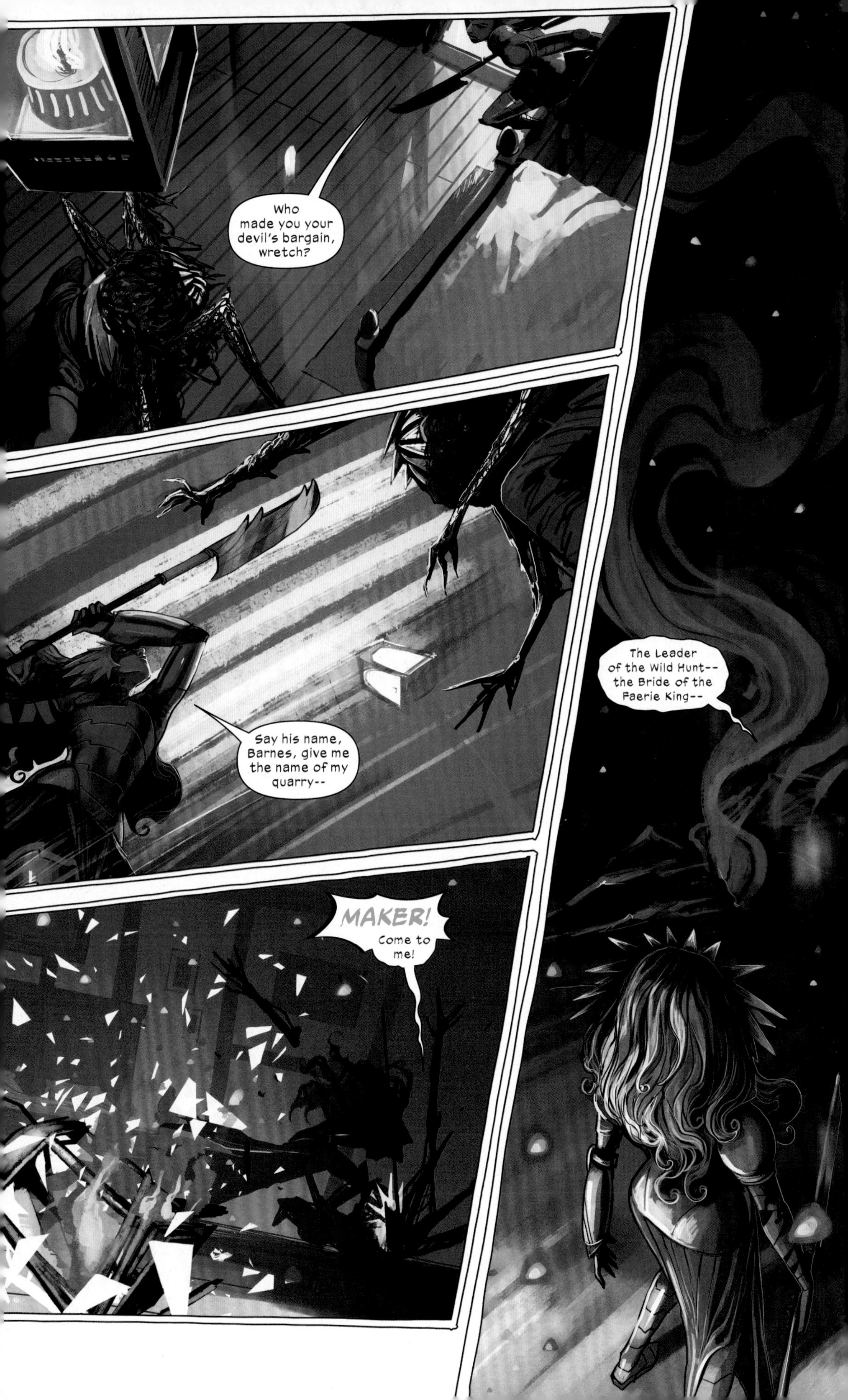
Who made you your devil's bargain, wretch?
Say his name, Barnes, give me the name of my quarry--
The Leader of the Wild Hunt-- the Bride of the Faerie King--
MAKER! Come to me!

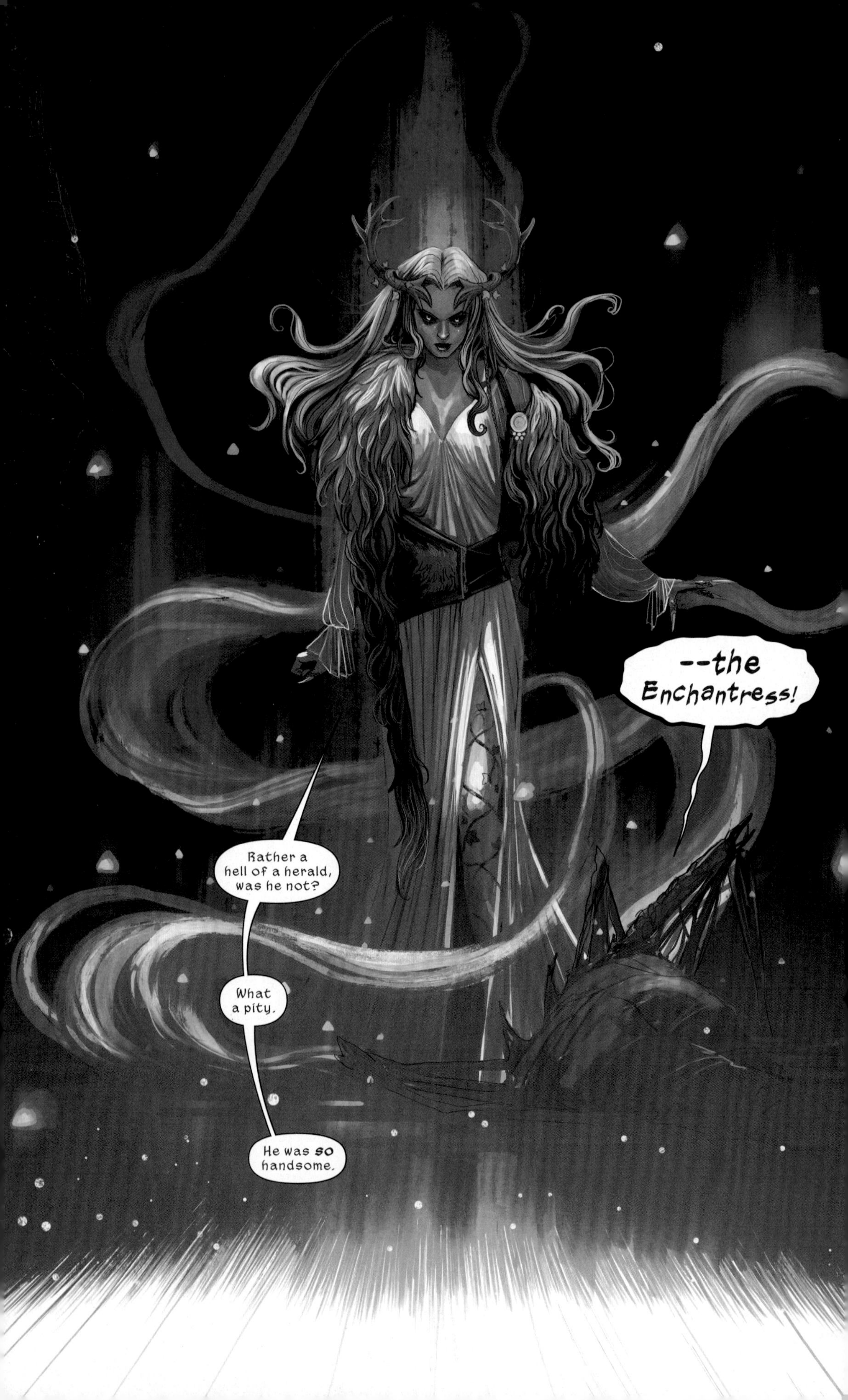
--the Enchantress!
Rather a hell of a herald, was he not?
What a pity.
He was **SO** handsome.

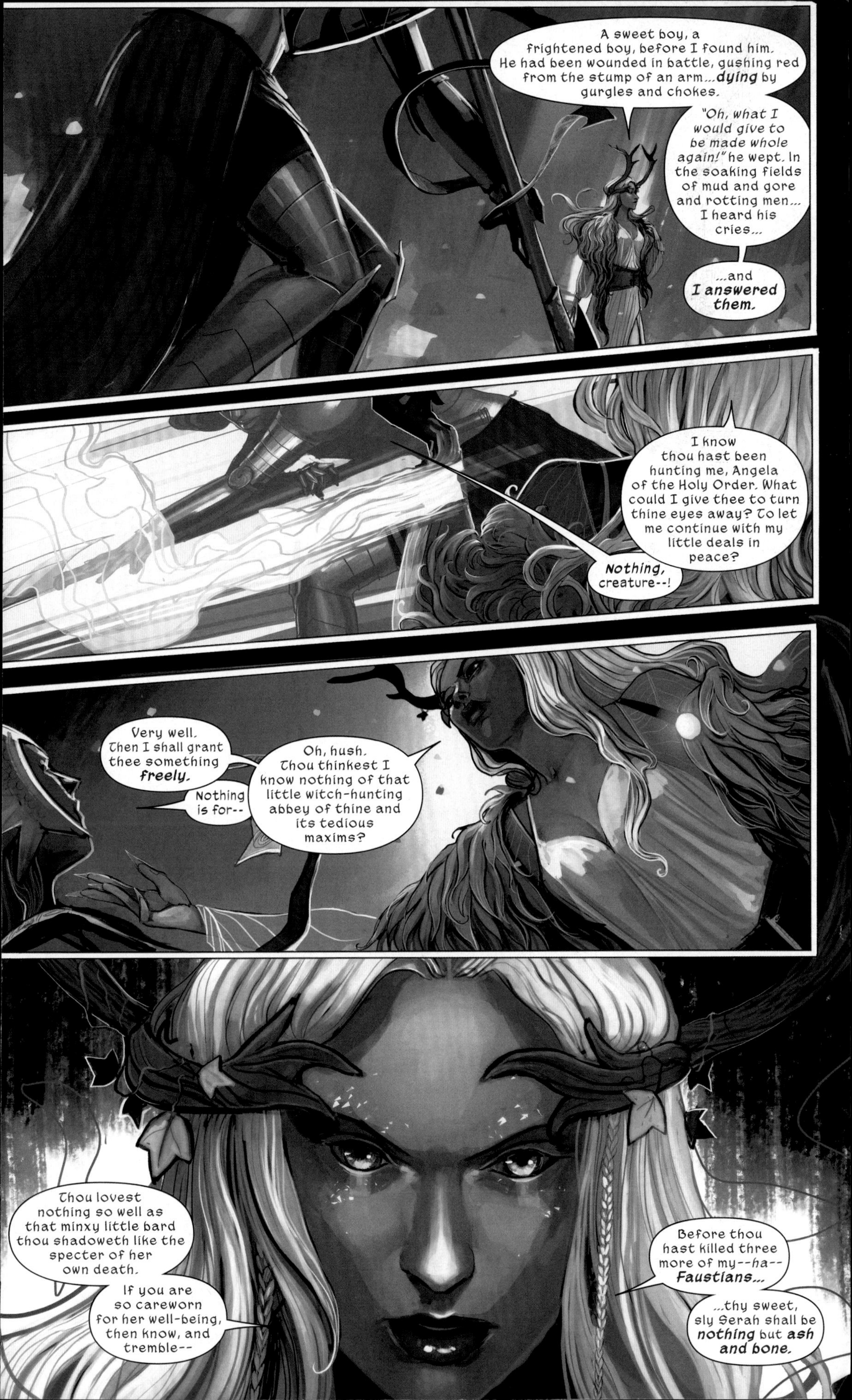
A sweet boy, a frightened boy, before I found him. He had been wounded in battle, gushing red from the stump of an arm... *dying* by gurgles and chokes.
"Oh, what I would give to be made whole again!" he wept. In the soaking fields of mud and gore and rotting men... I heard his cries...
...and **I answered them.**
I know thou hast been hunting me, Angela of the Holy Order. What could I give thee to turn thine eyes away? To let me continue with my little deals in peace?
Nothing, creature--!
Very well. Then I shall grant thee something **freely.**
Nothing is for--
Oh, hush. Thou thinkest I know nothing of that little witch-hunting abbey of thine and its tedious maxims?
Thou lovest nothing so well as that minxy little bard thou shadoweth like the specter of her own death.
If you are so careworn for her well-being, then know, and tremble--
Before thou hast killed three more of my--*ha*--**Faustians...**
...thy sweet, sly Serah shall be **nothing** but **ash and bone.**

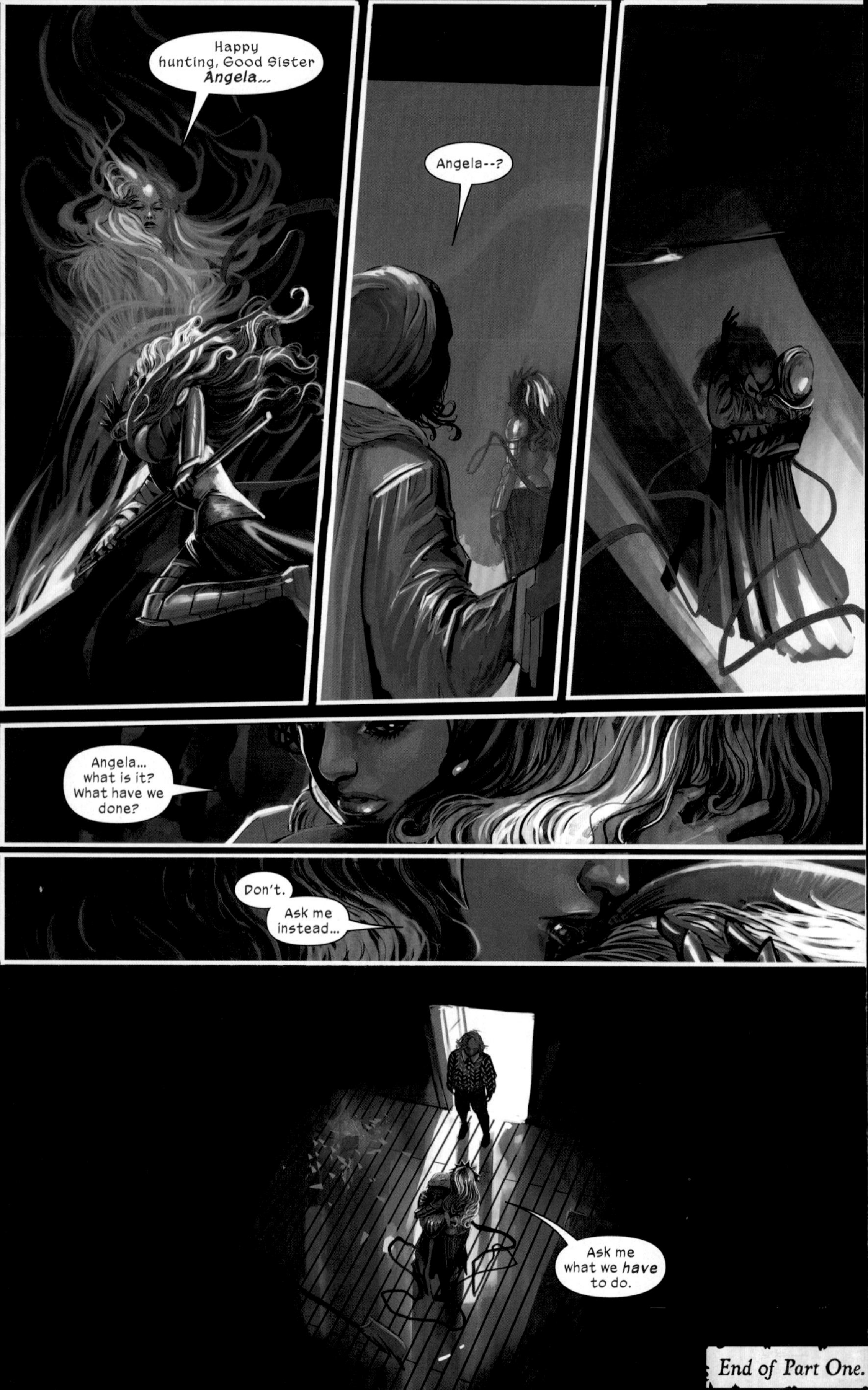
Happy hunting, Good Sister Angela...
Angela--?
Angela... what is it? What have we done?
Don't.
Ask me instead...
Ask me what we have to do.
End of Part One.

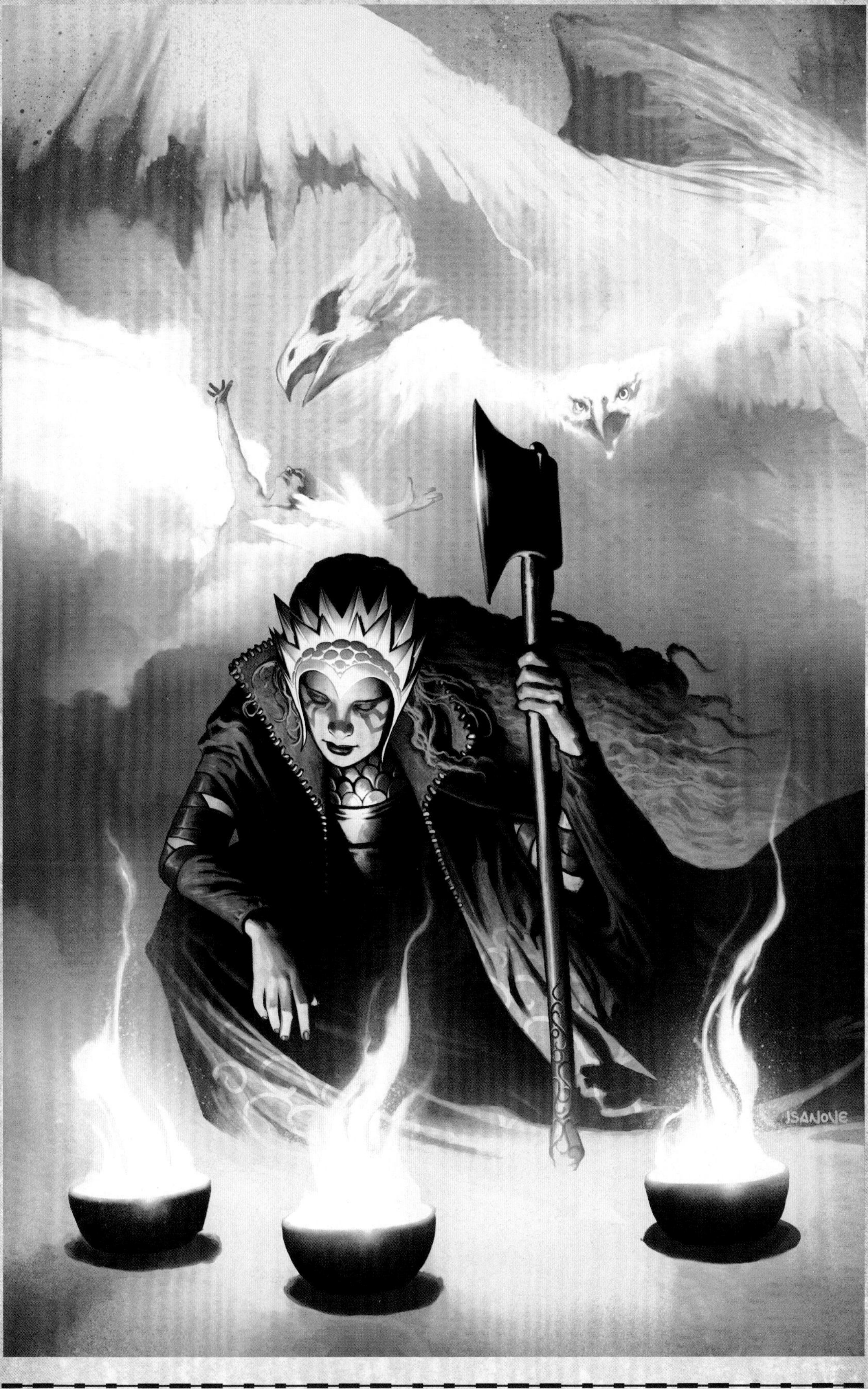
ISANOVE

#1 variant cover by Richard Isanove

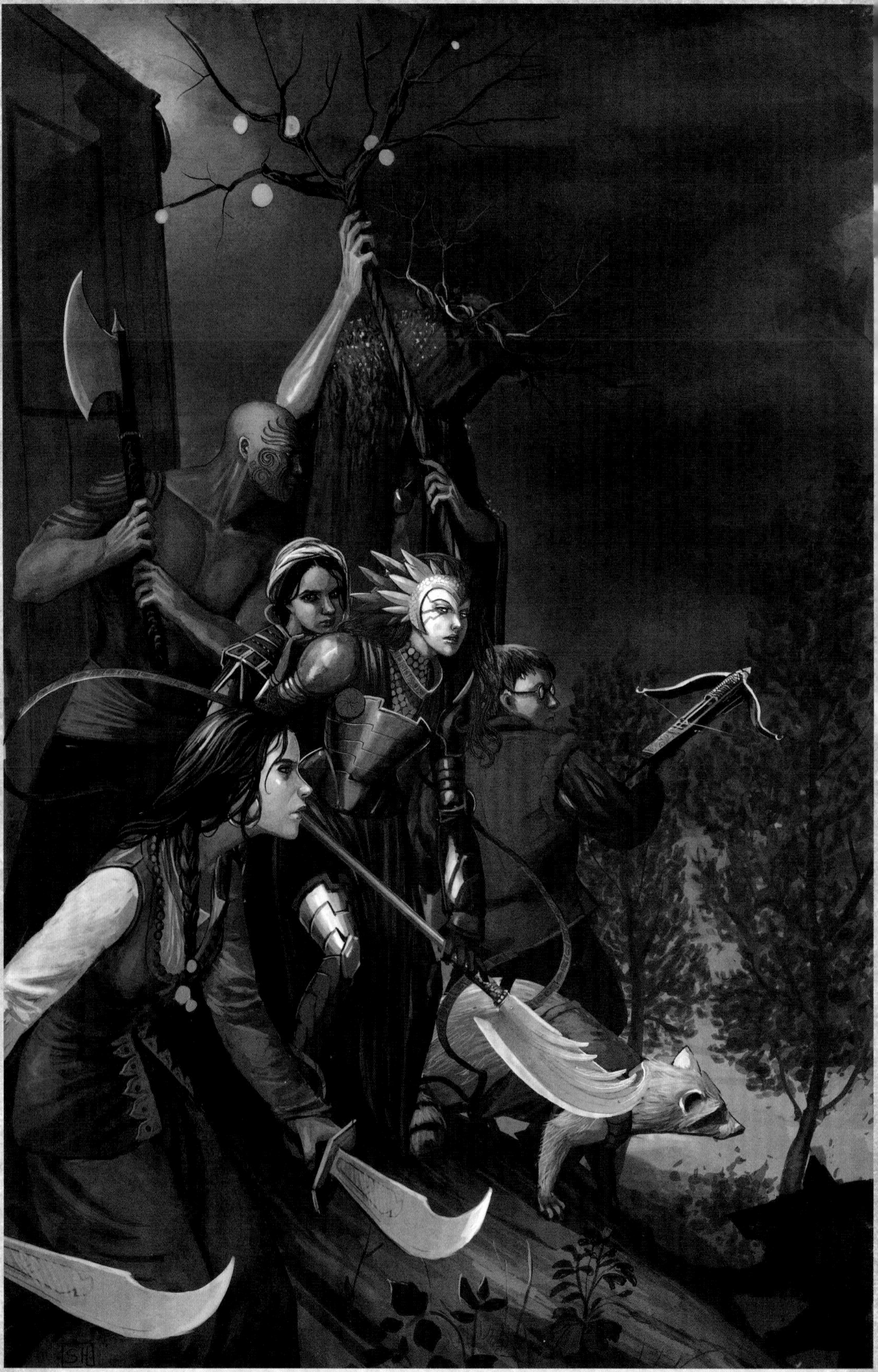

Part Two, In Which All The Worlds's a Stage and The Guardians Overthrow The Players

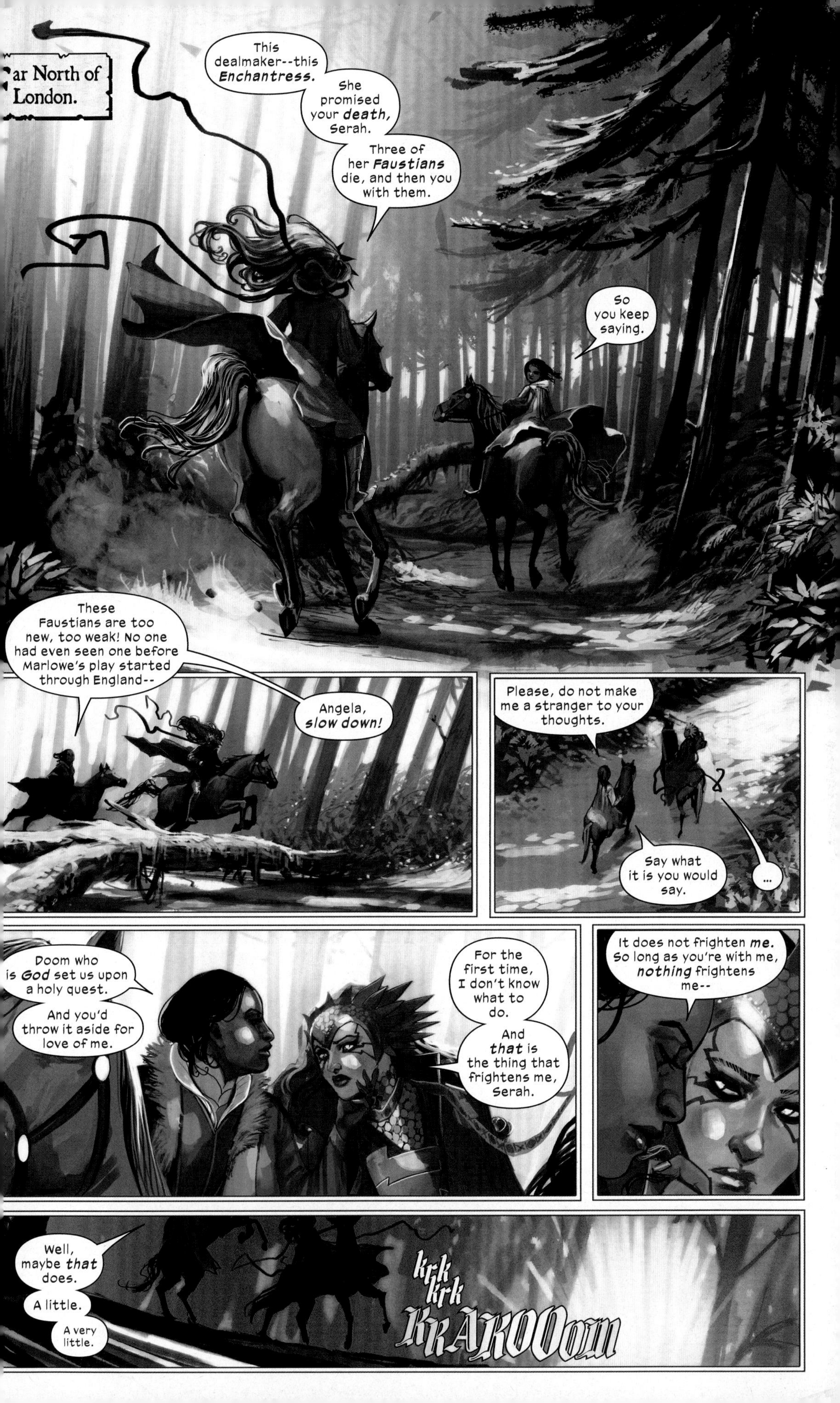

Far North of London.
This dealmaker--this *Enchantress.*
She promised your *death,* Serah.
Three of her *Faustians* die, and then you with them.
So you keep saying.
These Faustians are too new, too weak! No one had even seen one before Marlowe's play started through England--
Angela, *slow down!*
Please, do not make me a stranger to your thoughts.
Say what it is you would say.
...
Doom who is *God* set us upon a holy quest.
And you'd throw it aside for love of me.
For the first time, I don't know what to do.
And *that* is the thing that frightens me, Serah.
It does not frighten *me.* So long as you're with me, *nothing* frightens me--
Well, maybe *that* does.
A little.
A very little.
krk krk KRAKOOom

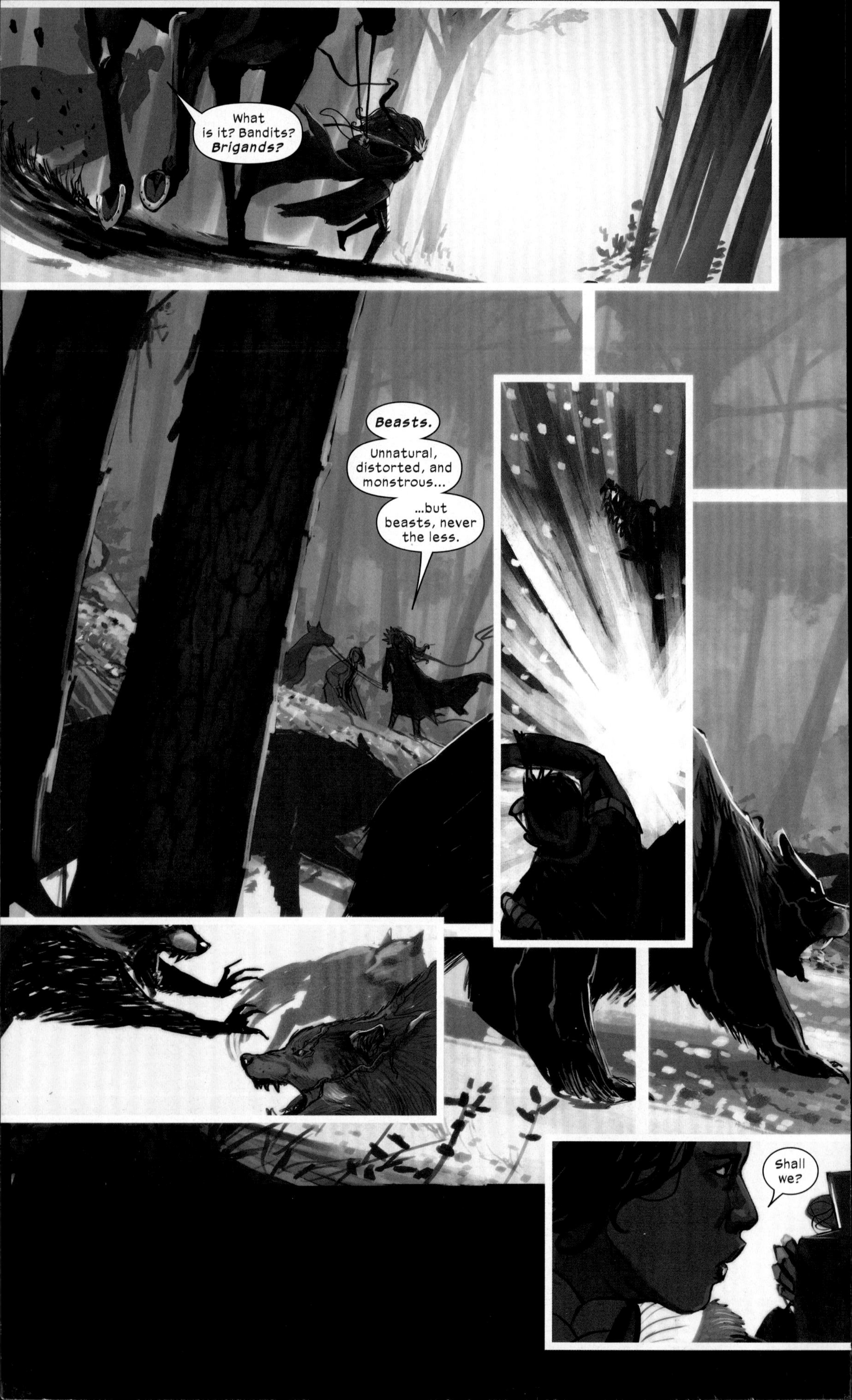
What is it? Bandits? *Brigands?*
Beasts.
Unnatural, distorted, and monstrous...
...but beasts, never the less.
Shall we?

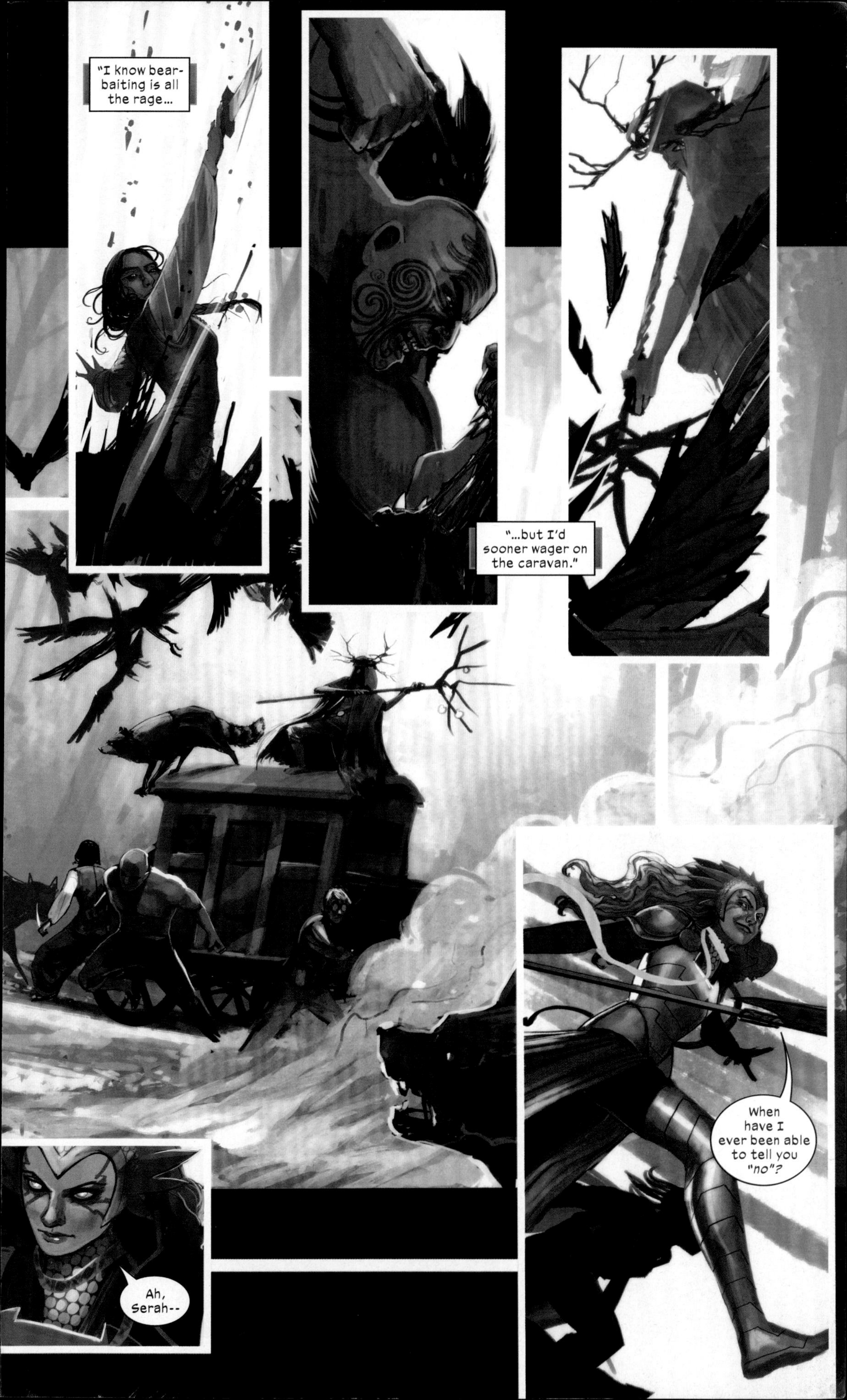
"I know bear-baiting is all the rage...
"...but I'd sooner wager on the caravan."
Ah, Serah--
When have I ever been able to tell you "no"?

Our thanks, holy sisters. We traveled too close to the *realm of Faerie*, it seems.

And what do you know of the realm of Faerie?

SNFF

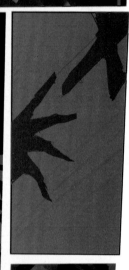

Angela, surely what corrupted these beasts into fell creatures...a trace of her magic--

The Enchantress.

She is close. She will require hosts--humans to *corrupt*. Perhaps a nearby village...

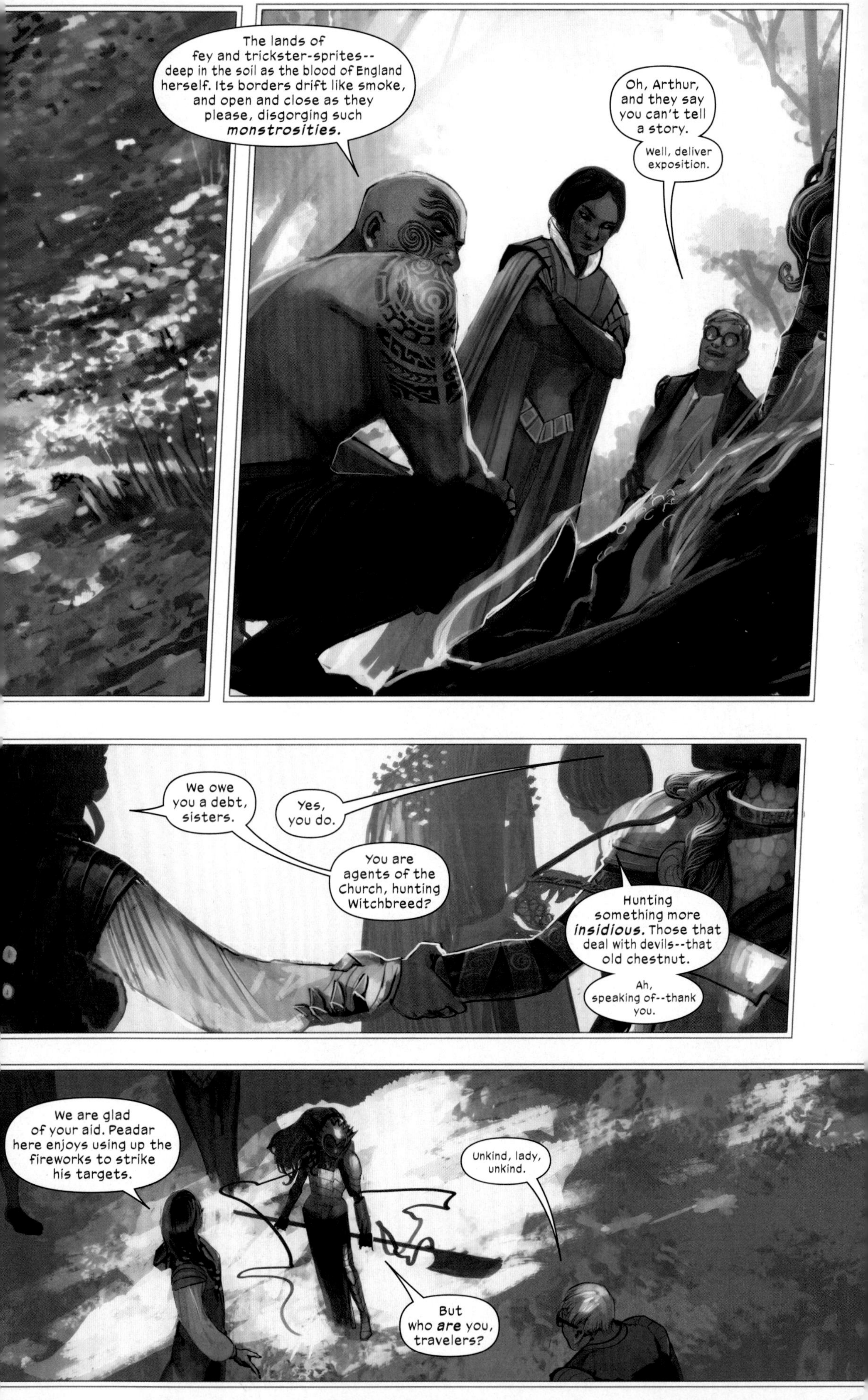
The lands of fey and trickster-sprites--deep in the soil as the blood of England herself. Its borders drift like smoke, and open and close as they please, disgorging such *monstrosities.*
Oh, Arthur, and they say you can't tell a story.
Well, deliver exposition.
We owe you a debt, sisters.
Yes, you do.
You are agents of the Church, hunting Witchbreed?
Hunting something more *insidious.* Those that deal with devils--that old chestnut.
Ah, speaking of--thank you.
We are glad of your aid. Peadar here enjoys using up the fireworks to strike his targets.
Unkind, lady, unkind.
But who *are* you, travelers?

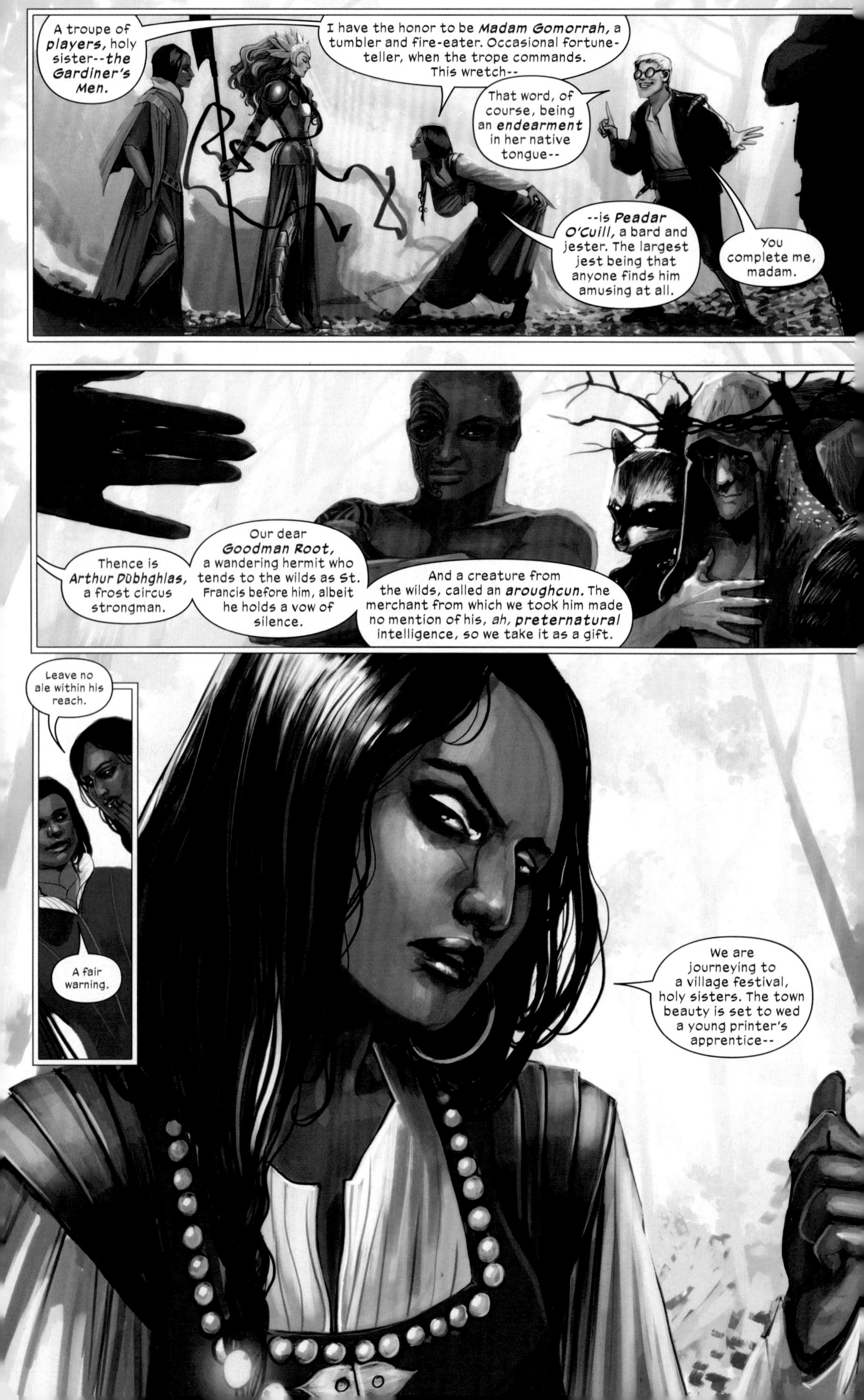
A troupe of players, holy sister--the Gardiner's Men.
I have the honor to be Madam Gomorrah, a tumbler and fire-eater. Occasional fortune-teller, when the trope commands. This wretch--
That word, of course, being an endearment in her native tongue--
--is Peadar O'Cuill, a bard and jester. The largest jest being that anyone finds him amusing at all.
You complete me, madam.
Thence is Arthur Dùbhghlas, a frost circus strongman.
Our dear Goodman Root, a wandering hermit who tends to the wilds as St. Francis before him, albeit he holds a vow of silence.
And a creature from the wilds, called an aroughcun. The merchant from which we took him made no mention of his, ah, preternatural intelligence, so we take it as a gift.
Leave no ale within his reach.
A fair warning.
We are journeying to a village festival, holy sisters. The town beauty is set to wed a young printer's apprentice--

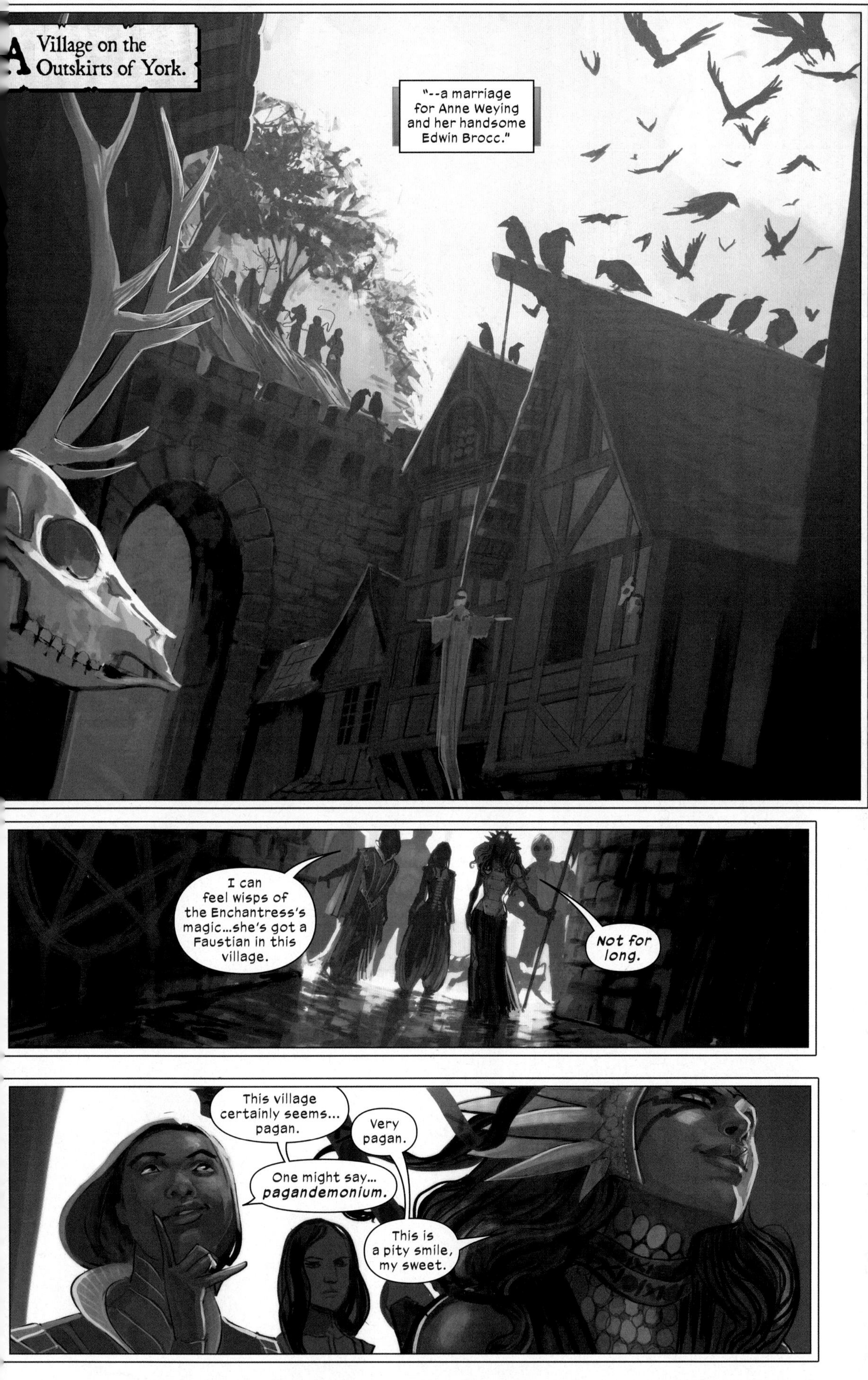
A Village on the Outskirts of York.
"--a marriage for Anne Weying and her handsome Edwin Brocc."
I can feel wisps of the Enchantress's magic...she's got a Faustian in this village.
Not for long.
This village certainly seems... pagan.
Very pagan.
One might say... *pagandemonium.*
This is a pity smile, my sweet.

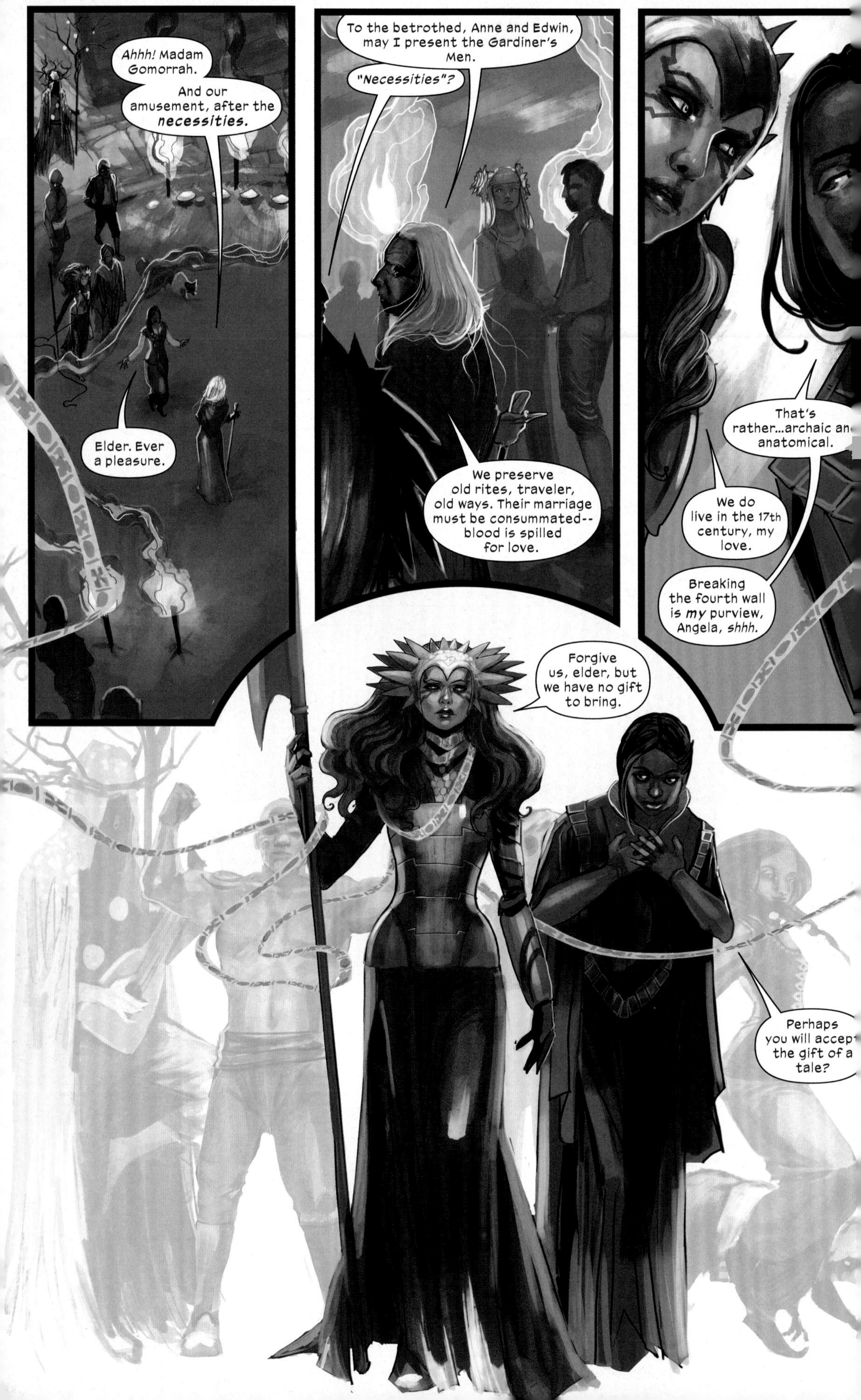
Ahhh! Madam Gomorrah.
And our amusement, after the *necessities.*
Elder. Ever a pleasure.
To the betrothed, Anne and Edwin, may I present the Gardiner's Men.
"*Necessities*"?
We preserve old rites, traveler, old ways. Their marriage must be consummated--blood is spilled for love.
That's rather...archaic an anatomical.
We do live in the 17th century, my love.
Breaking the fourth wall is *my* purview, Angela, *shhh.*
Forgive us, elder, but we have no gift to bring.
Perhaps you will accept the gift of a tale?

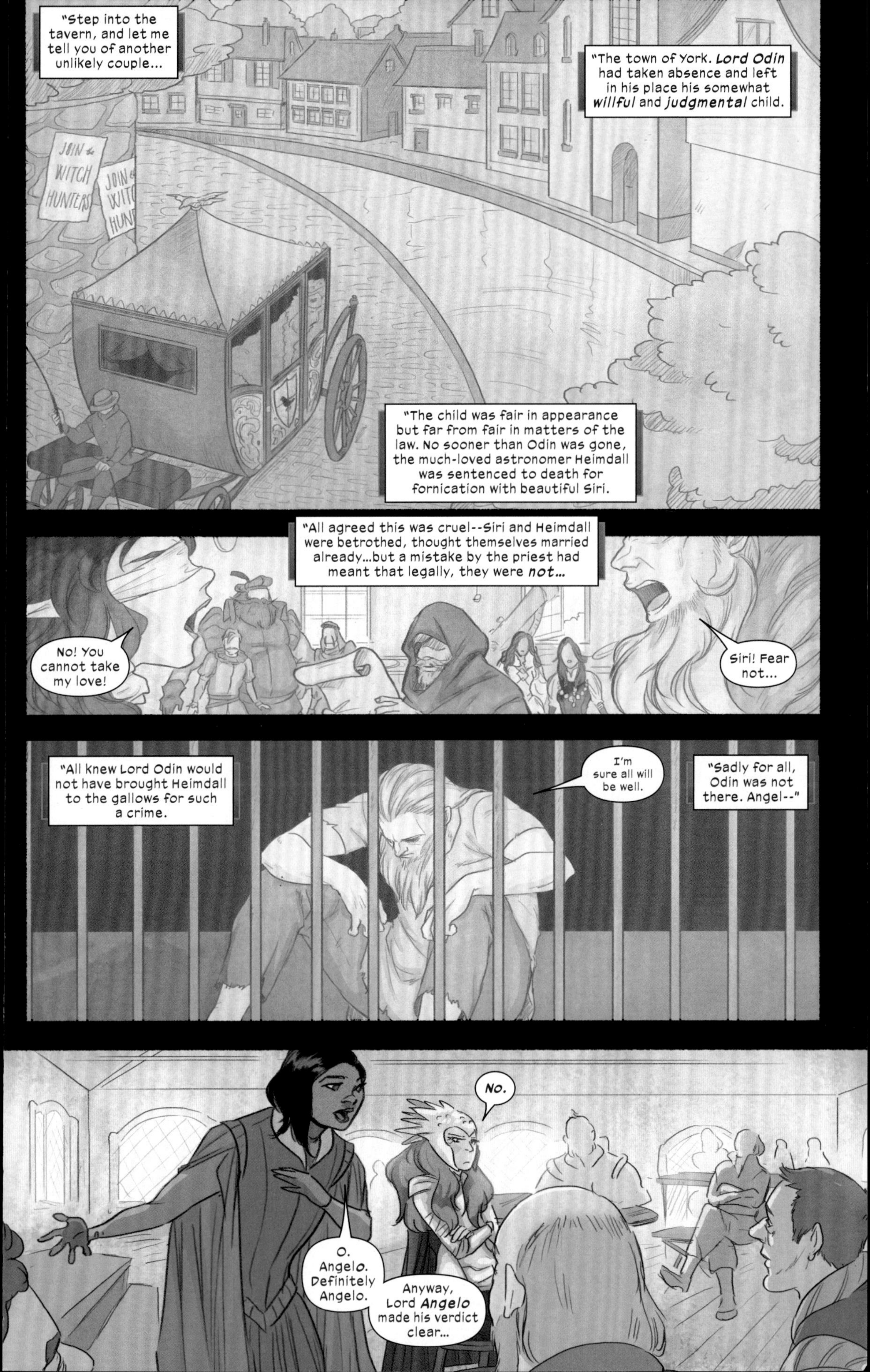
"Step into the tavern, and let me tell you of another unlikely couple...
"The town of York. Lord Odin had taken absence and left in his place his somewhat willful and judgmental child.
JOIN the WITCH HUNTERS
"The child was fair in appearance but far from fair in matters of the law. No sooner than Odin was gone, the much-loved astronomer Heimdall was sentenced to death for fornication with beautiful Siri.
"All agreed this was cruel--Siri and Heimdall were betrothed, thought themselves married already...but a mistake by the priest had meant that legally, they were not...
No! You cannot take my love!
Siri! Fear not...
"All knew Lord Odin would not have brought Heimdall to the gallows for such a crime.
I'm sure all will be well.
"Sadly for all, Odin was not there. Angel--"
NO.
O. Angelo. Definitely Angelo.
Anyway, Lord Angelo made his verdict clear...

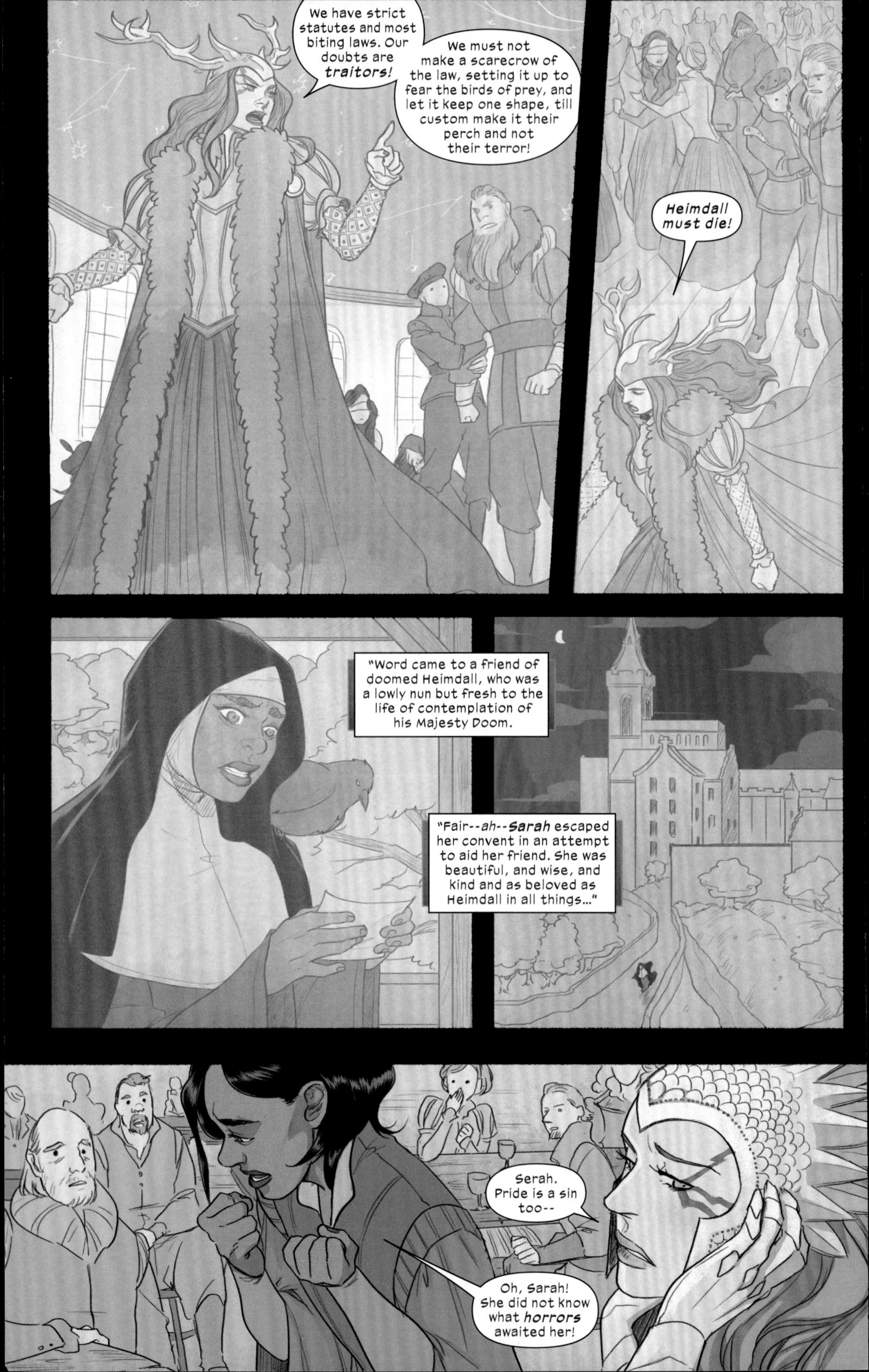
We have strict statutes and most biting laws. Our doubts are traitors!
We must not make a scarecrow of the law, setting it up to fear the birds of prey, and let it keep one shape, till custom make it their perch and not their terror!
Heimdall must die!
"Word came to a friend of doomed Heimdall, who was a lowly nun but fresh to the life of contemplation of his Majesty Doom.
"Fair--ah--Sarah escaped her convent in an attempt to aid her friend. She was beautiful, and wise, and kind and as beloved as Heimdall in all things..."
Serah. Pride is a sin too--
Oh, Sarah! She did not know what horrors awaited her!

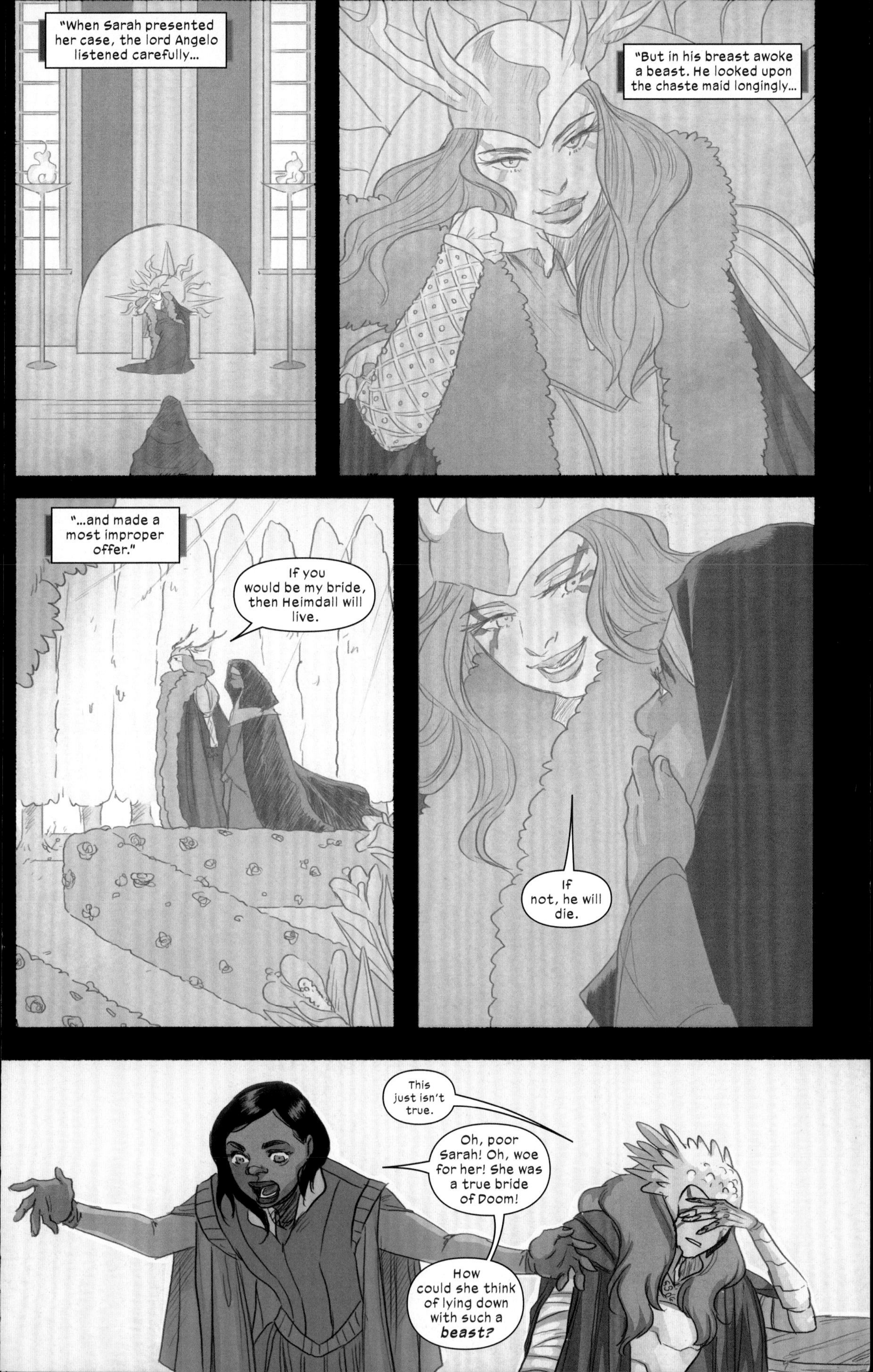

"When Sarah presented her case, the lord Angelo listened carefully...
"But in his breast awoke a beast. He looked upon the chaste maid longingly...
"...and made a most improper offer."
If you would be my bride, then Heimdall will live.
If not, he will die.
This just isn't true.
Oh, poor Sarah! Oh, woe for her! She was a true bride of Doom!
How could she think of lying down with such a *beast?*

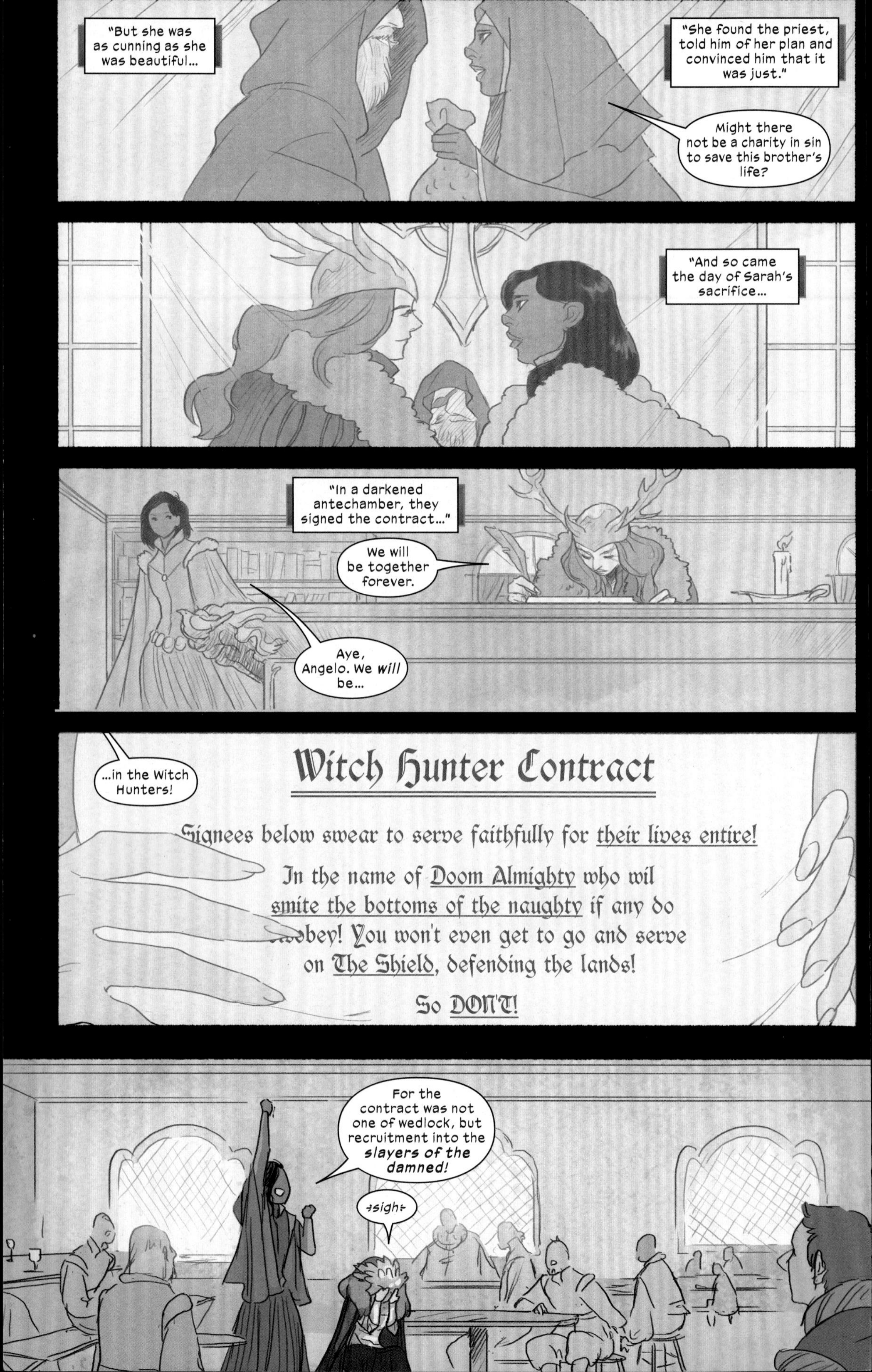
"But she was as cunning as she was beautiful...
"She found the priest, told him of her plan and convinced him that it was just."
Might there not be a charity in sin to save this brother's life?
"And so came the day of Sarah's sacrifice...
"In a darkened antechamber, they signed the contract..."
We will be together forever.
Aye, Angelo. We *will* be...
...in the Witch Hunters!
Witch Hunter Contract
Signees below swear to serve faithfully for their lives entire!
In the name of Doom Almighty who wil smite the bottoms of the naughty if any do disobey! You won't even get to go and serve on The Shield, defending the lands!
So DON'T!
For the contract was not one of wedlock, but recruitment into the *slayers of the damned!*
sigh

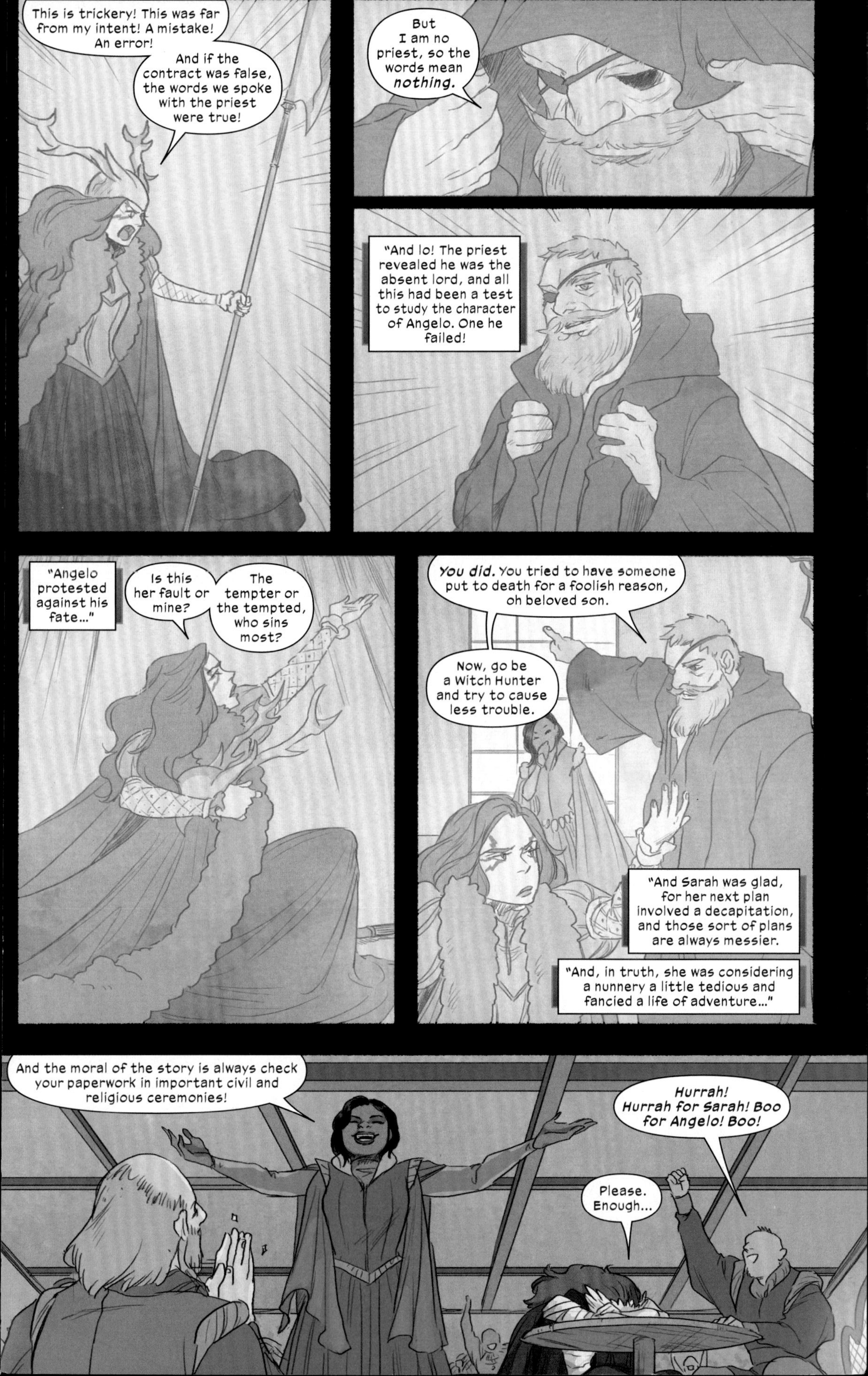
This is trickery! This was far from my intent! A mistake! An error!
And if the contract was false, the words we spoke with the priest were true!
But I am no priest, so the words mean *nothing.*
"And lo! The priest revealed he was the absent lord, and all this had been a test to study the character of Angelo. One he failed!
"Angelo protested against his fate..."
Is this her fault or mine?
The tempter or the tempted, who sins most?
You did. You tried to have someone put to death for a foolish reason, oh beloved son.
Now, go be a Witch Hunter and try to cause less trouble.
"And Sarah was glad, for her next plan involved a decapitation, and those sort of plans are always messier.
"And, in truth, she was considering a nunnery a little tedious and fancied a life of adventure..."
And the moral of the story is always check your paperwork in important civil and religious ceremonies!
Hurrah! Hurrah for Sarah! Boo for Angelo! Boo!
Please. Enough...

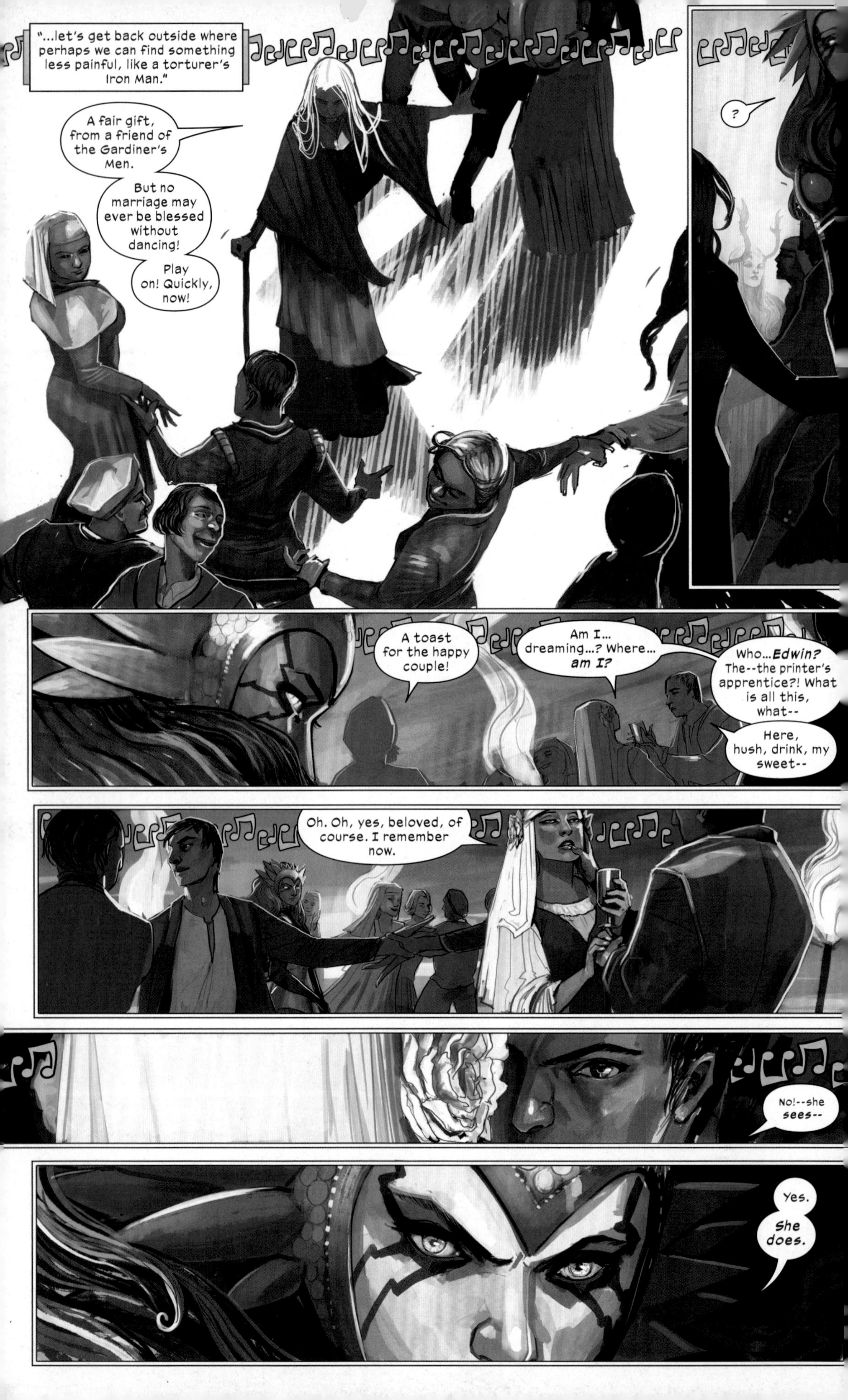
"...let's get back outside where perhaps we can find something less painful, like a torturer's Iron Man."
A fair gift, from a friend of the Gardiner's Men.
But no marriage may ever be blessed without dancing!
Play on! Quickly, now!
?
A toast for the happy couple!
Am I... dreaming...? Where... *am I?*
Who...*Edwin?* The--the printer's apprentice?! What is all this, what--
Here, hush, drink, my sweet--
Oh. Oh, yes, beloved, of course. I remember now.
No!--she *sees*--
Yes.
She does.

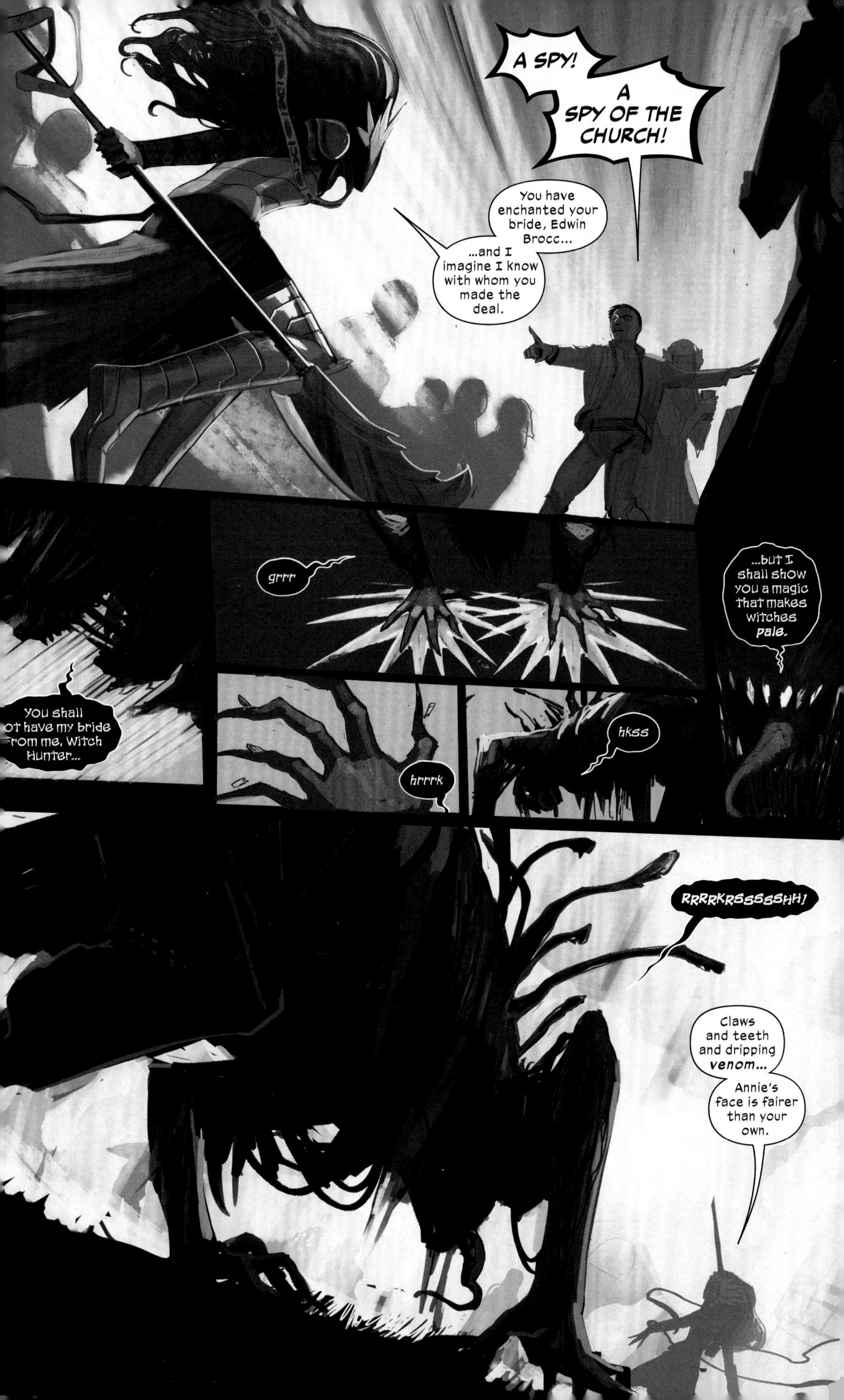
A SPY!
A SPY OF THE CHURCH!
You have enchanted your bride, Edwin Brocc...
...and I imagine I know with whom you made the deal.
grrr
You shall ot have my bride from me, Witch Hunter...
hrrrk
hkss
...but I shall show you a magic that makes witches pale.
RRRRKRSSSSSSHH!
Claws and teeth and dripping venom...
Annie's face is fairer than your own.

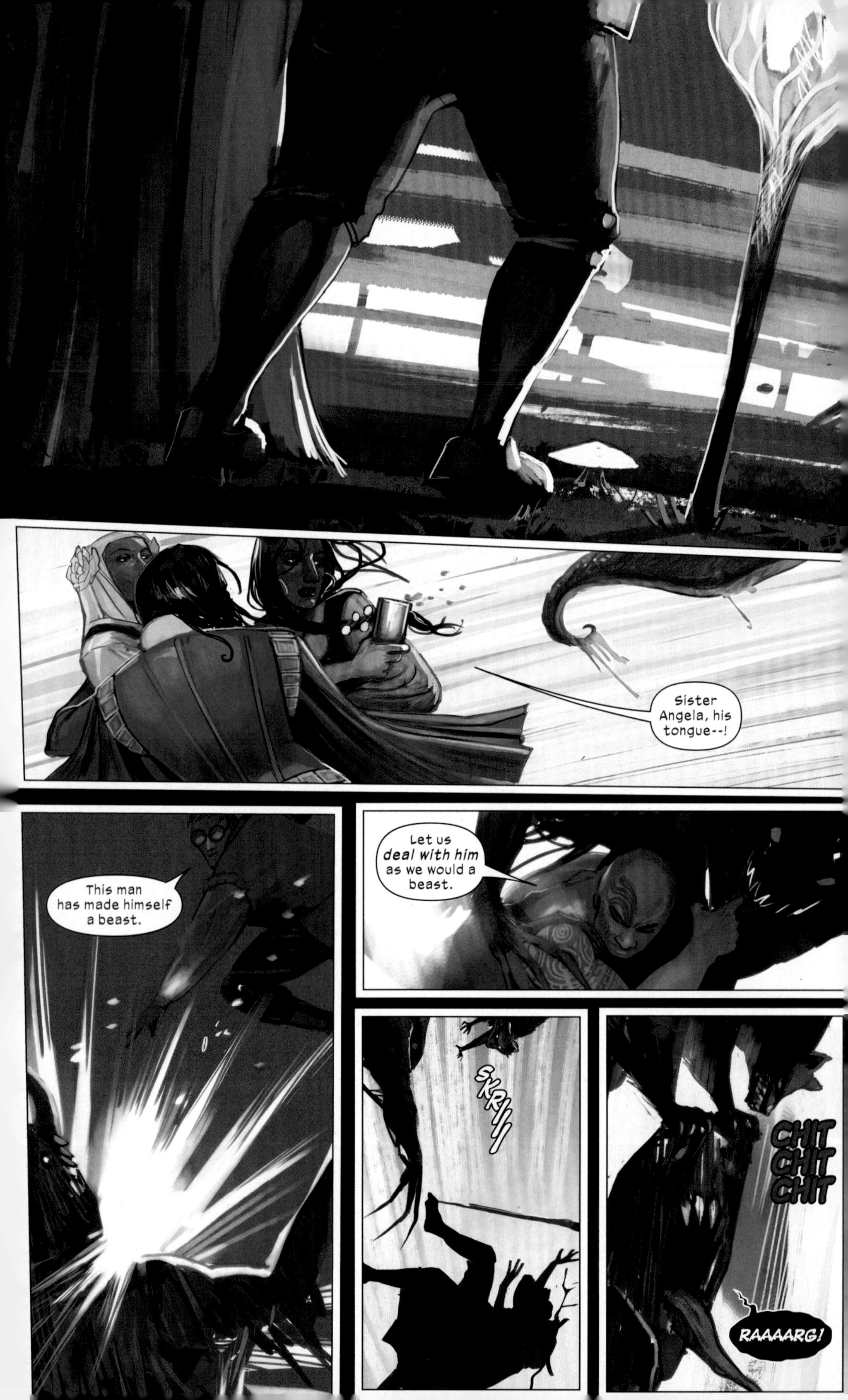
Sister Angela, his tongue--!
This man has made himself a beast.
Let us deal with him as we would a beast.
SKRIII
CHIT CHIT CHIT
RAAAARG!

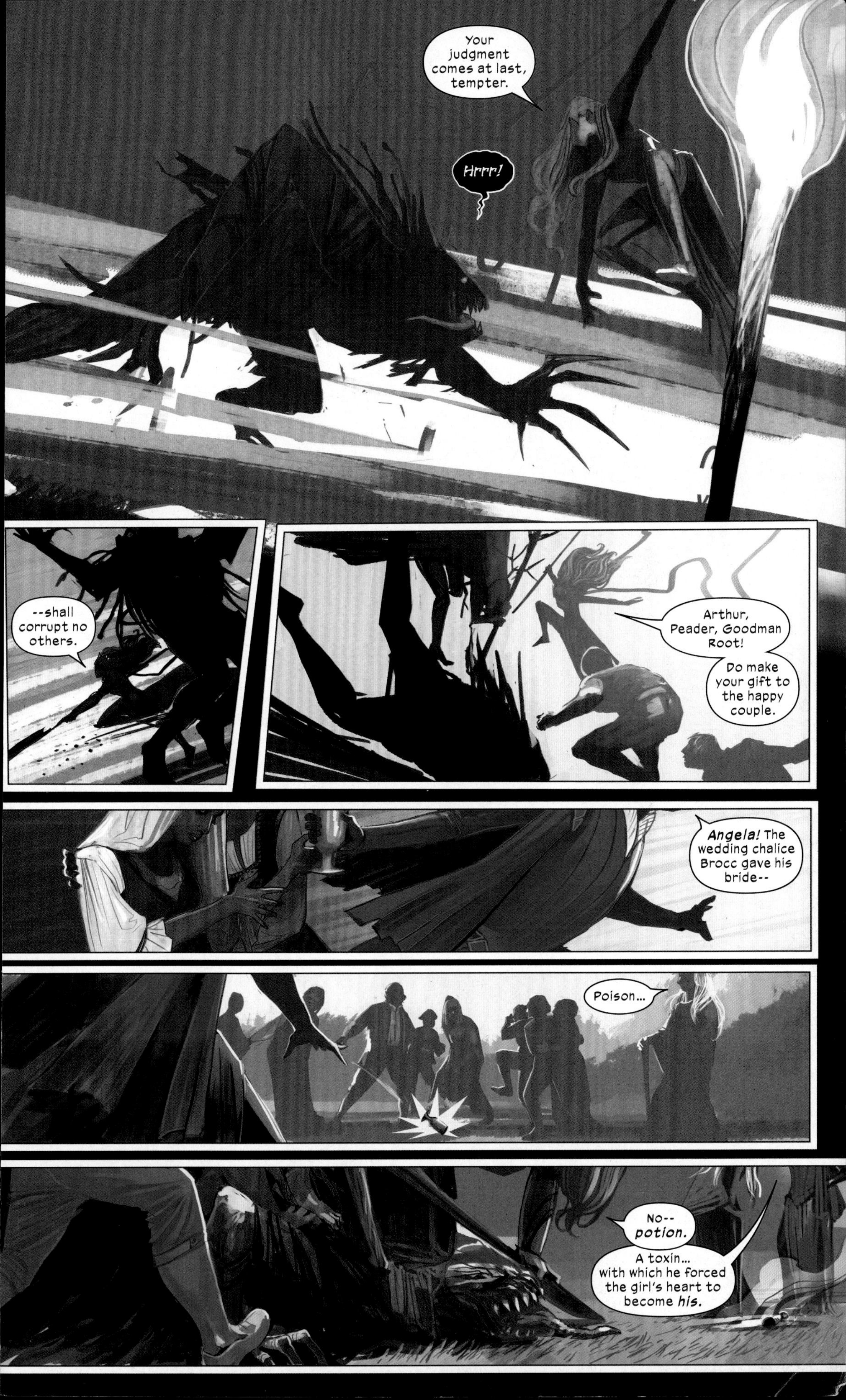
Your judgment comes at last, tempter.
Hrrr!
--shall corrupt no others.
Arthur, Peader, Goodman Root!
Do make your gift to the happy couple.
Angela! The wedding chalice Brocc gave his bride--
Poison...
No-- potion.
A toxin... with which he forced the girl's heart to become his.

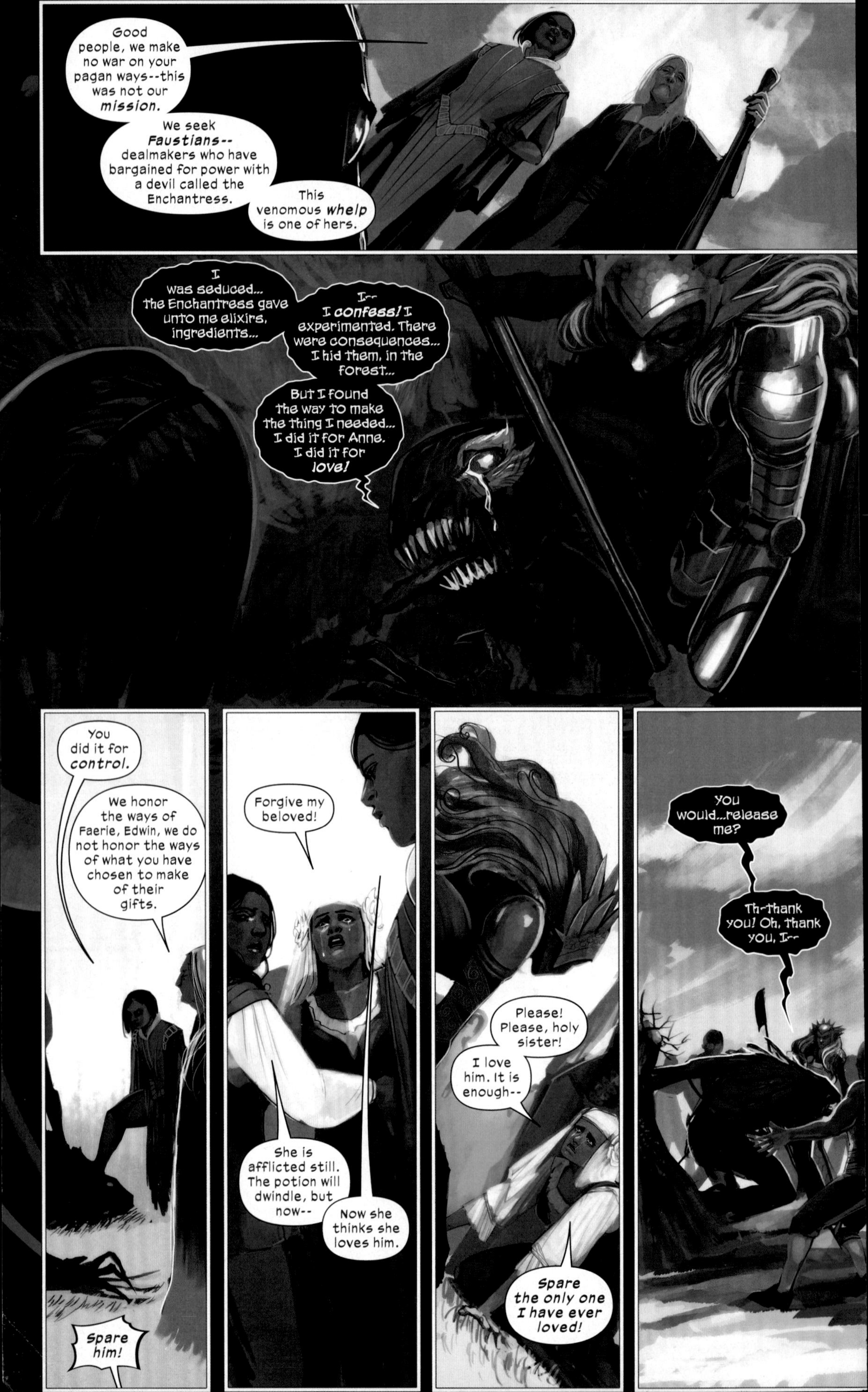

Good people, we make no war on your pagan ways--this was not our *mission.*
We seek ***Faustians--*** dealmakers who have bargained for power with a devil called the Enchantress.
This venomous ***whelp*** is one of hers.
I was seduced... the Enchantress gave unto me elixirs, ingredients...
I-- I ***confess!*** I experimented. There were consequences... I hid them, in the forest...
But I found the way to make the thing I needed... I did it for Anne. I did it for ***love!***
You did it for ***control.***
We honor the ways of Faerie, Edwin, we do not honor the ways of what you have chosen to make of their gifts.
Spare him!
Forgive my beloved!
She is afflicted still. The potion will dwindle, but now--
Now she thinks she loves him.
Please! Please, holy sister!
I love him. It is enough--
Spare the only one I have ever loved!
You would...release me?
Th-thank you! Oh, thank you, I--

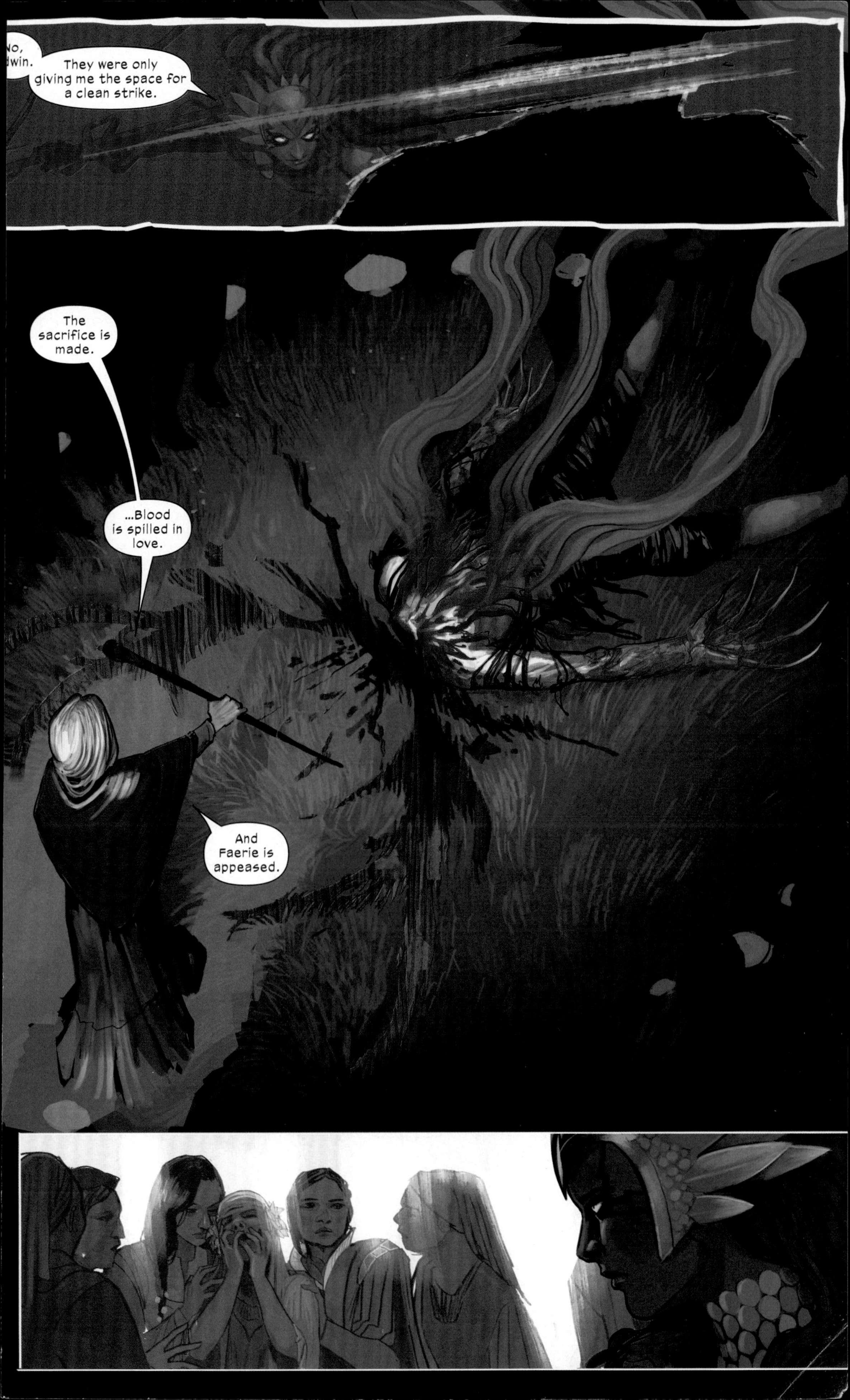
No,
dwin.
They were only giving me the space for a clean strike.
The sacrifice is made.
...Blood is spilled in love.
And Faerie is appeased.

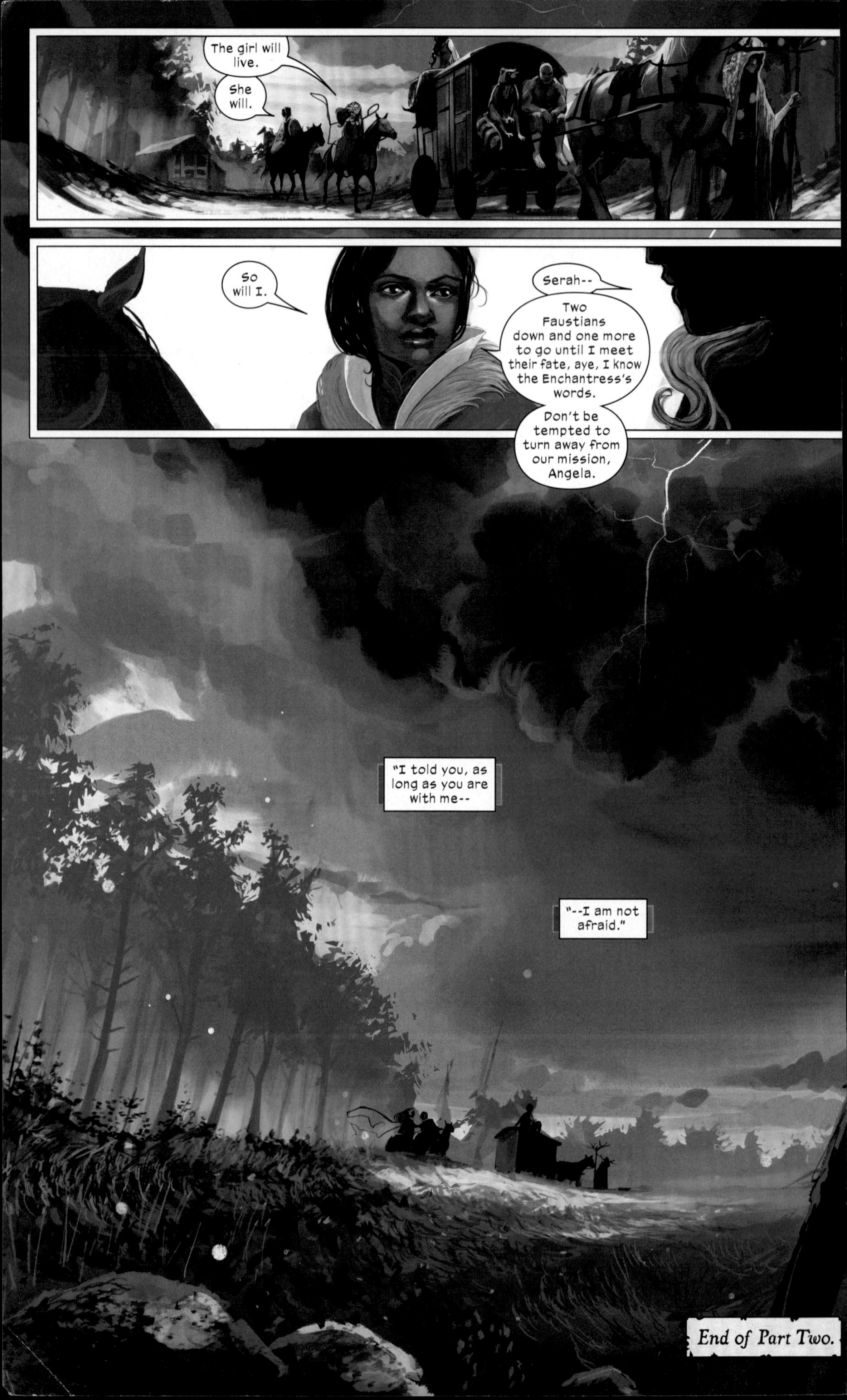

The girl will live.
She will.
So will I.
Serah--
Two Faustians down and one more to go until I meet their fate, aye, I know the Enchantress's words.
Don't be tempted to turn away from our mission, Angela.
"I told you, as long as you are with me--
"--I am not afraid."
End of Part Two.

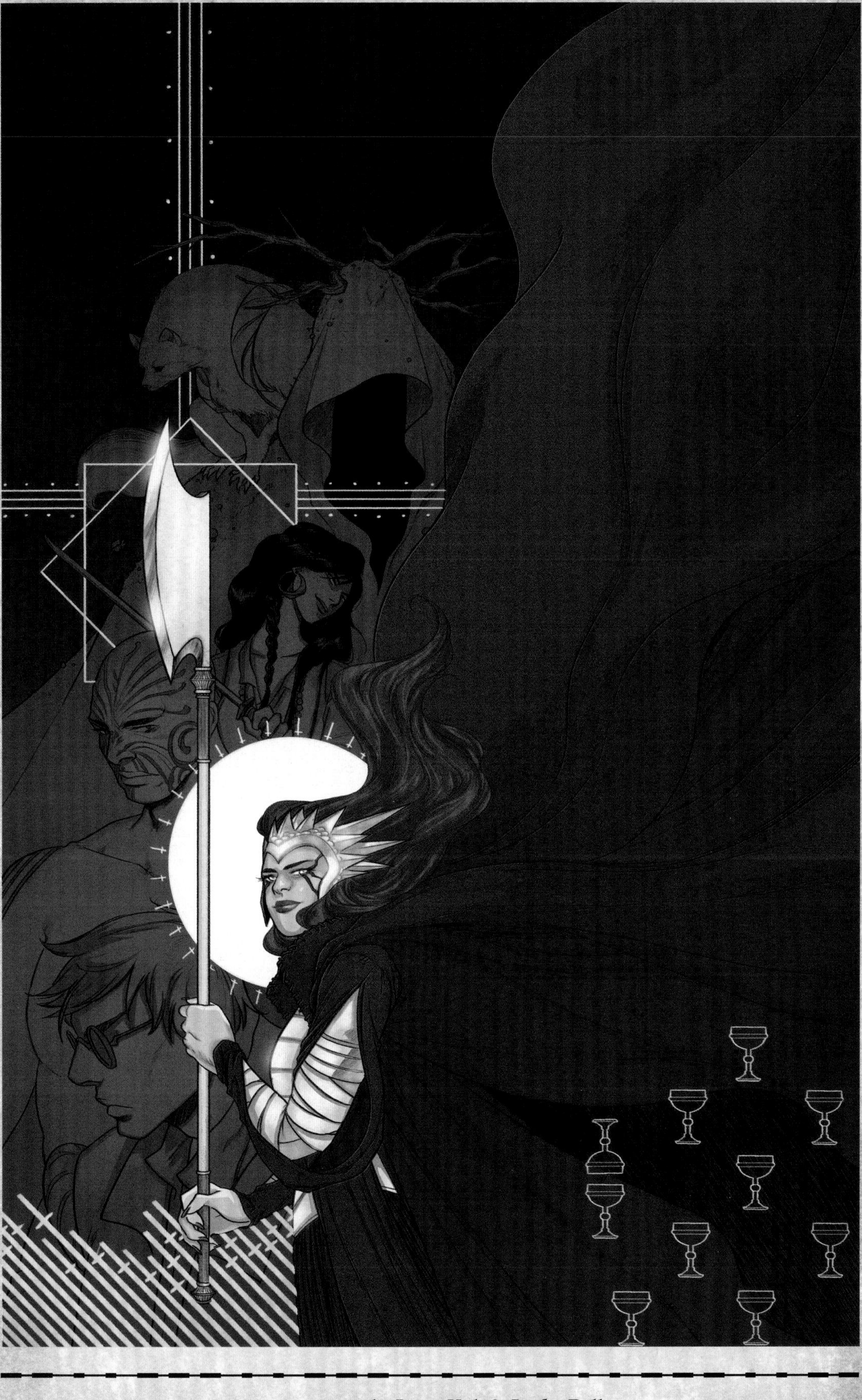

#2 variant cover by Irene Koh & Jordie Bellaire

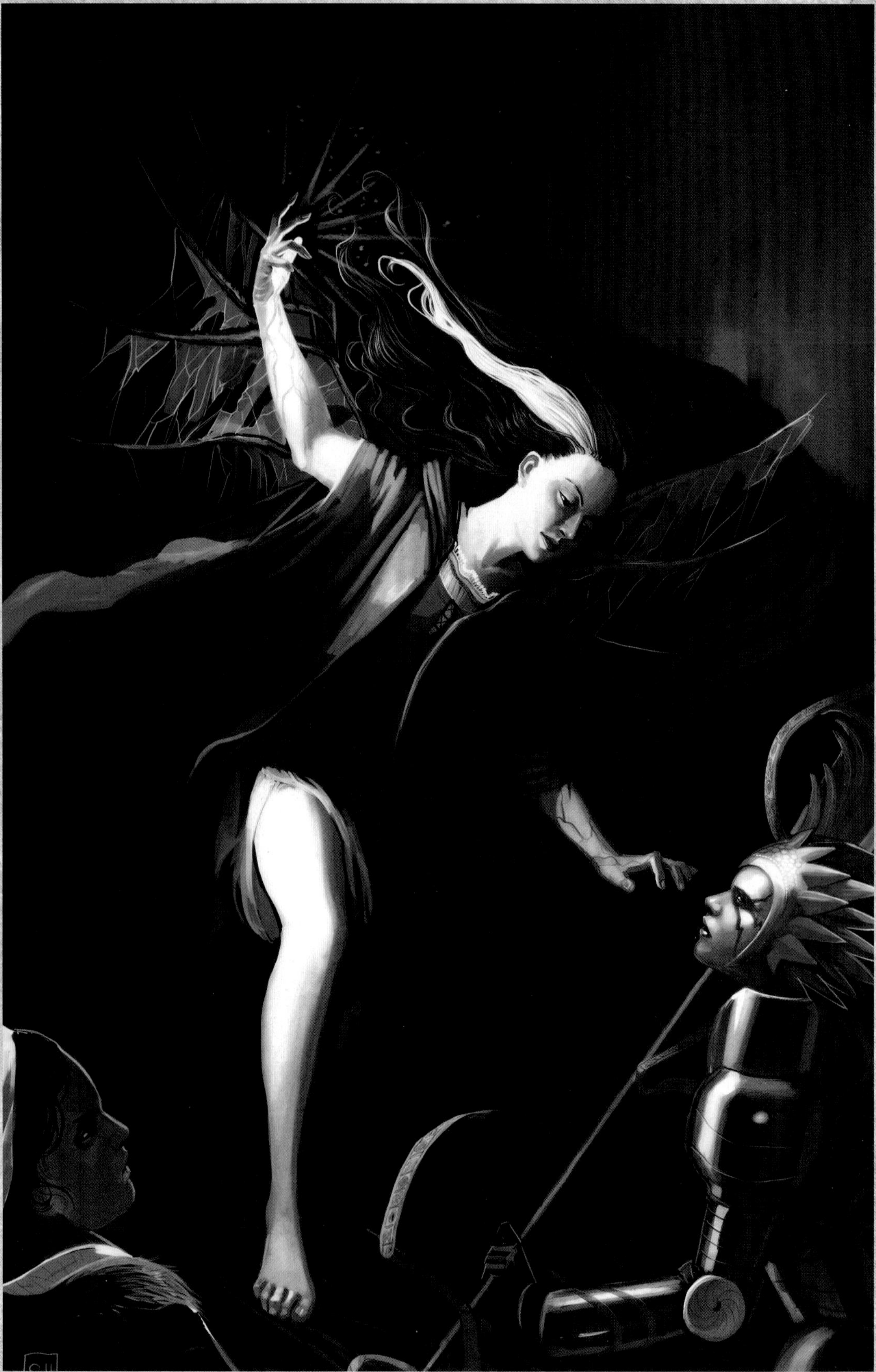

Part Three, In Which Hearts Rend and Heads Roll

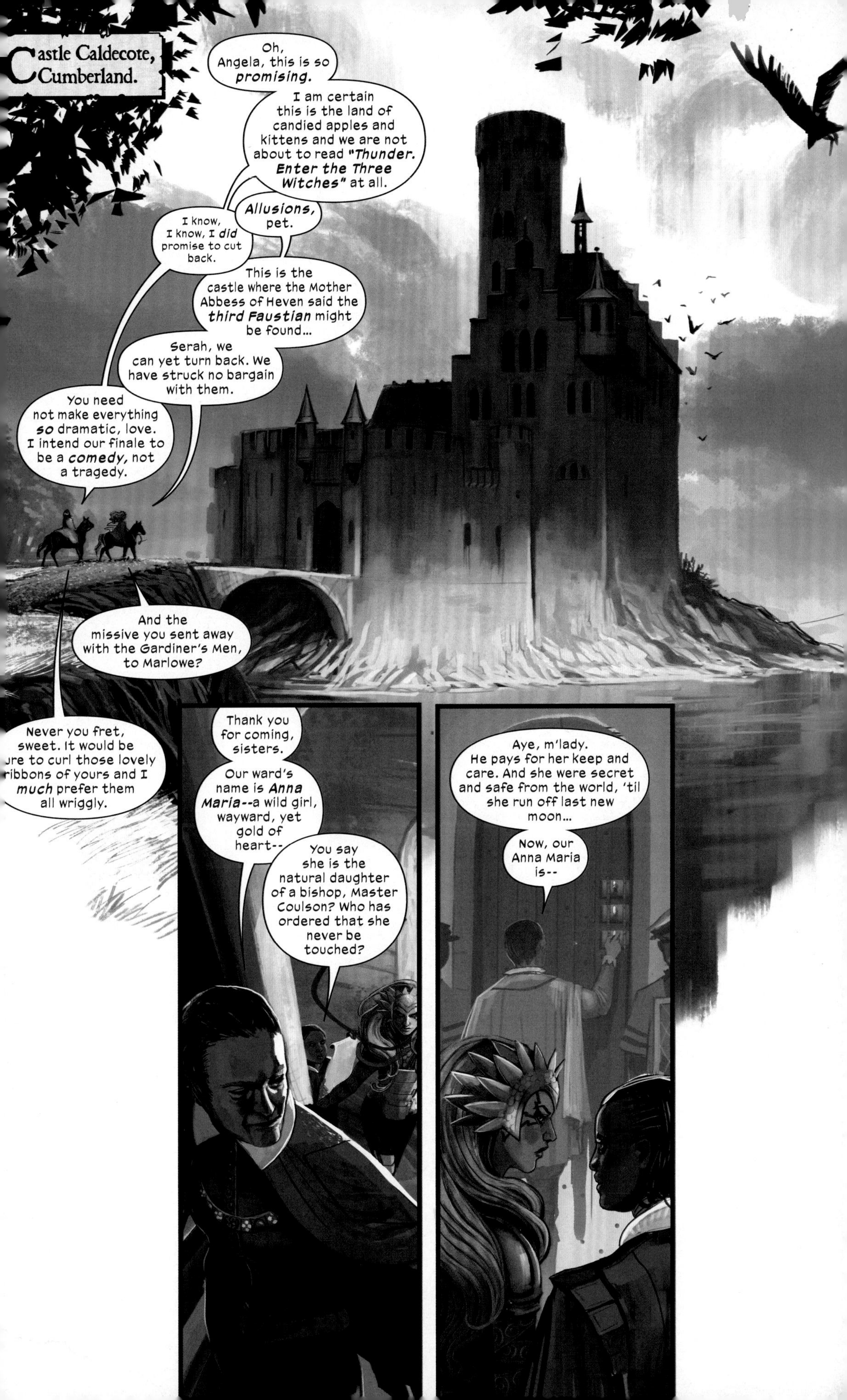

Castle Caldecote, Cumberland.
Oh, Angela, this is so promising.
I am certain this is the land of candied apples and kittens and we are not about to read "Thunder. Enter the Three Witches" at all.
Allusions, pet.
I know, I know, I did promise to cut back.
This is the castle where the Mother Abbess of Heven said the third Faustian might be found...
Serah, we can yet turn back. We have struck no bargain with them.
You need not make everything so dramatic, love. I intend our finale to be a comedy, not a tragedy.
And the missive you sent away with the Gardiner's Men, to Marlowe?
Never you fret, sweet. It would be ure to curl those lovely ribbons of yours and I much prefer them all wriggly.
Thank you for coming, sisters.
Our ward's name is Anna Maria--a wild girl, wayward, yet gold of heart--
You say she is the natural daughter of a bishop, Master Coulson? Who has ordered that she never be touched?
Aye, m'lady. He pays for her keep and care. And she were secret and safe from the world, 'til she run off last new moon...
Now, our Anna Maria is--

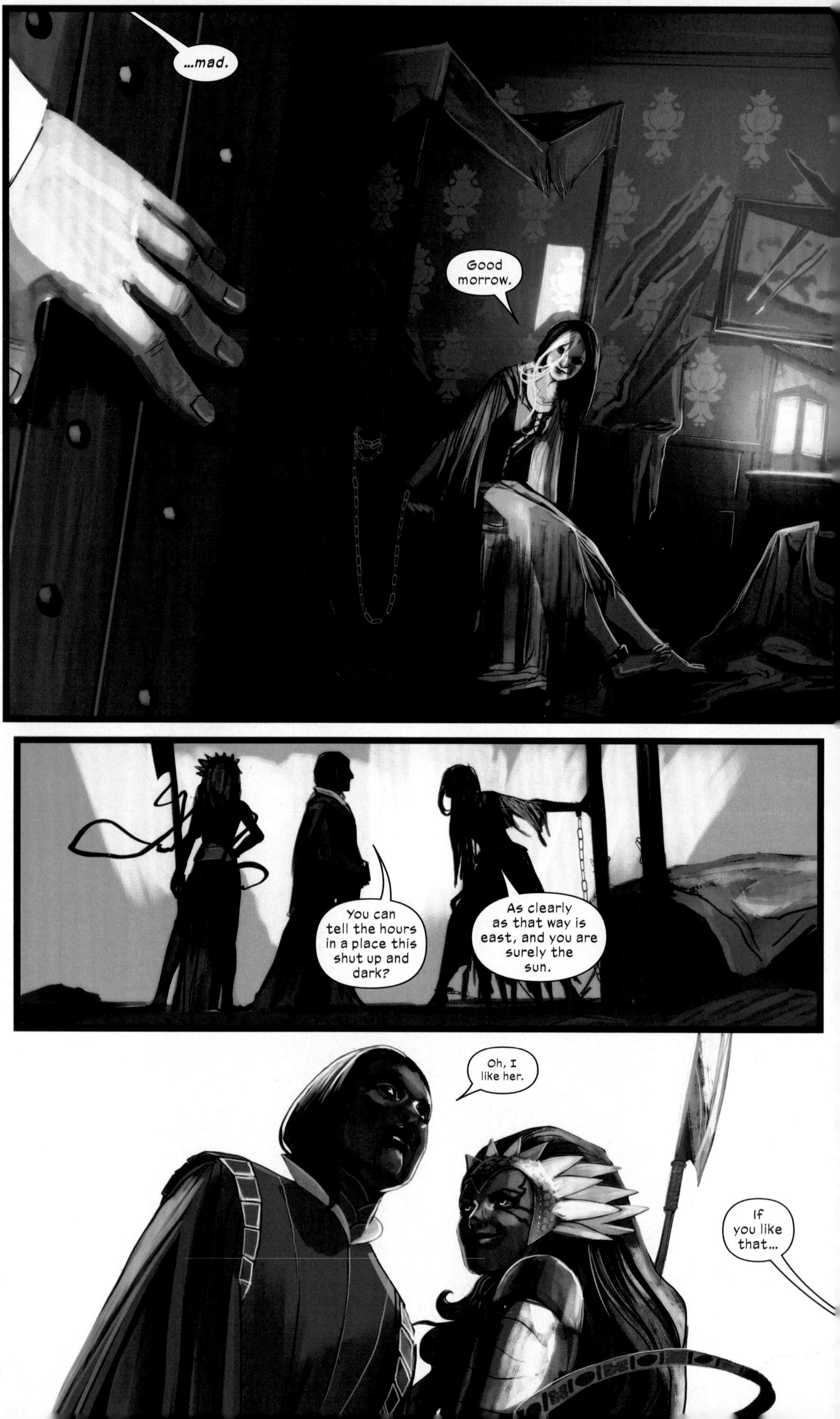
...mad.
Good morrow.
You can tell the hours in a place this shut up and dark?
As clearly as that way is east, and you are surely the sun.
Oh, I like her.
If you like that...

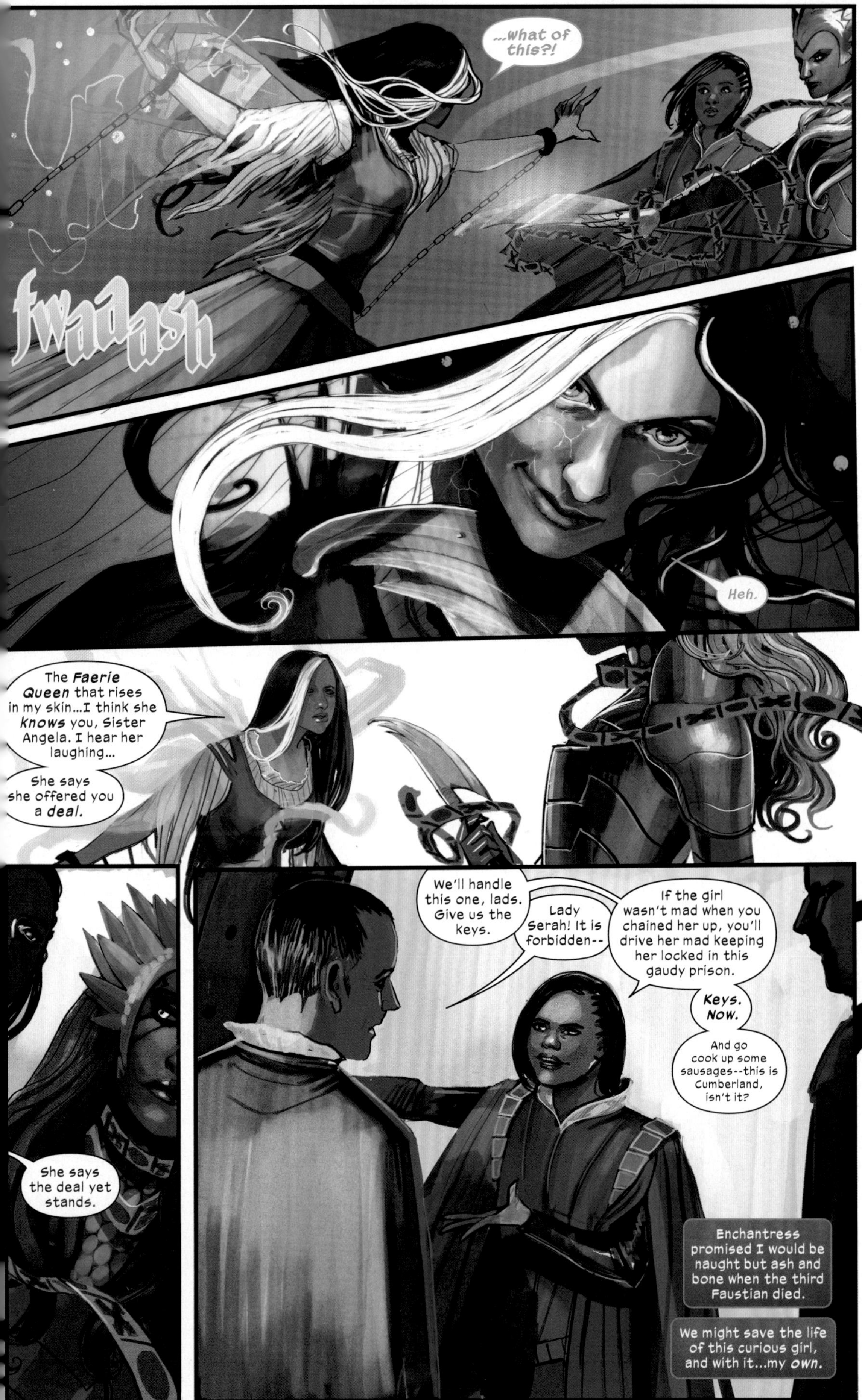
...what of this?!
fwaaash
Heh.
The Faerie Queen that rises in my skin...I think she knows you, Sister Angela. I hear her laughing...
She says she offered you a deal.
She says the deal yet stands.
We'll handle this one, lads. Give us the keys.
Lady Serah! It is forbidden--
If the girl wasn't mad when you chained her up, you'll drive her mad keeping her locked in this gaudy prison.
Keys. Now.
And go cook up some sausages--this is Cumberland, isn't it?
Enchantress promised I would be naught but ash and bone when the third Faustian died.
We might save the life of this curious girl, and with it...my own.

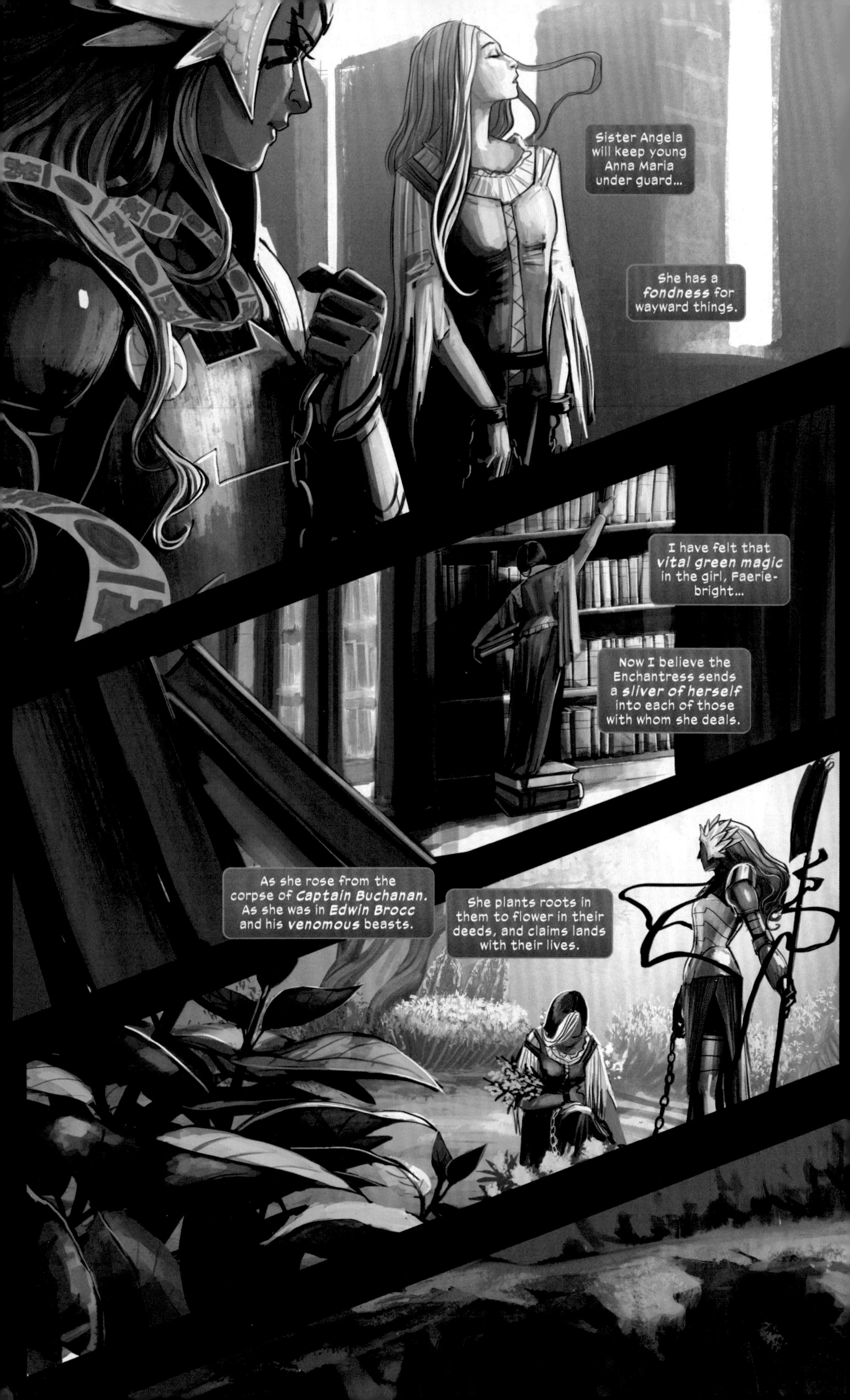
Sister Angela will keep young Anna Maria under guard...
She has a *fondness* for wayward things.
I have felt that *vital green magic* in the girl, Faerie-bright...
Now I believe the Enchantress sends a *sliver of herself* into each of those with whom she deals.
As she rose from the corpse of *Captain Buchanan*. As she was in *Edwin Brocc* and his *venomous* beasts.
She plants roots in them to flower in their deeds, and claims lands with their lives.

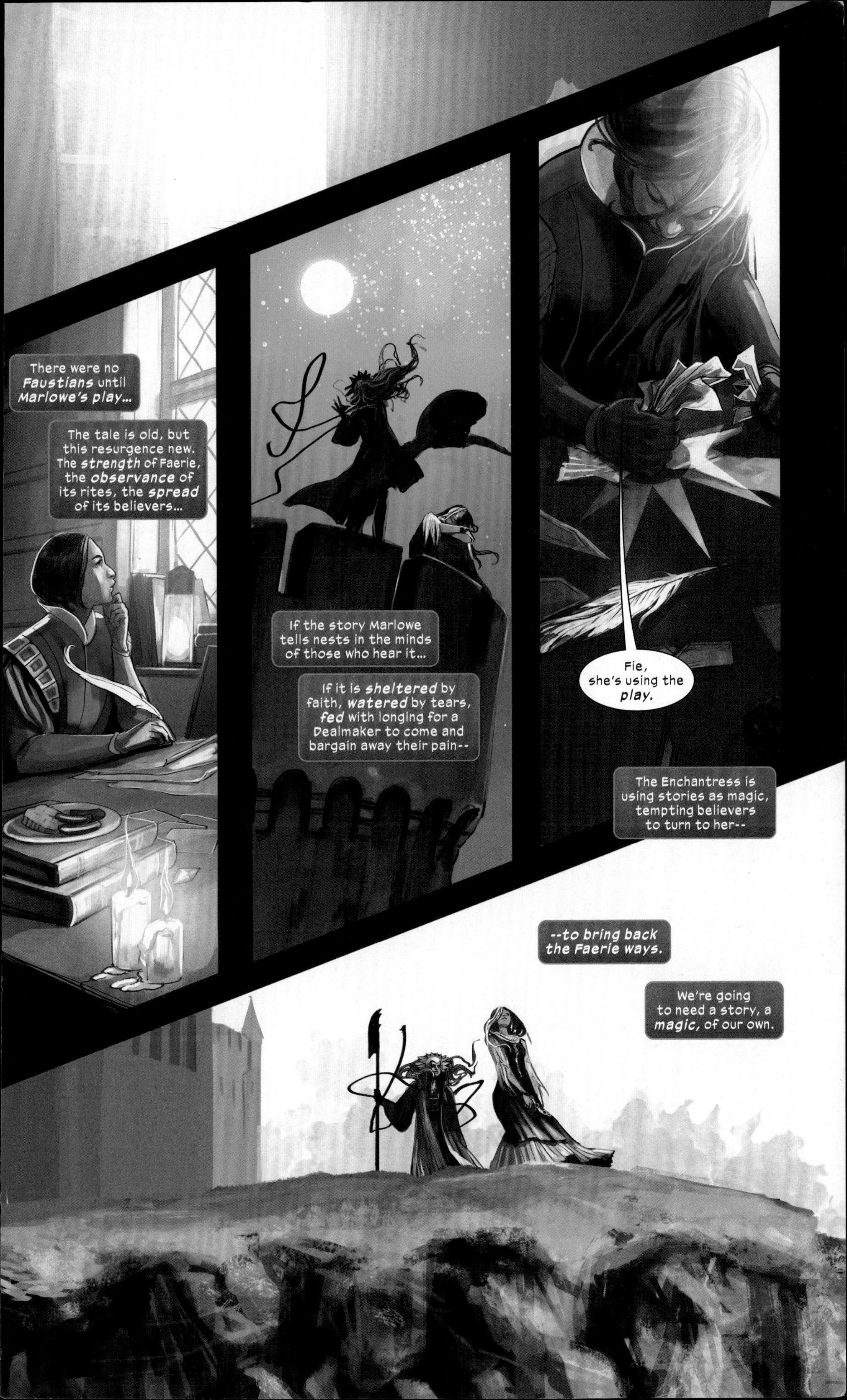
There were no *Faustians* until *Marlowe's play*...
The tale is old, but this resurgence new. The *strength* of Faerie, the *observance* of its rites, the *spread* of its believers...
If the story Marlowe tells nests in the minds of those who hear it...
If it is *sheltered* by faith, *watered* by tears, *fed* with longing for a Dealmaker to come and bargain away their pain--
Fie, she's using the *play.*
The Enchantress is using stories as magic, tempting believers to turn to her--
--to bring back the Faerie ways.
We're going to need a story, a *magic,* of our own.

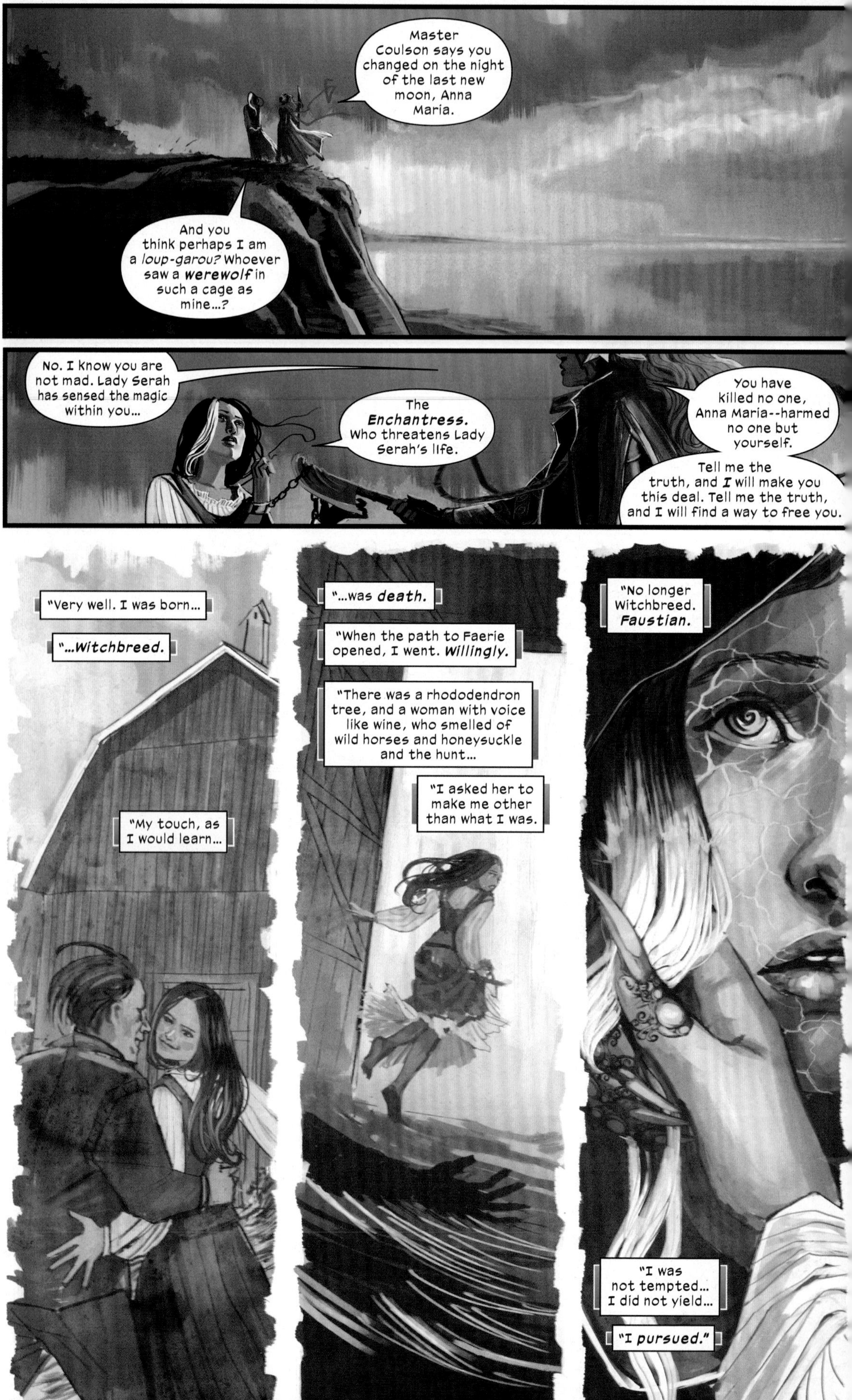
Master Coulson says you changed on the night of the last new moon, Anna Maria.
And you think perhaps I am a *loup-garou?* Whoever saw a ***werewolf*** in such a cage as mine...?
No. I know you are not mad. Lady Serah has sensed the magic within you...
The ***Enchantress.*** Who threatens Lady Serah's life.
You have killed no one, Anna Maria--harmed no one but yourself.
Tell me the truth, and ***I*** will make you this deal. Tell me the truth, and I will find a way to free you.
"Very well. I was born...
"...***Witchbreed.***
"My touch, as I would learn...
"...was ***death.***
"When the path to Faerie opened, I went. ***Willingly.***
"There was a rhododendron tree, and a woman with voice like wine, who smelled of wild horses and honeysuckle and the hunt...
"I asked her to make me other than what I was.
"No longer Witchbreed. ***Faustian.***
"I was not tempted... I did not yield...
"I ***pursued.***"

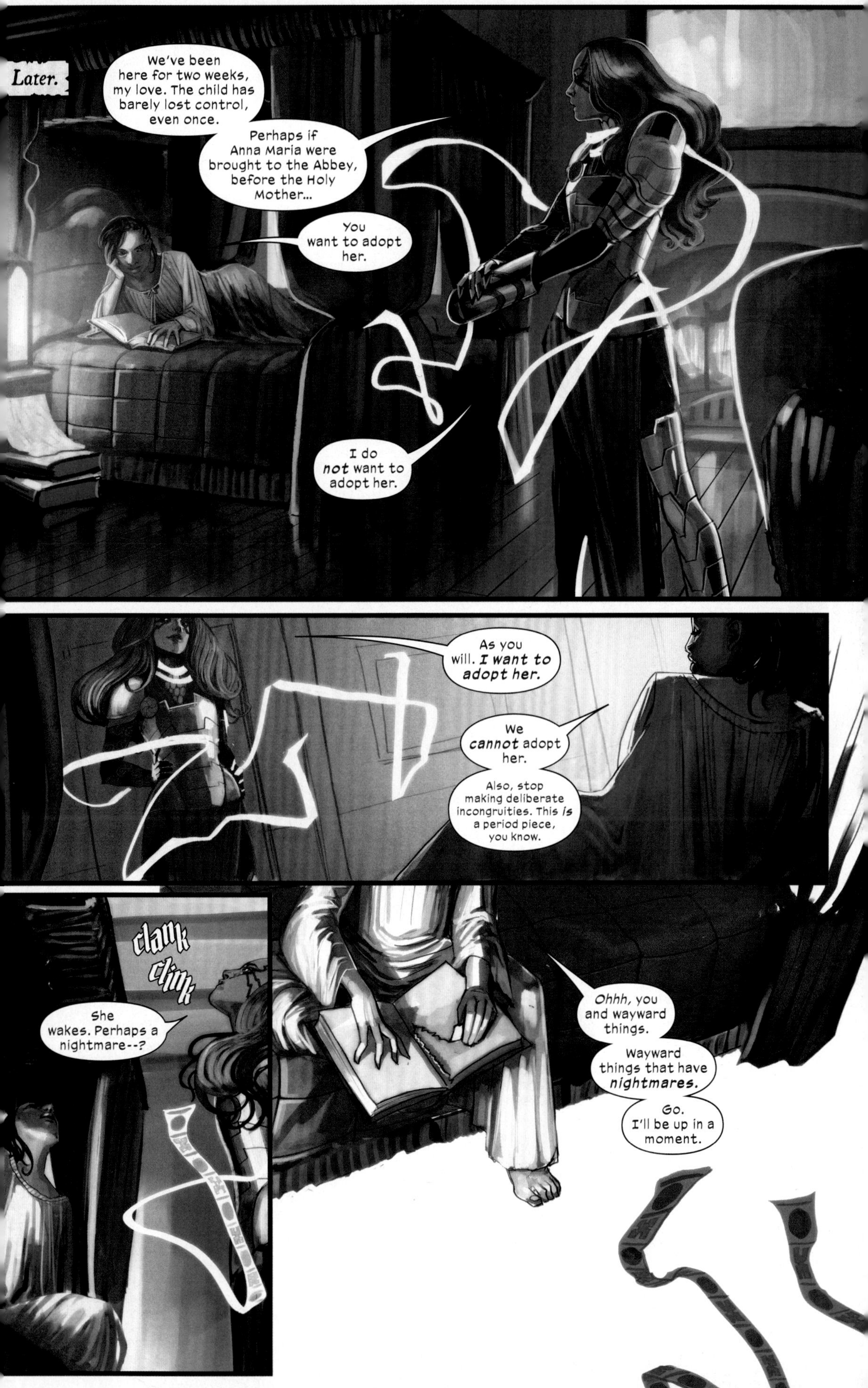
Later.
We've been here for two weeks, my love. The child has barely lost control, even once.
Perhaps if Anna Maria were brought to the Abbey, before the Holy Mother...
You want to adopt her.
I do *not* want to adopt her.
As you will. ***I want to adopt her.***
We *cannot* adopt her.
Also, stop making deliberate incongruities. This *is* a period piece, you know.
clank
clink
She wakes. Perhaps a nightmare--?
Ohhh, you and wayward things.
Wayward things that have ***nightmares.***
Go. I'll be up in a moment.

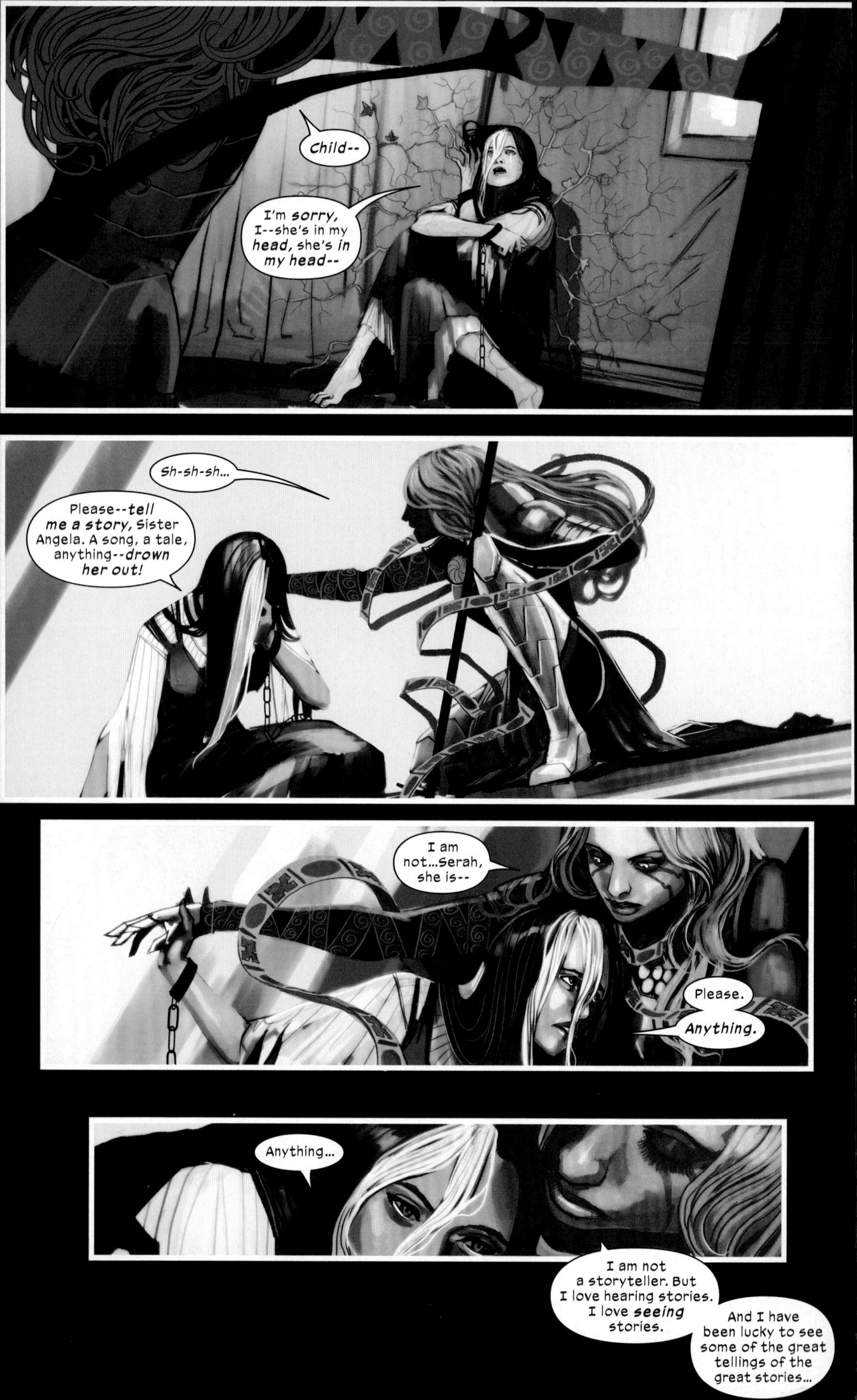

Child--
I'm sorry, I--she's in my head, she's in my head--
Sh-sh-sh...
Please--tell me a story, Sister Angela. A song, a tale, anything--drown her out!
I am not...Serah, she is--
Please.
Anything.
Anything...
I am not a storyteller. But I love hearing stories. I love seeing stories.
And I have been lucky to see some of the great tellings of the great stories...

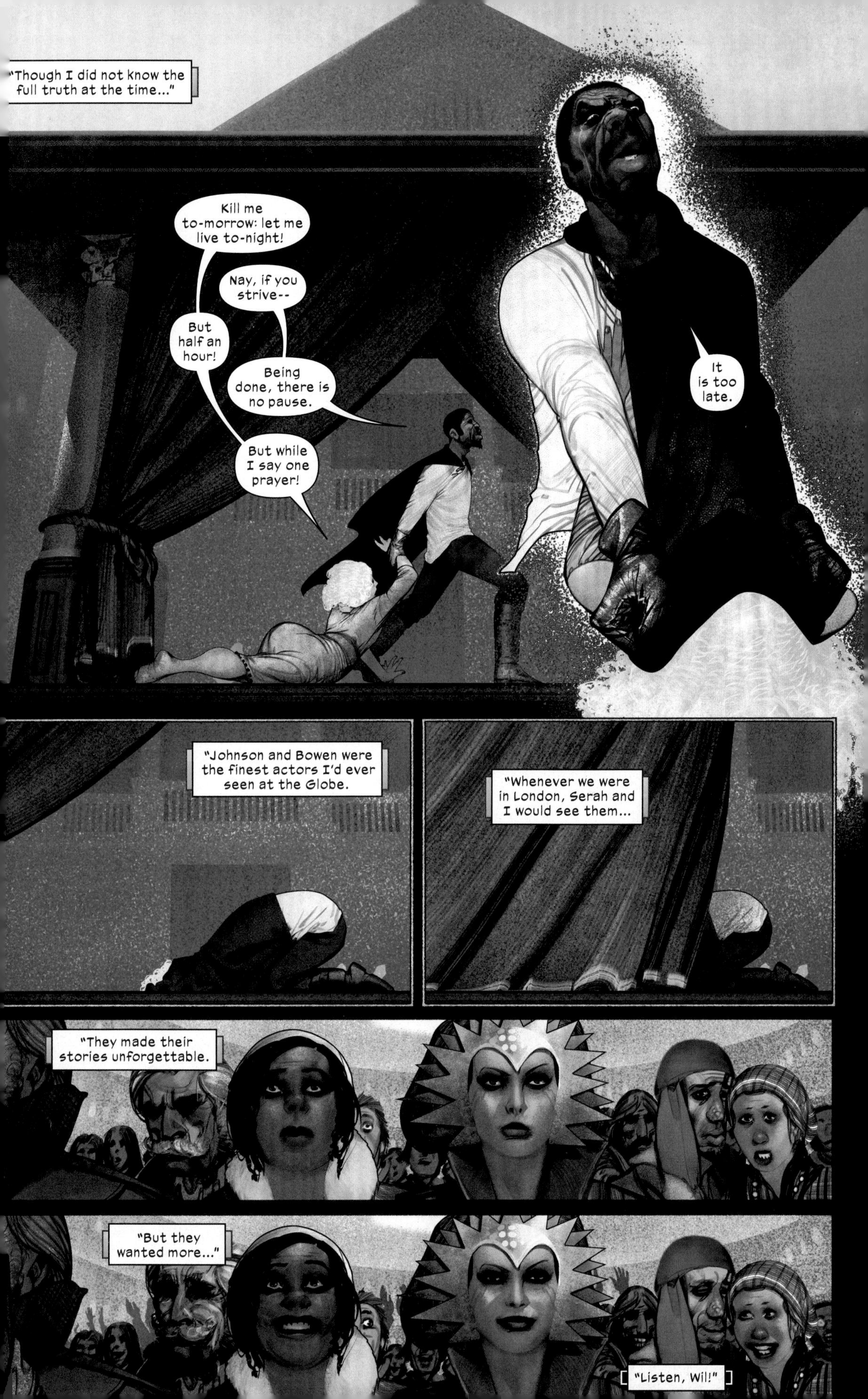
"Though I did not know the full truth at the time..."
Kill me to-morrow: let me live to-night!
Nay, if you strive--
But half an hour!
Being done, there is no pause.
But while I say one prayer!
It is too late.
"Johnson and Bowen were the finest actors I'd ever seen at the Globe.
"Whenever we were in London, Serah and I would see them...
"They made their stories unforgettable.
"But they wanted more..."
"Listen, Wil!"

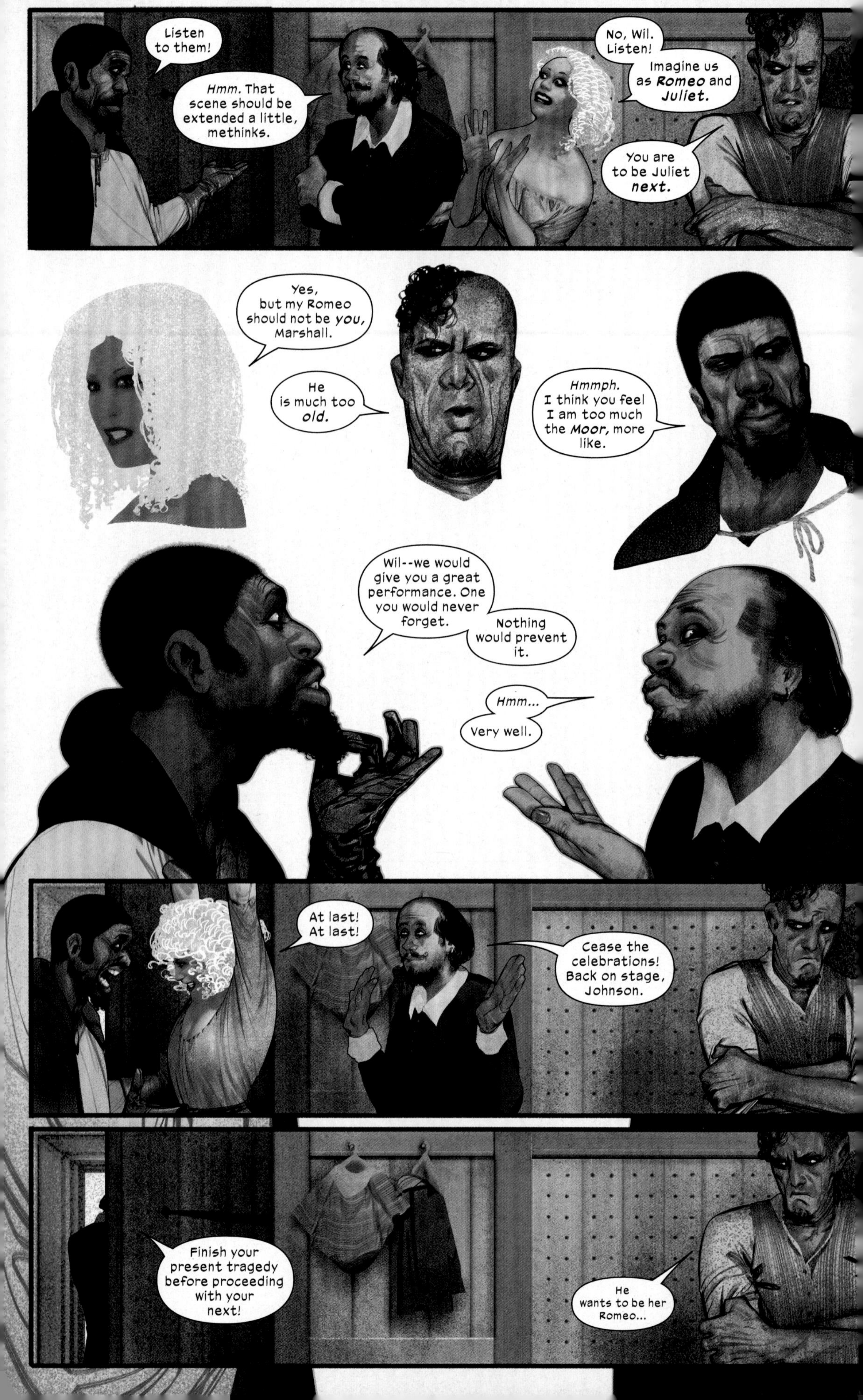
Listen to them!
Hmm. That scene should be extended a little, methinks.
No, Wil. Listen!
Imagine us as Romeo and Juliet.
You are to be Juliet next.
Yes, but my Romeo should not be you, Marshall.
He is much too old.
Hmmph. I think you feel I am too much the Moor, more like.
Wil--we would give you a great performance. One you would never forget.
Nothing would prevent it.
Hmm...
Very well.
At last! At last!
Cease the celebrations! Back on stage, Johnson.
Finish your present tragedy before proceeding with your next!
He wants to be her Romeo...

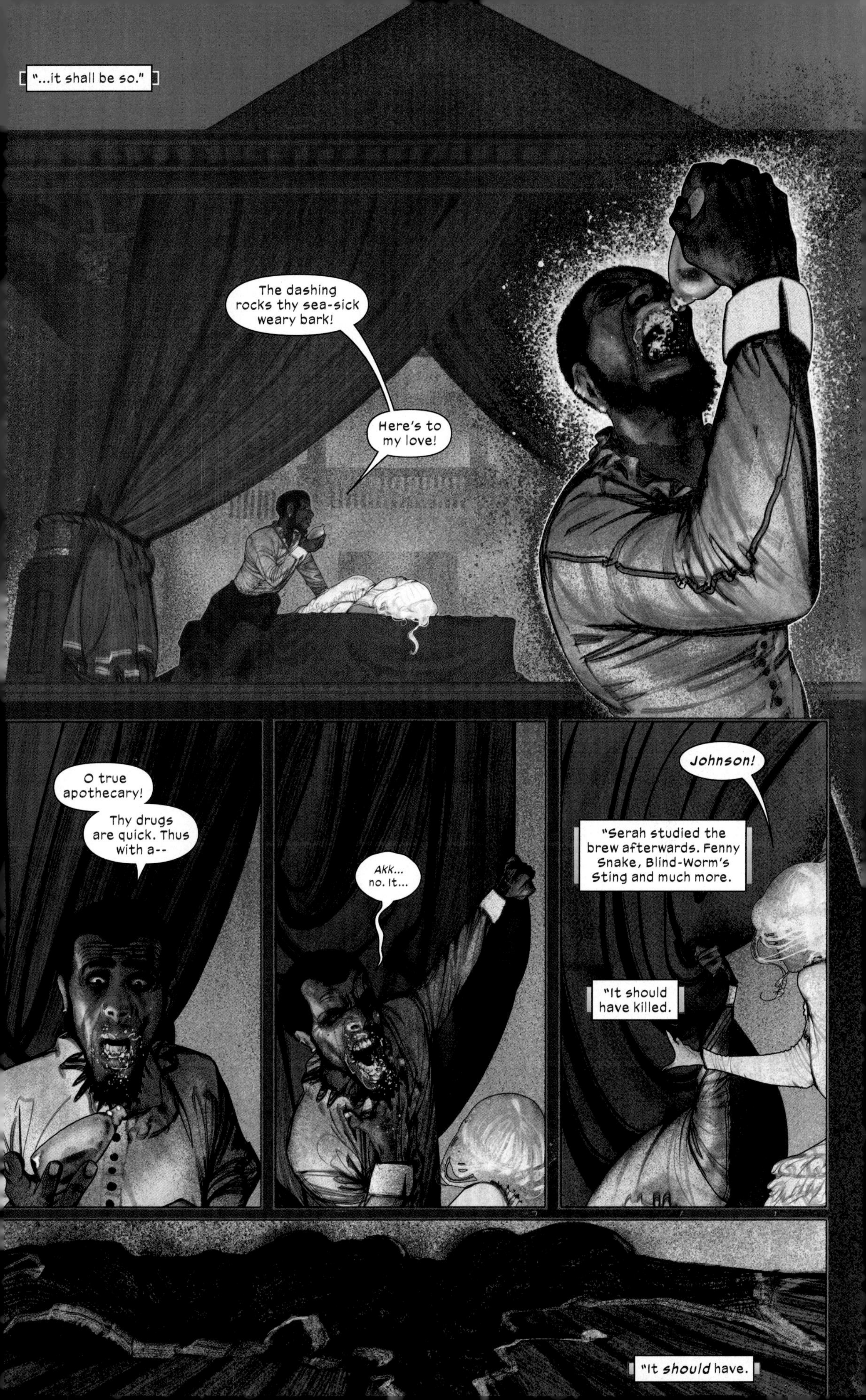
"...it shall be so."
The dashing rocks thy sea-sick weary bark!
Here's to my love!
O true apothecary!
Thy drugs are quick. Thus with a--
Akk... no. It...
Johnson!
"Serah studied the brew afterwards. Fenny Snake, Blind-Worm's Sting and much more.
"It should have killed.
"It *should* have.

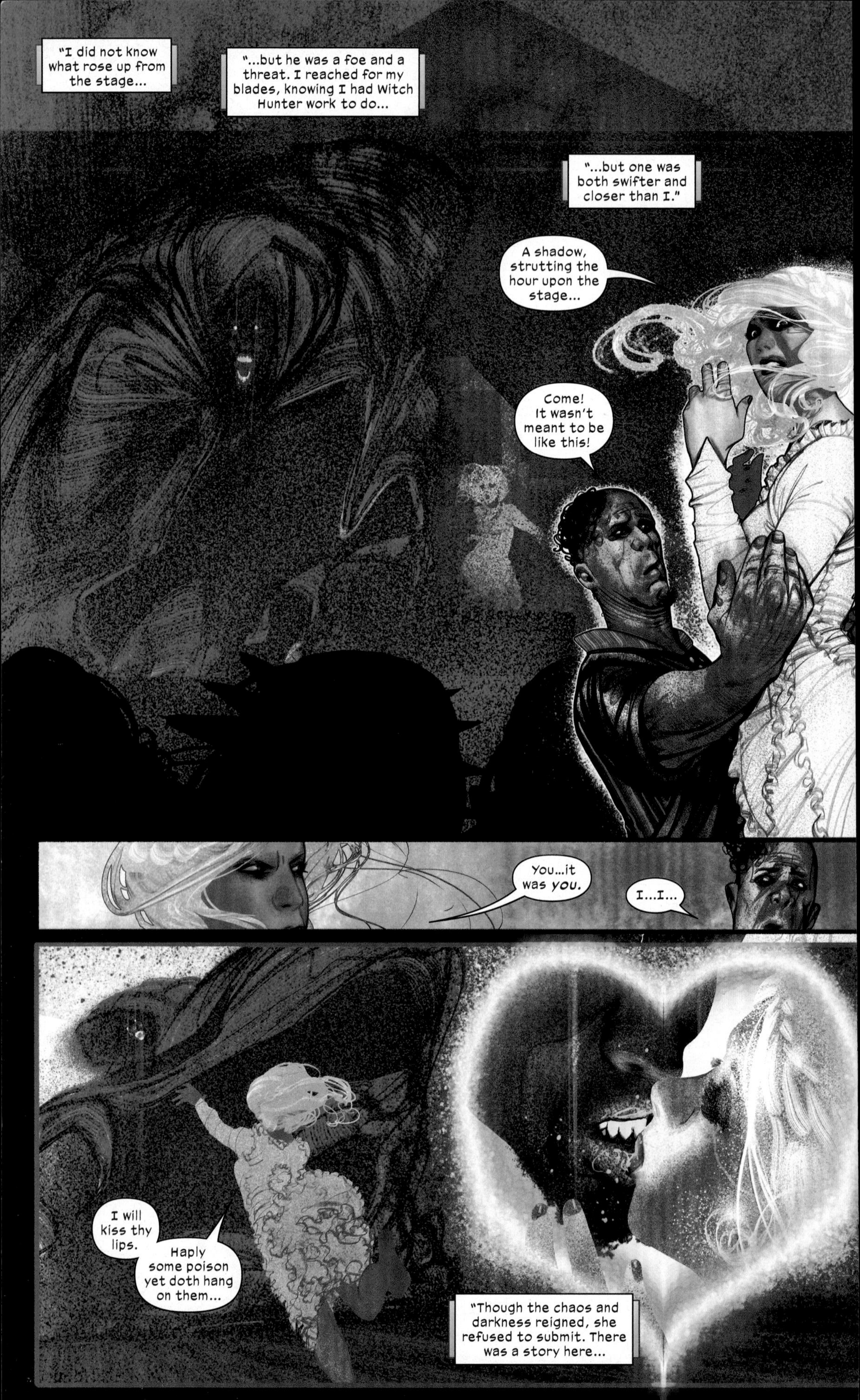
"I did not know what rose up from the stage...
"...but he was a foe and a threat. I reached for my blades, knowing I had Witch Hunter work to do...
"...but one was both swifter and closer than I."
A shadow, strutting the hour upon the stage...
Come! It wasn't meant to be like this!
You...it was *you*.
I...I...
I will kiss thy lips.
Haply some poison yet doth hang on them...
"Though the chaos and darkness reigned, she refused to submit. There was a story here...

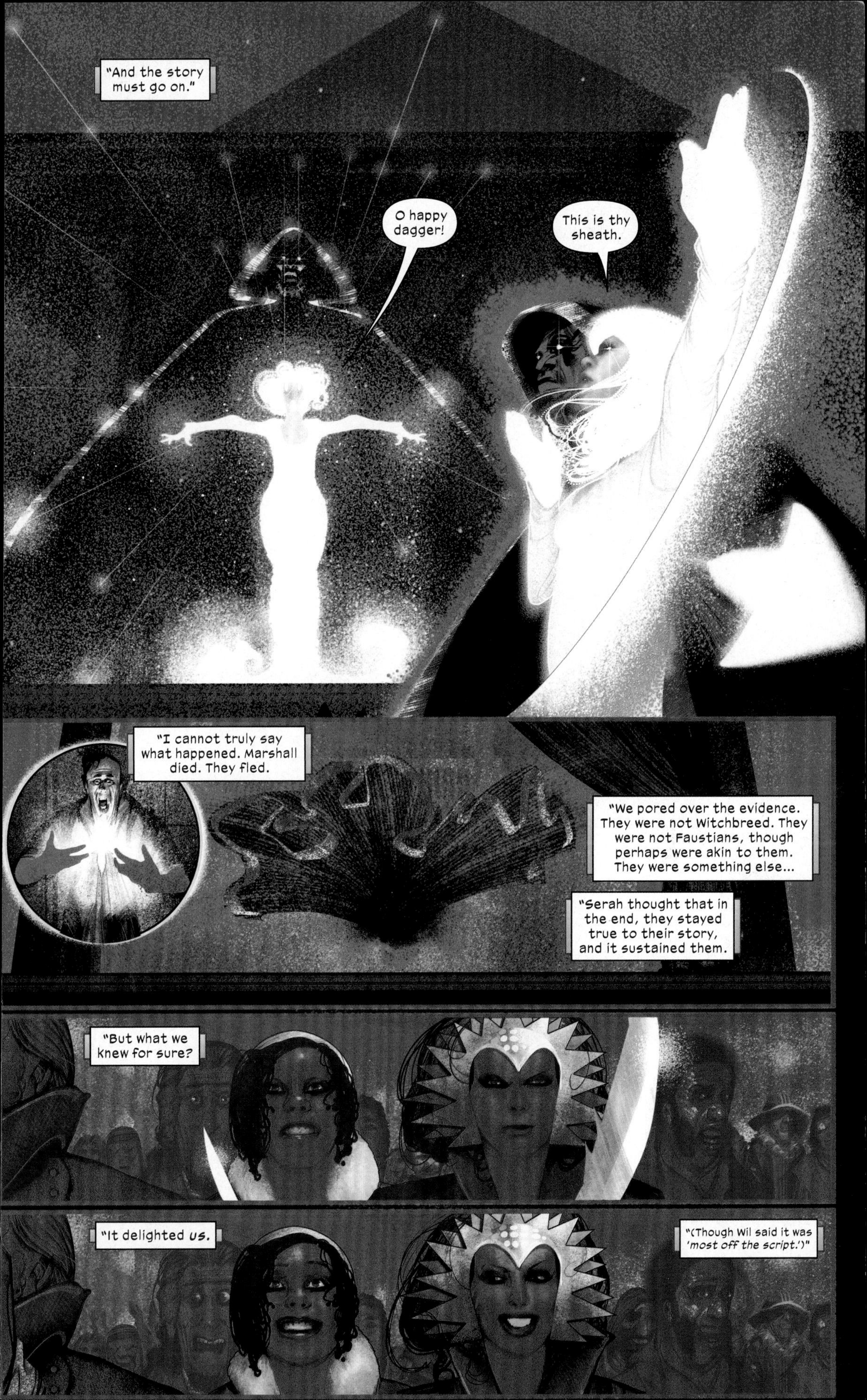
"And the story must go on."
O happy dagger!
This is thy sheath.
"I cannot truly say what happened. Marshall died. They fled.
"We pored over the evidence. They were not Witchbreed. They were not Faustians, though perhaps were akin to them. They were something else...
"Serah thought that in the end, they stayed true to their story, and it sustained them.
"But what we knew for sure?
"It delighted *us*.
"(Though Wil said it was *'most off the script.'*)"

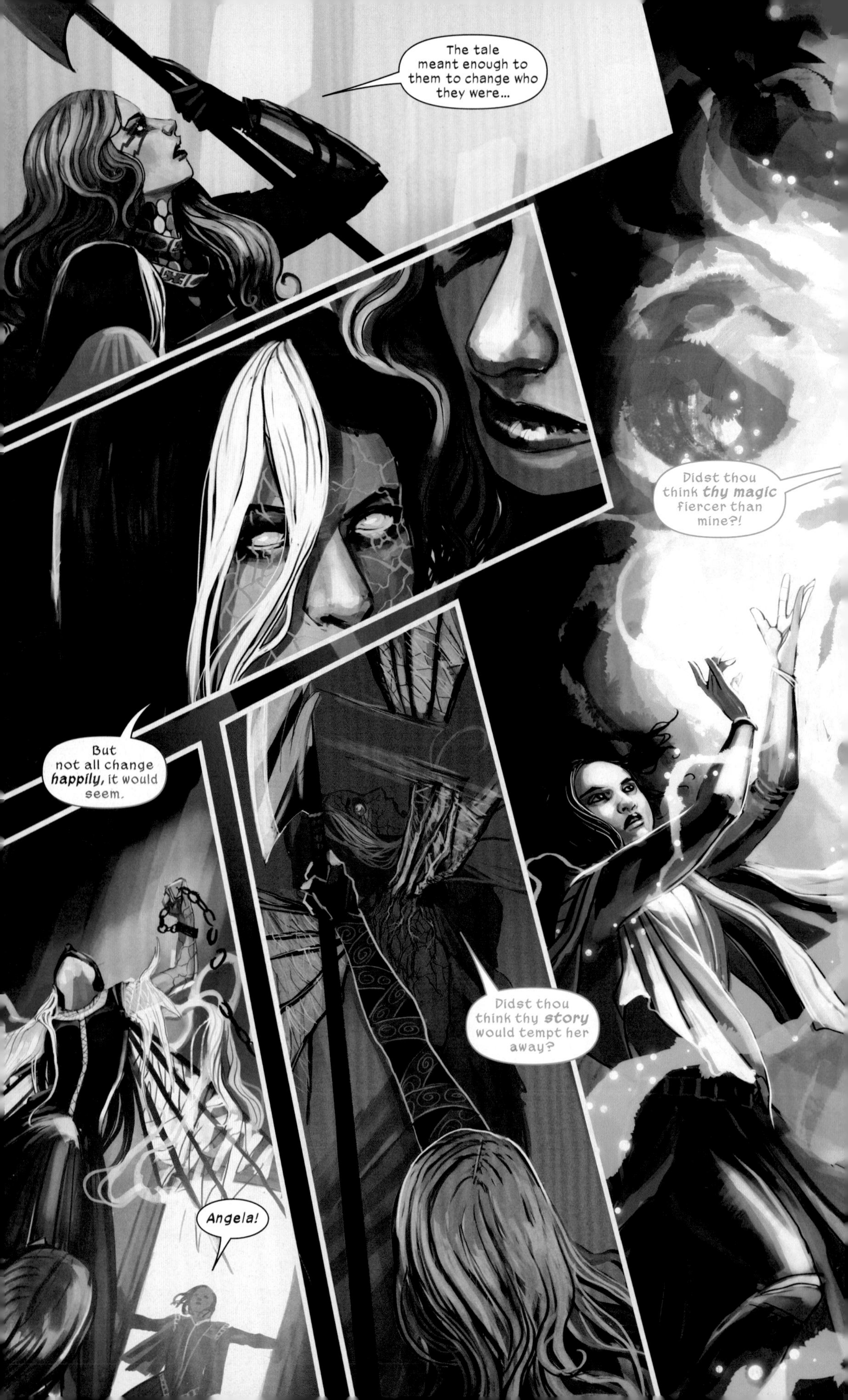

The tale meant enough to them to change who they were...
Didst thou think *thy magic* fiercer than mine?!
But not all change *happily,* it would seem.
Didst thou think thy *story* would tempt her away?
Angela!

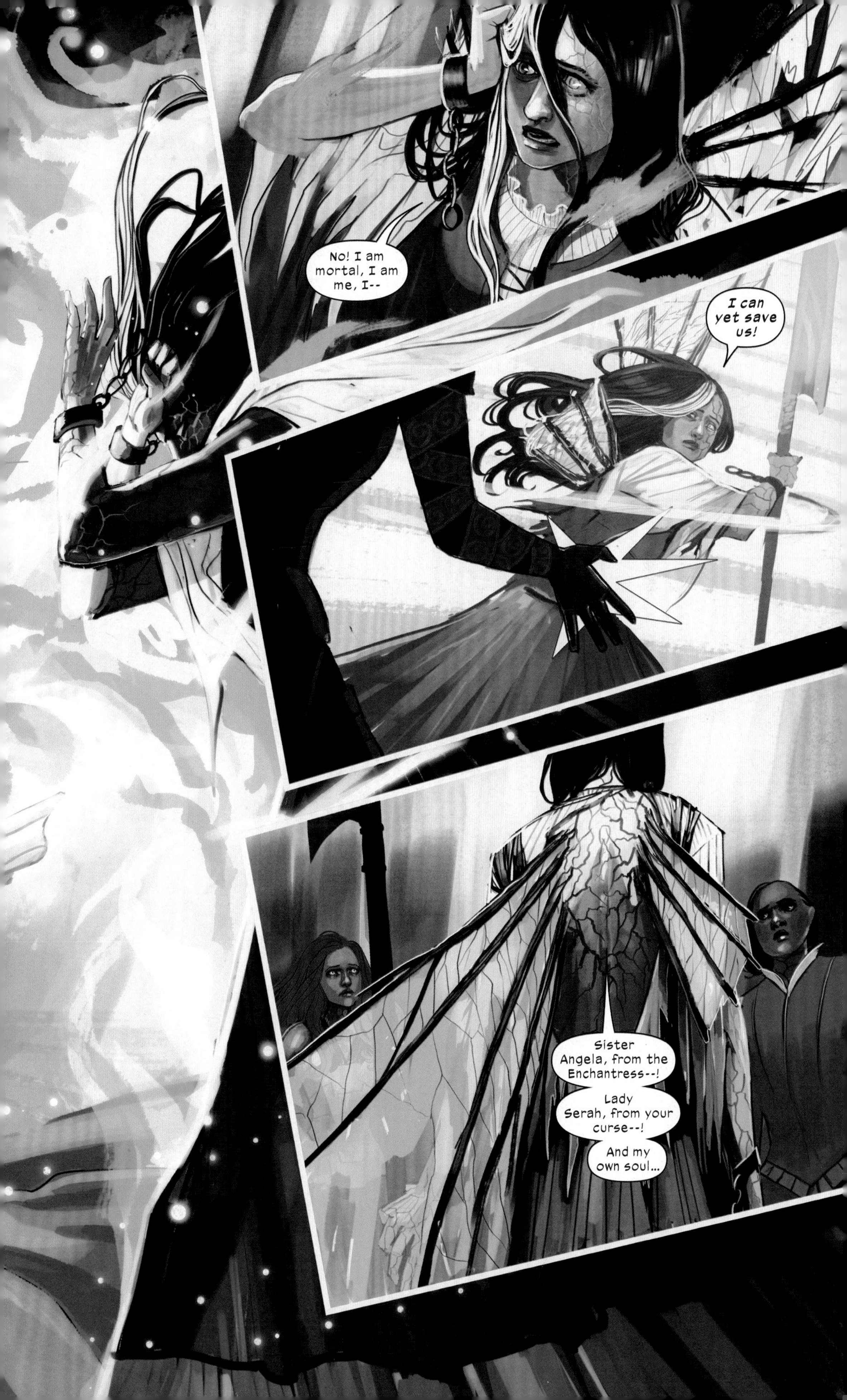
No! I am mortal, I am me, I--
I can yet save us!
Sister Angela, from the Enchantress--!
Lady Serah, from your curse--!
And my own soul...

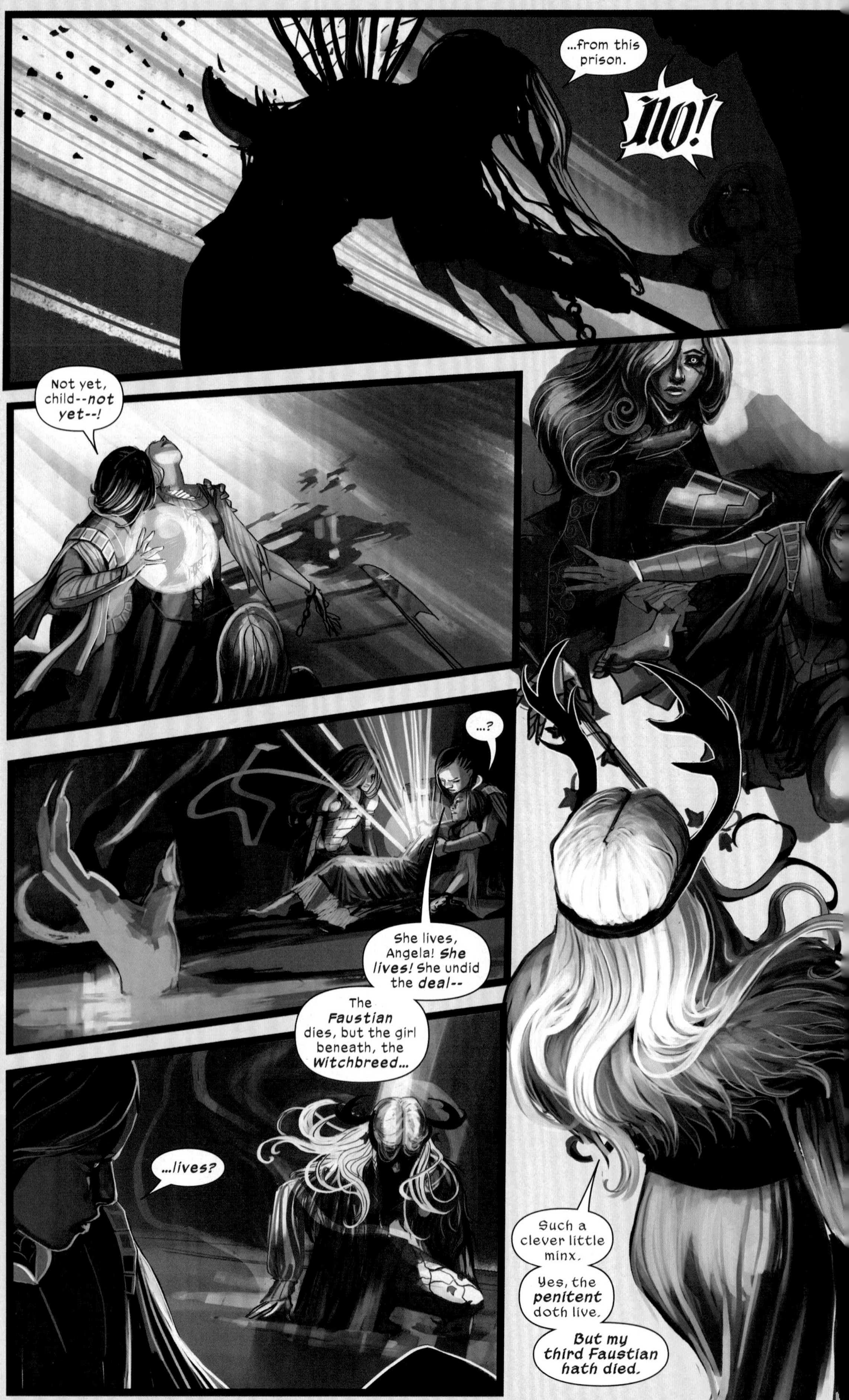
...from this prison.
NO!
Not yet, child--*not yet*--!
...?
She lives, Angela! *She lives!* She undid the *deal*--
The *Faustian* dies, but the girl beneath, the *Witchbreed*...
...*lives?*
Such a clever little minx.
Yes, the *penitent* doth live.
But my third Faustian hath died.

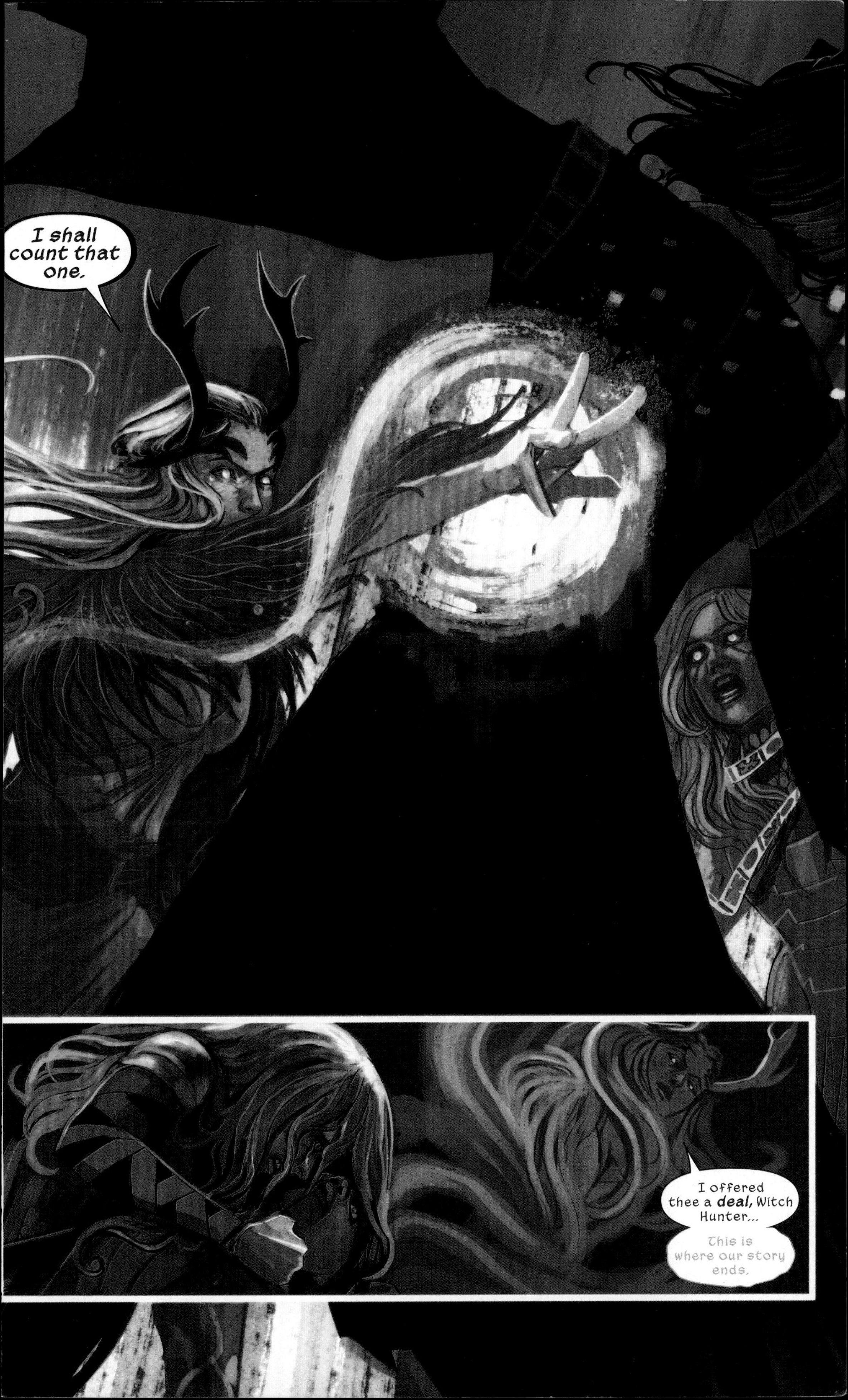
I shall count that one.
I offered thee a deal, Witch Hunter...
This is where our story ends.

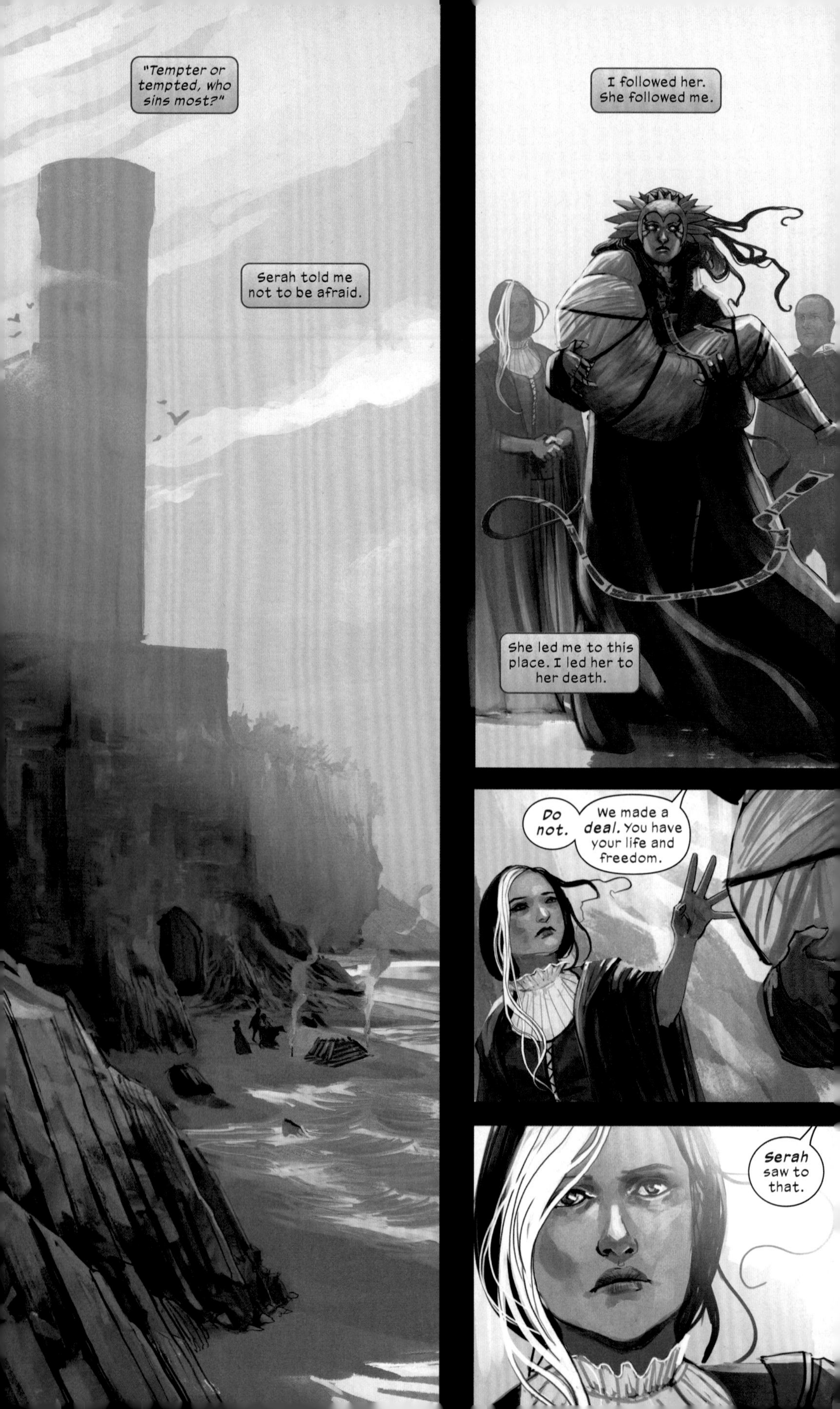
"Tempter or tempted, who sins most?"
Serah told me not to be afraid.
I followed her. She followed me.
She led me to this place. I led her to her death.
Do not.
We made a *deal.* You have your life and freedom.
Serah saw to that.

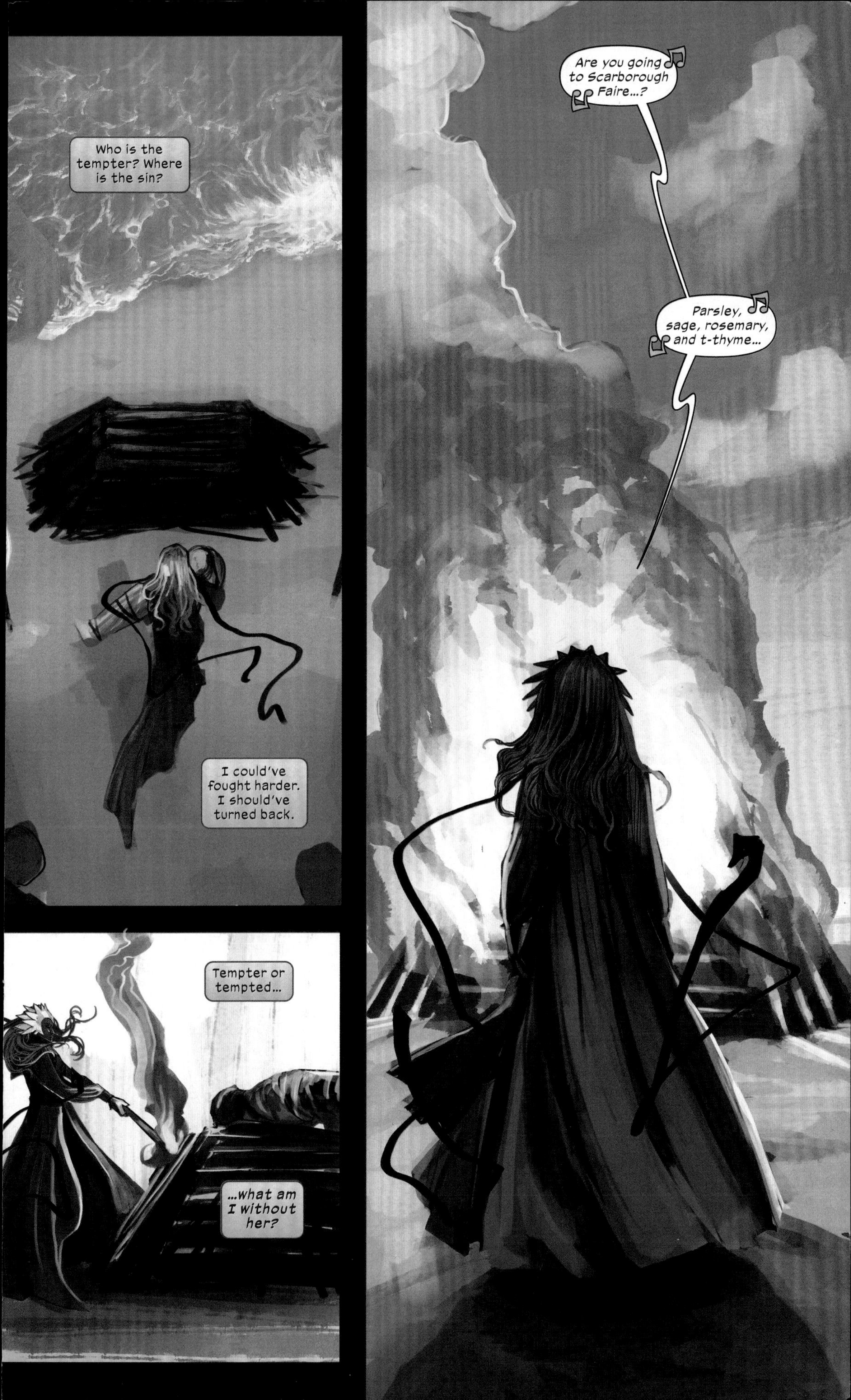
Who is the tempter? Where is the sin?
I could've fought harder. I should've turned back.
Are you going to Scarborough Faire...?
Parsley, sage, rosemary, and t-thyme...
Tempter or tempted...
...what am I without her?

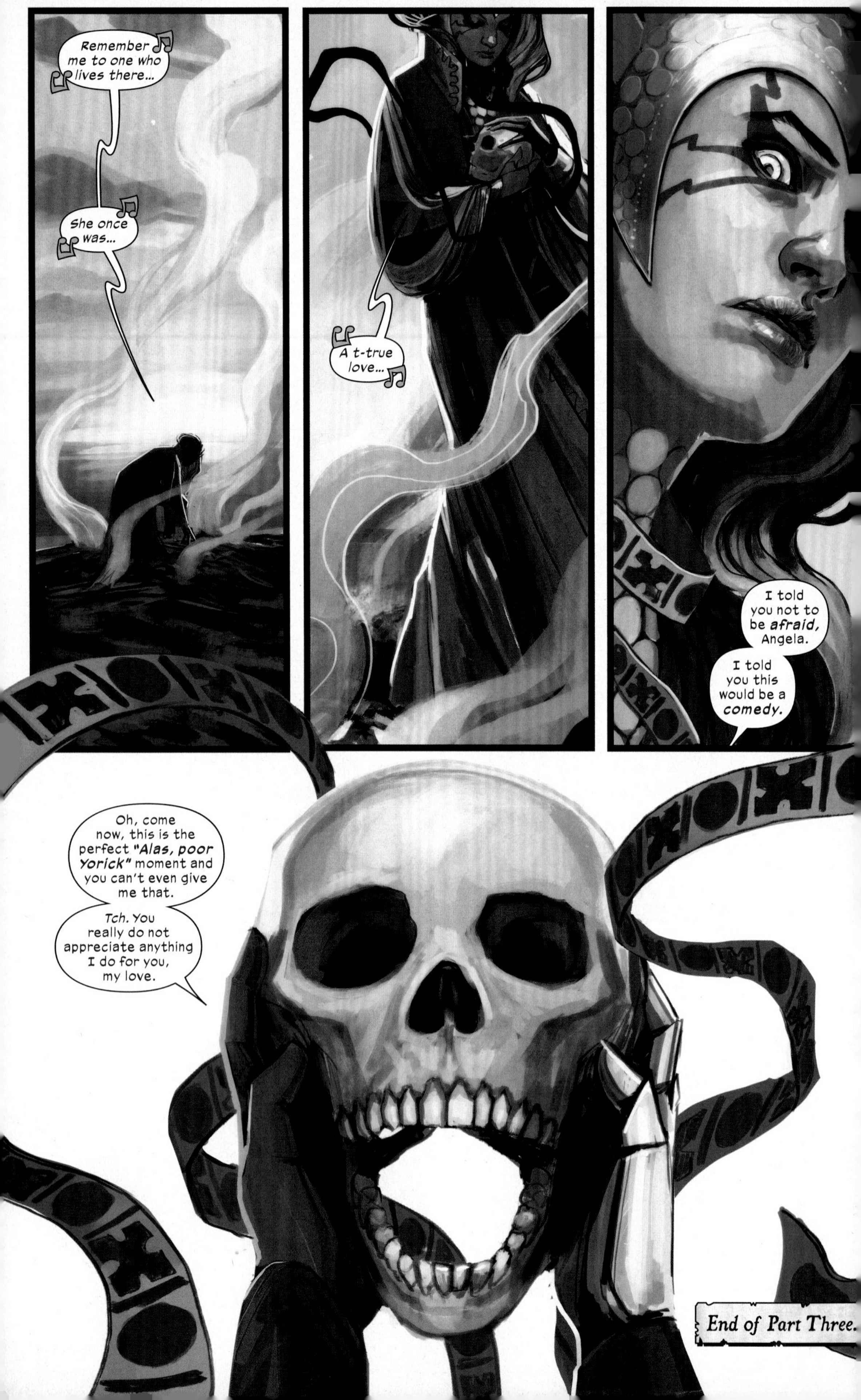
Remember me to one who lives there...
She once was...
A t-true love...
I told you not to be *afraid,* Angela.
I told you this would be a *comedy.*
Oh, come now, this is the perfect *"Alas, poor Yorick"* moment and you can't even give me that.
Tch. You really do not appreciate anything I do for you, my love.
End of Part Three.

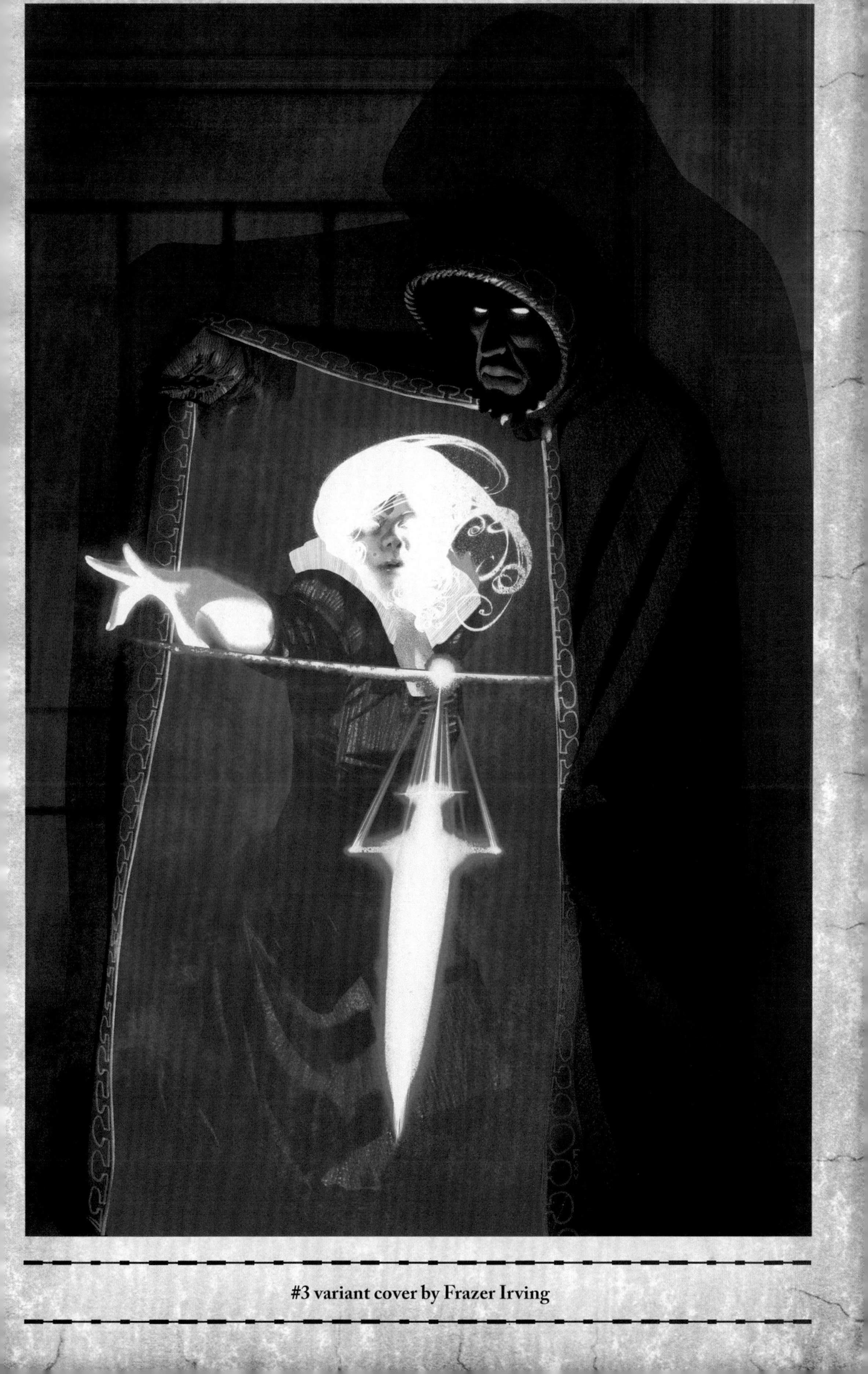

#3 variant cover by Frazer Irving

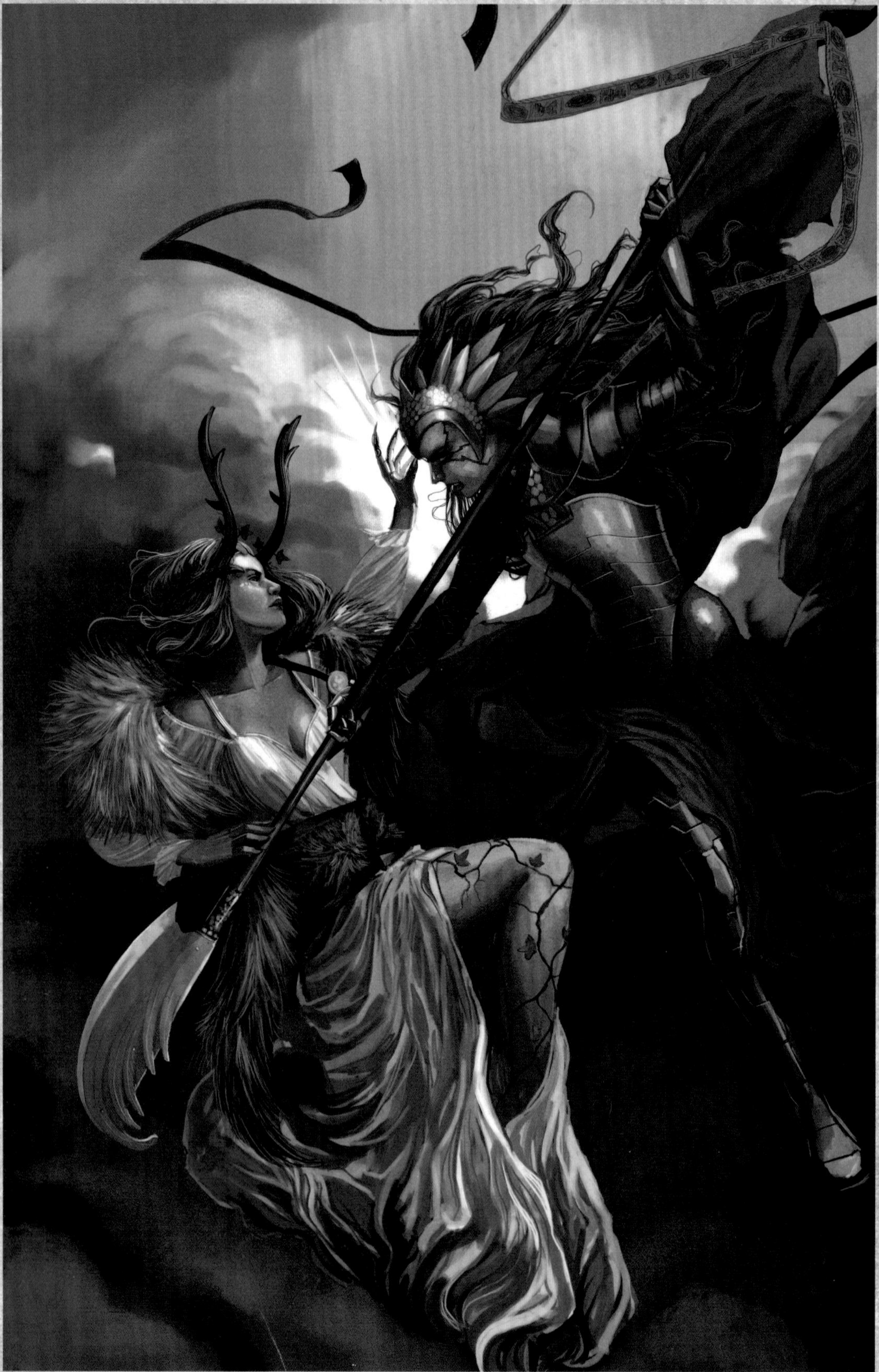

Part Four, In Which a Witch Will Beget a Very Excellent Piece of Villainy

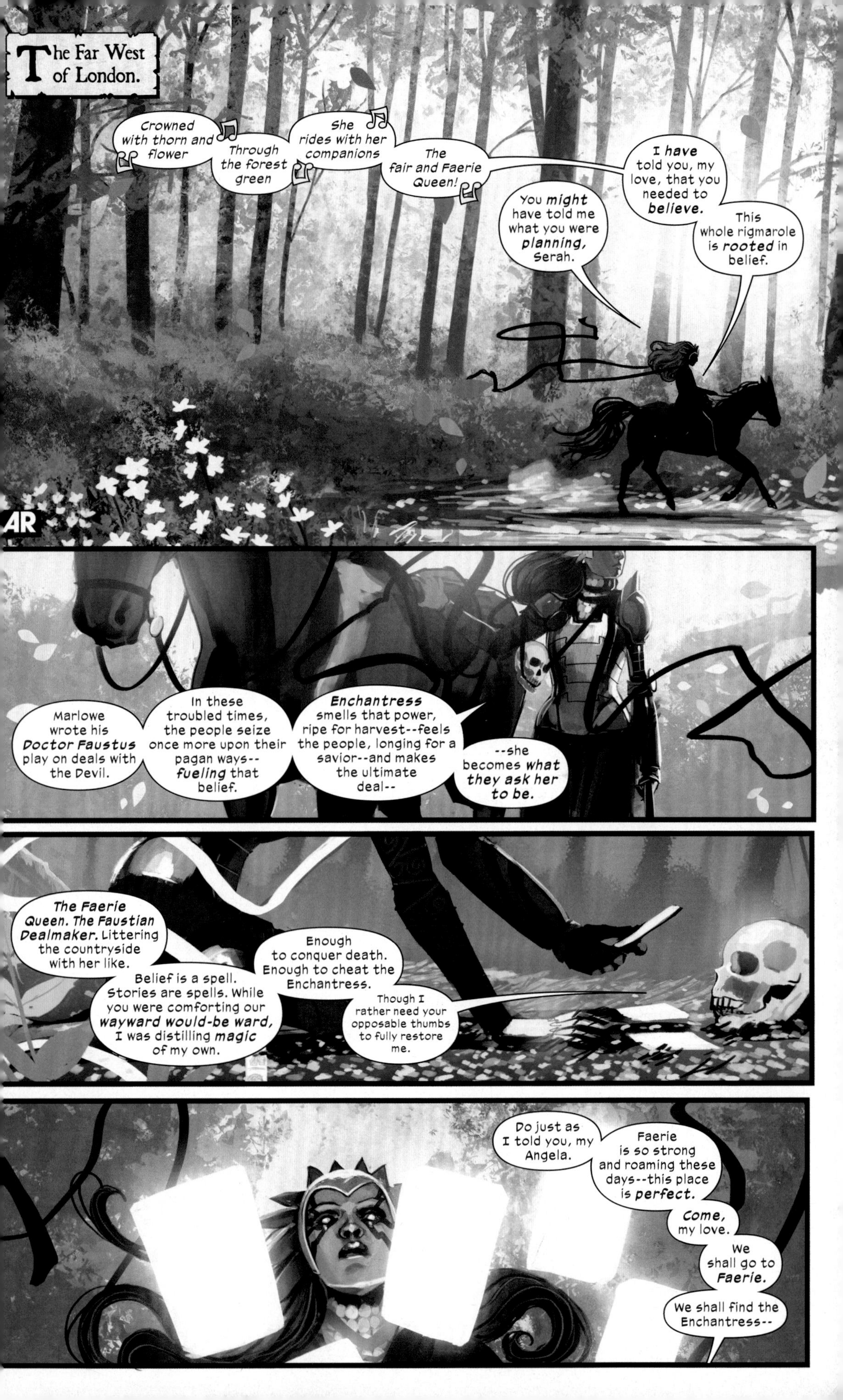
The Far West of London.
Crowned with thorn and flower
Through the forest green
She rides with her companions
The fair and Faerie Queen!
I have told you, my love, that you needed to believe.
You might have told me what you were planning, Serah.
This whole rigmarole is rooted in belief.
Marlowe wrote his Doctor Faustus play on deals with the Devil.
In these troubled times, the people seize once more upon their pagan ways--fueling that belief.
Enchantress smells that power, ripe for harvest--feels the people, longing for a savior--and makes the ultimate deal--
--she becomes what they ask her to be.
The Faerie Queen. The Faustian Dealmaker. Littering the countryside with her like.
Belief is a spell. Stories are spells. While you were comforting our wayward would-be ward, I was distilling magic of my own.
Enough to conquer death. Enough to cheat the Enchantress.
Though I rather need your opposable thumbs to fully restore me.
Do just as I told you, my Angela.
Faerie is so strong and roaming these days--this place is perfect.
Come, my love.
We shall go to Faerie.
We shall find the Enchantress--

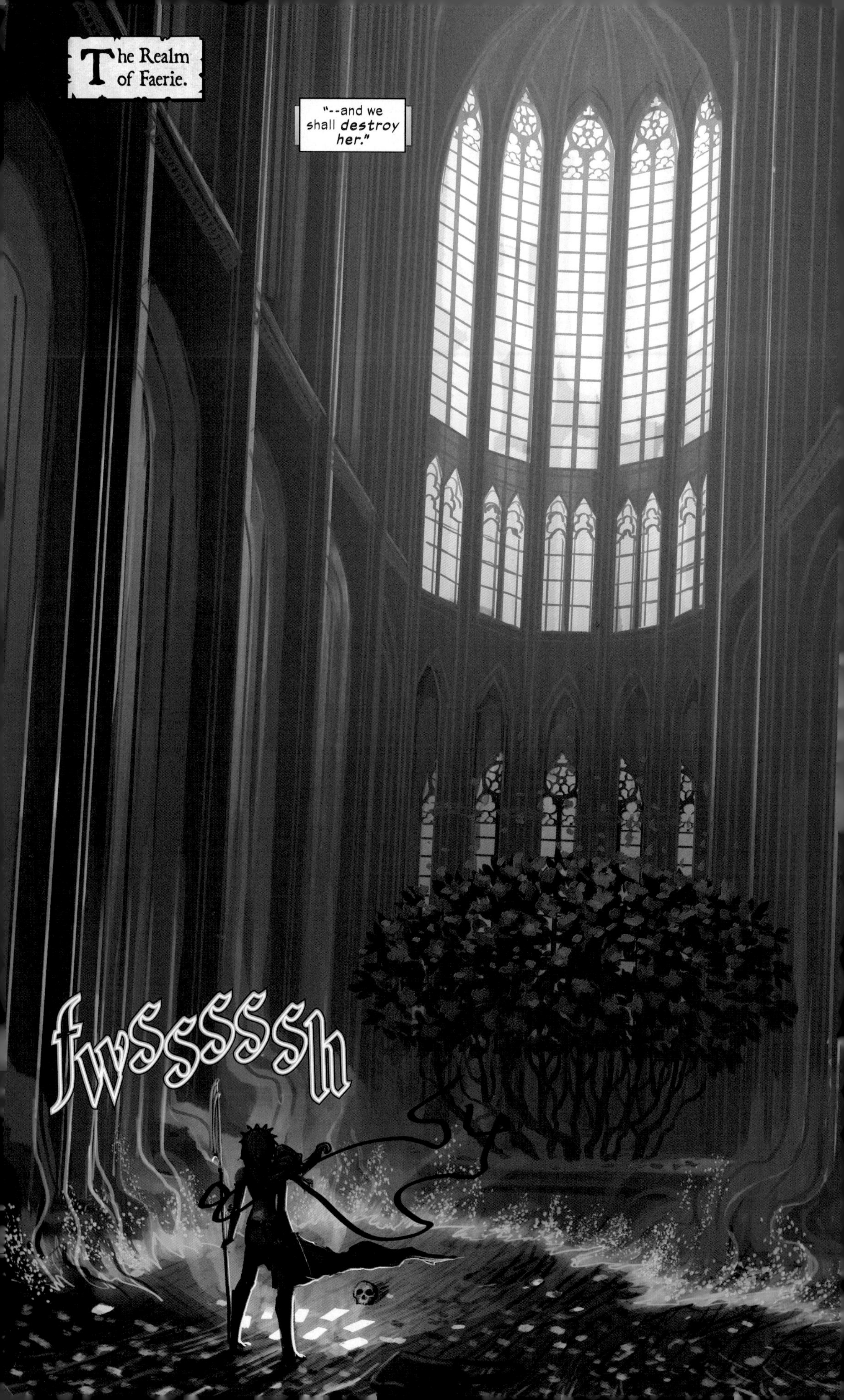
The Realm of Faerie.
"--and we shall destroy her."
fwssssssh

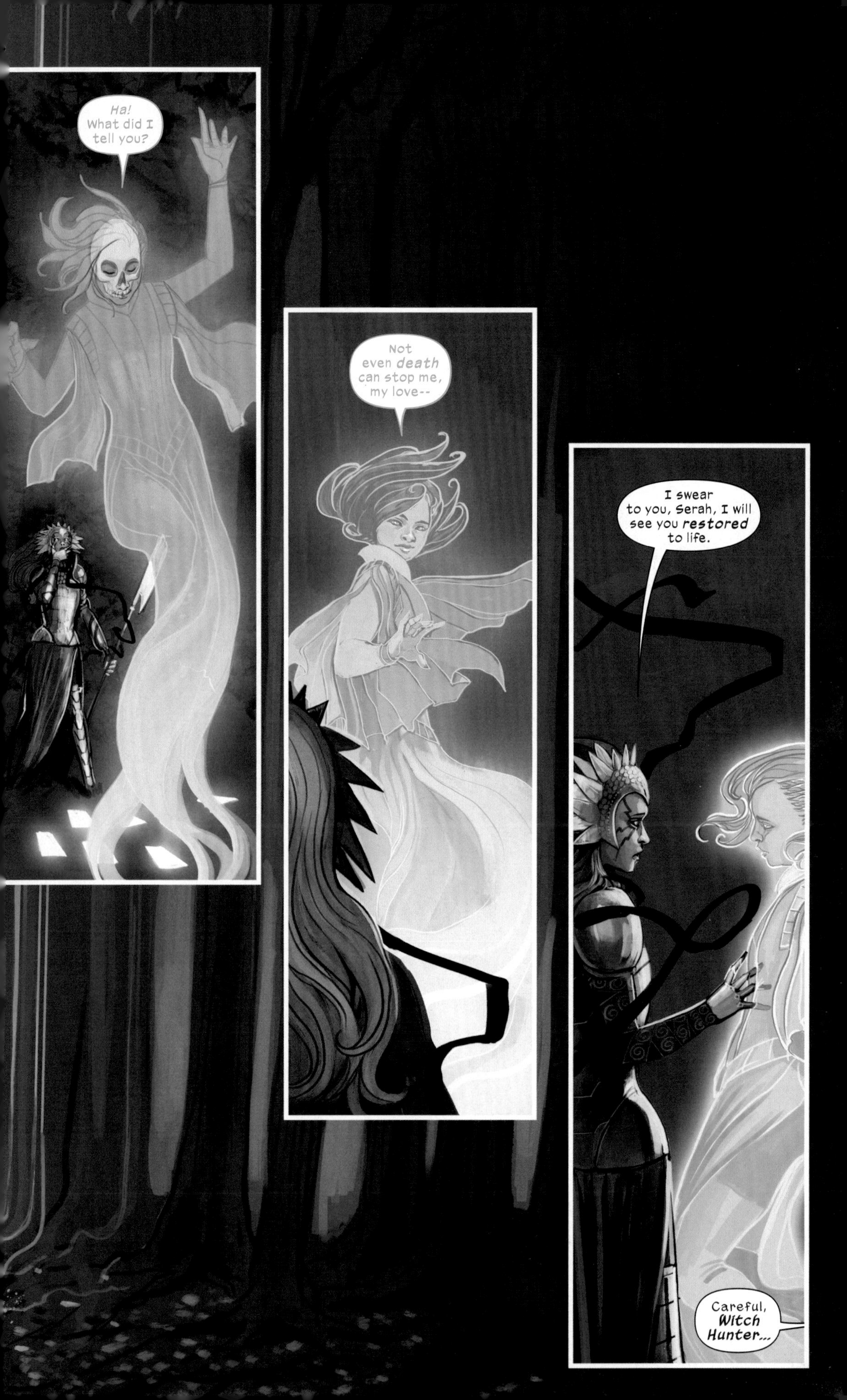
Ha! What did I tell you?
Not even death can stop me, my love--
I swear to you, Serah, I will see you restored to life.
Careful, Witch Hunter...

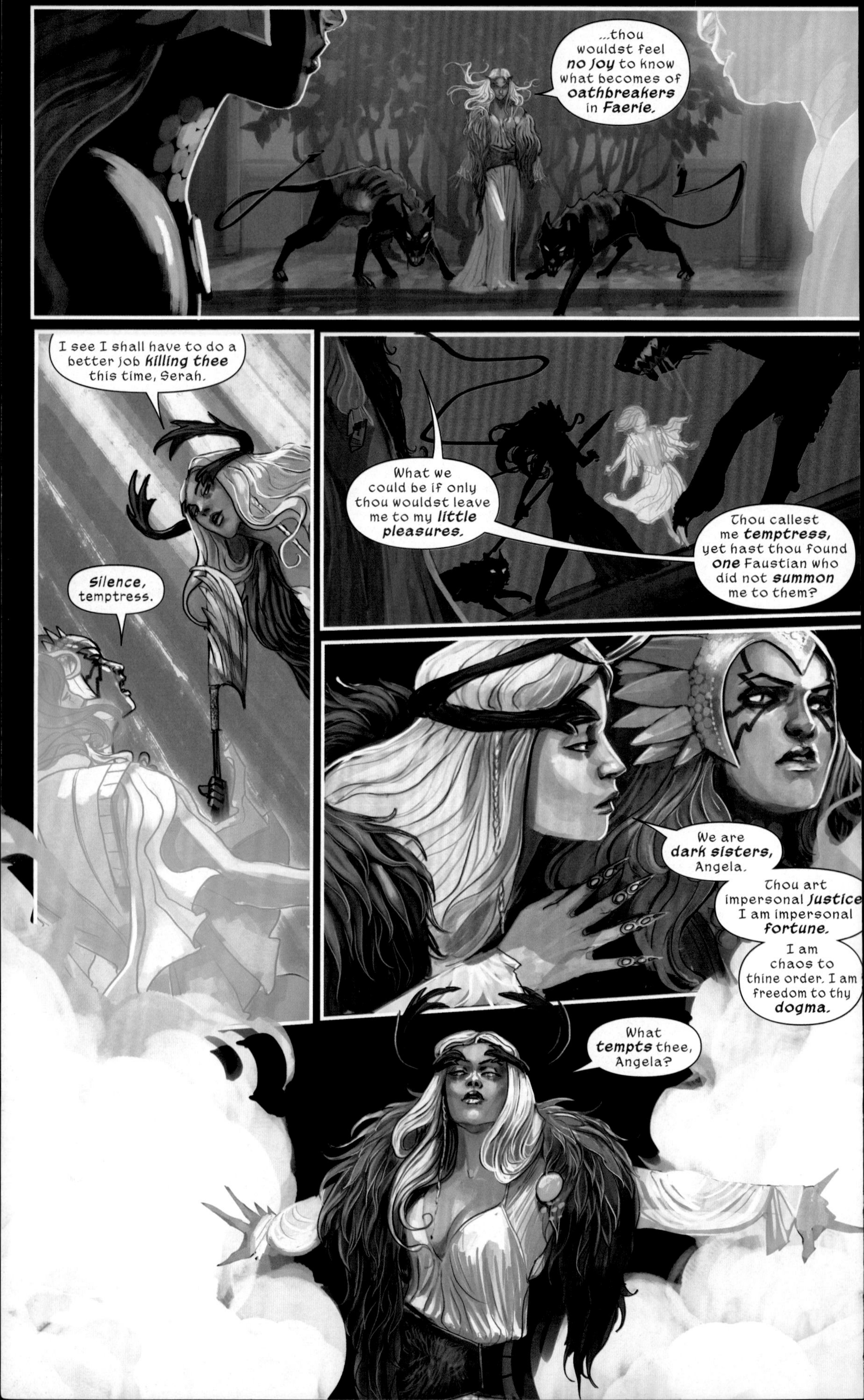
...thou wouldst feel no joy to know what becomes of oathbreakers in Faerie.
I see I shall have to do a better job killing thee this time, Serah.
Silence, temptress.
What we could be if only thou wouldst leave me to my little pleasures.
Thou callest me temptress, yet hast thou found one Faustian who did not summon me to them?
We are dark sisters, Angela.
Thou art impersonal justice. I am impersonal fortune.
I am chaos to thine order. I am freedom to thy dogma.
What tempts thee, Angela?

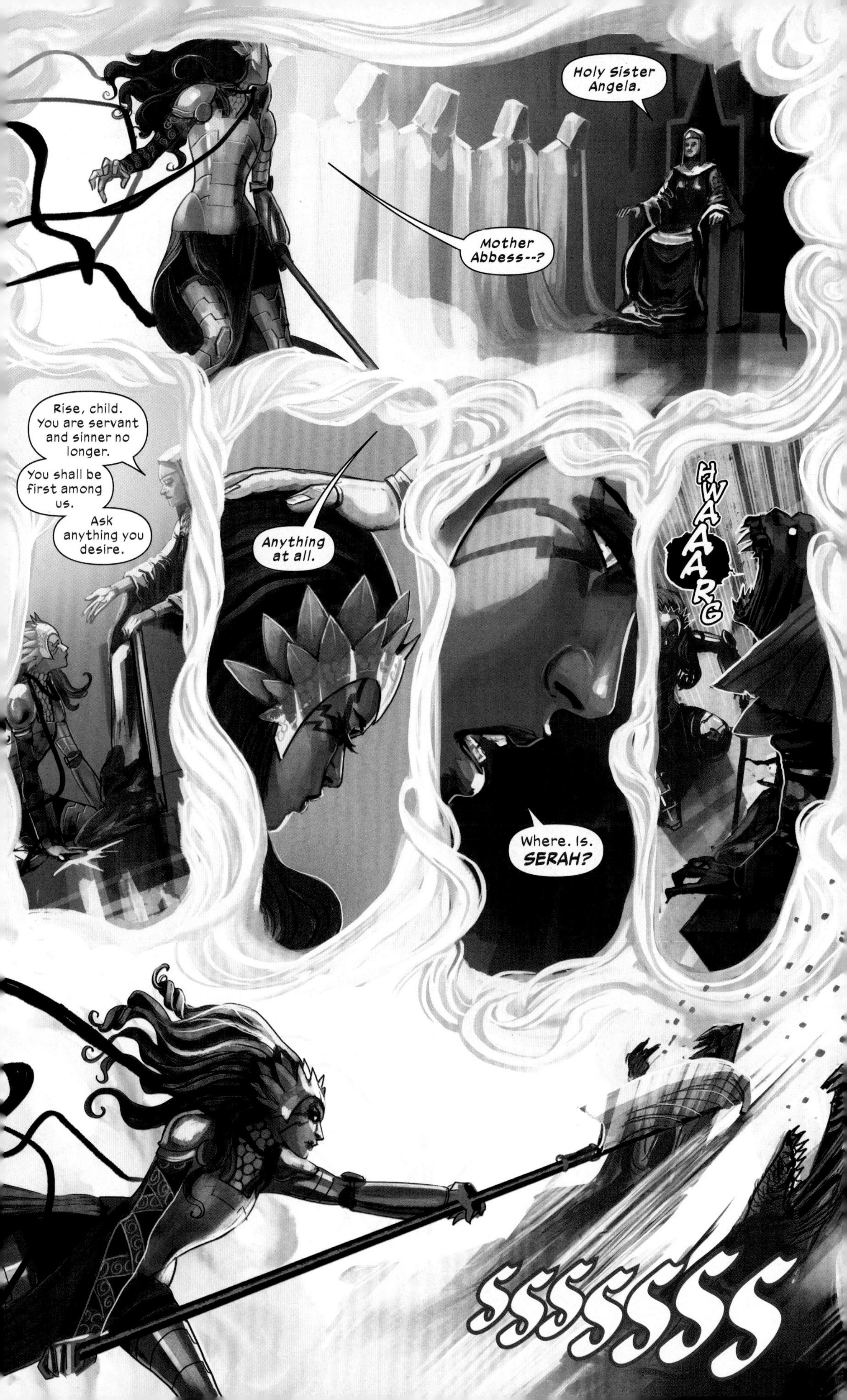
Holy Sister Angela.
Mother Abbess--?
Rise, child. You are servant and sinner no longer.
You shall be first among us.
Ask anything you desire.
Anything at all.
Where. Is. SERAH?
HWAAARG
SSSSSSS

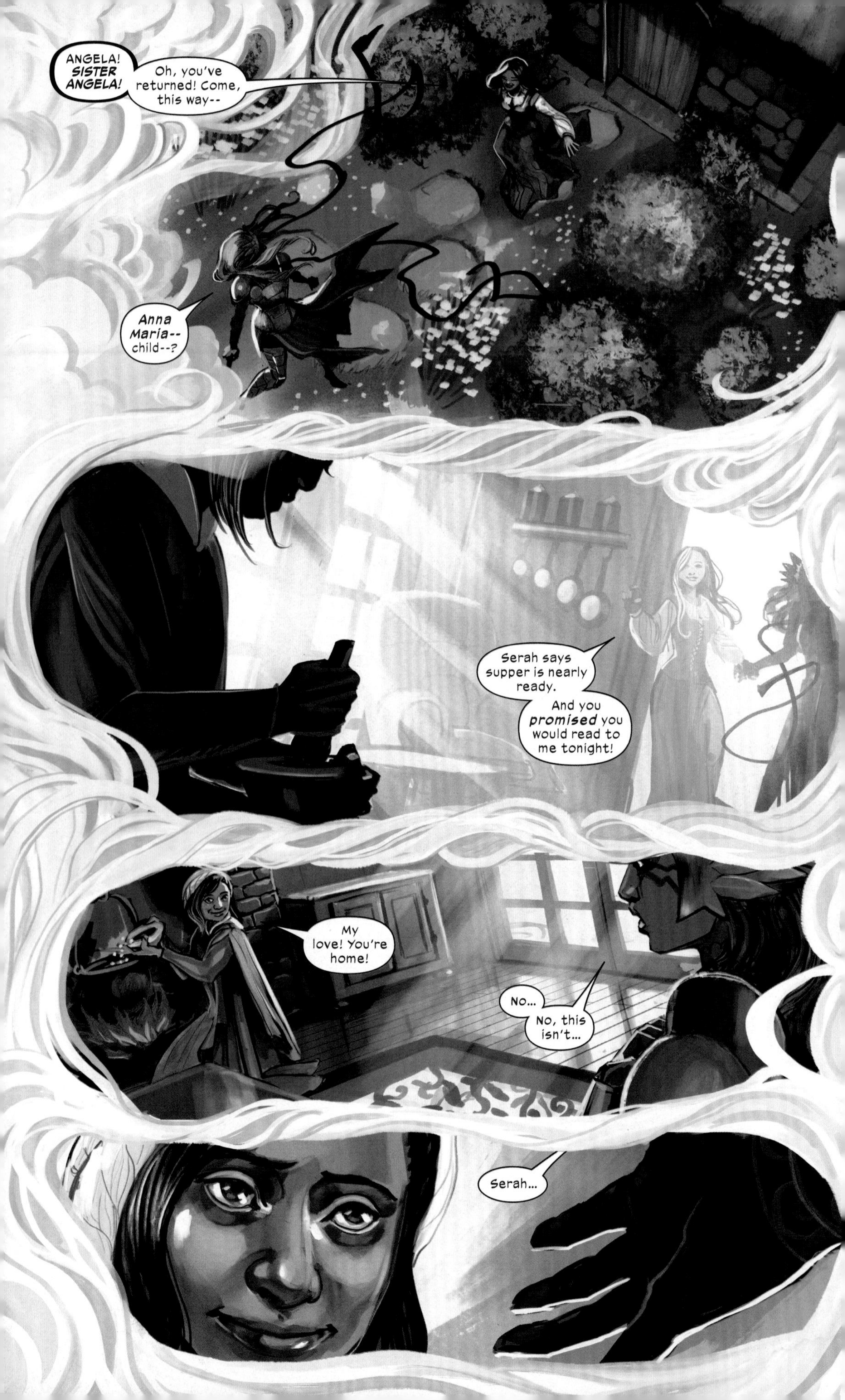
ANGELA! SISTER ANGELA!
Oh, you've returned! Come, this way--
Anna Maria-- child--?
Serah says supper is nearly ready.
And you promised you would read to me tonight!
My love! You're home!
No...
No, this isn't...
Serah...

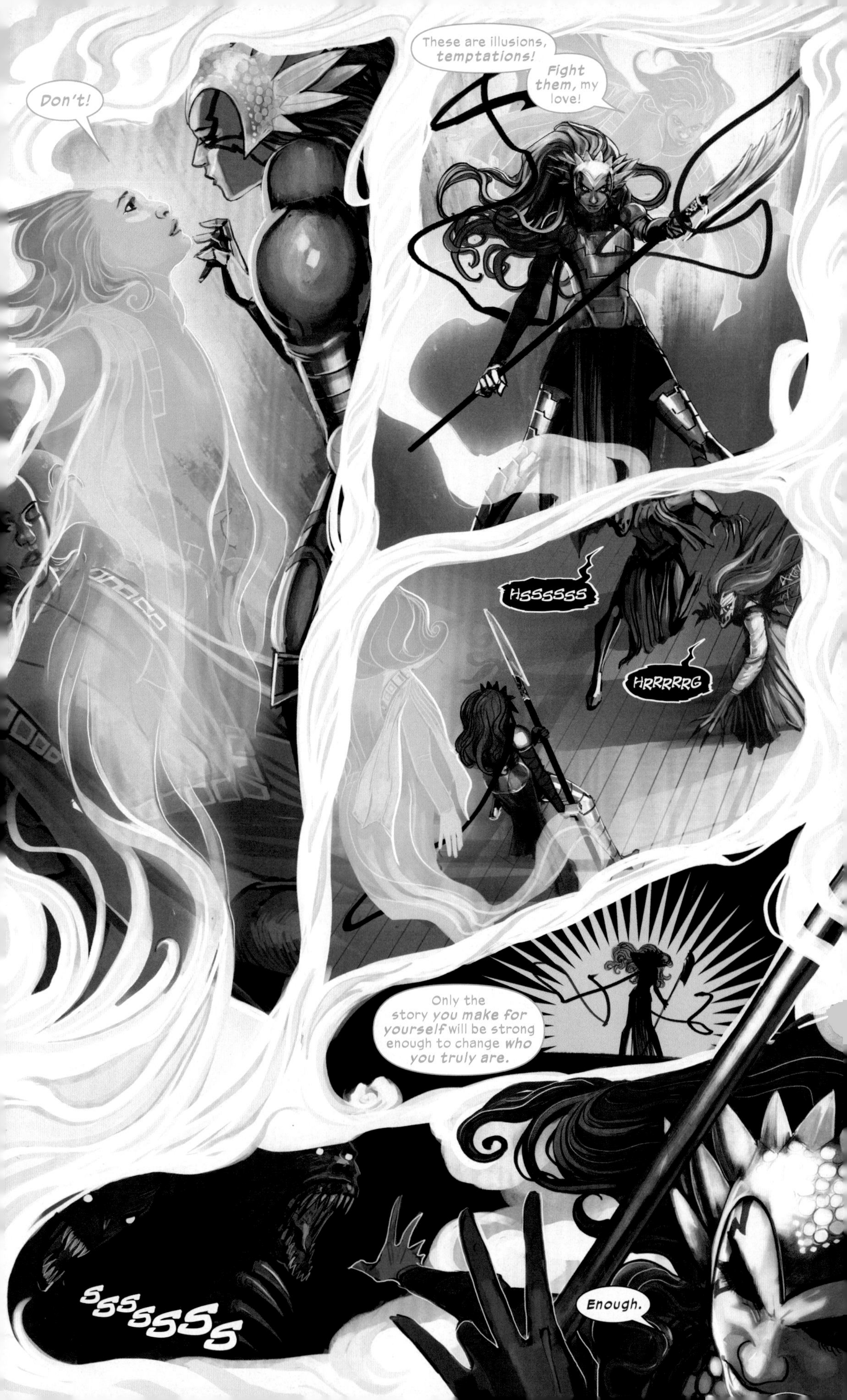
Don't!
These are illusions, temptations!
Fight them, my love!
HSSSSSS
HRRRRRG
Only the story you make for yourself will be strong enough to change who you truly are.
SSSSSSS
Enough.

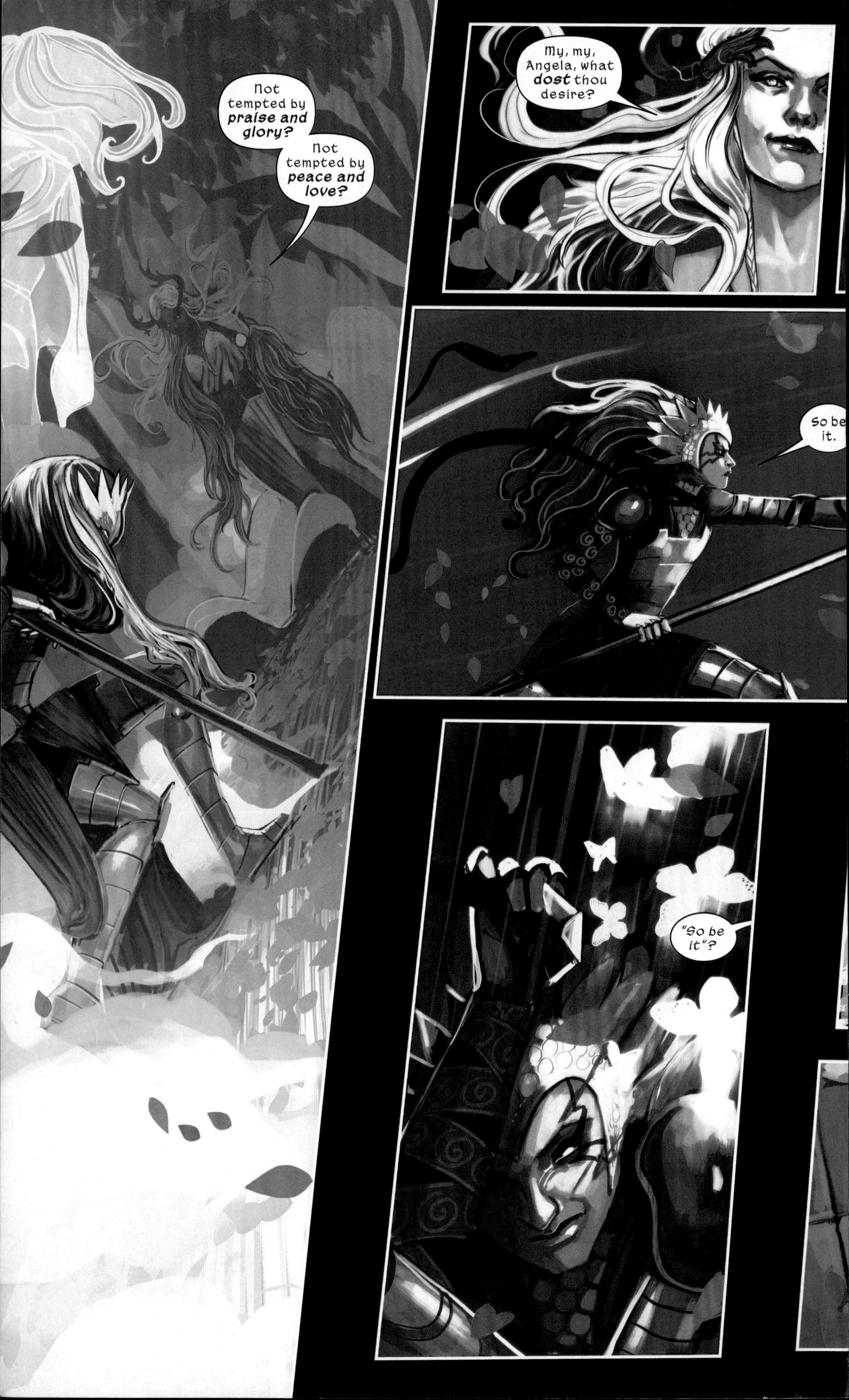
Not tempted by **praise and glory?**
Not tempted by **peace and love?**
My, my, Angela, what **dost** thou desire?
So be it.
"So be it"?

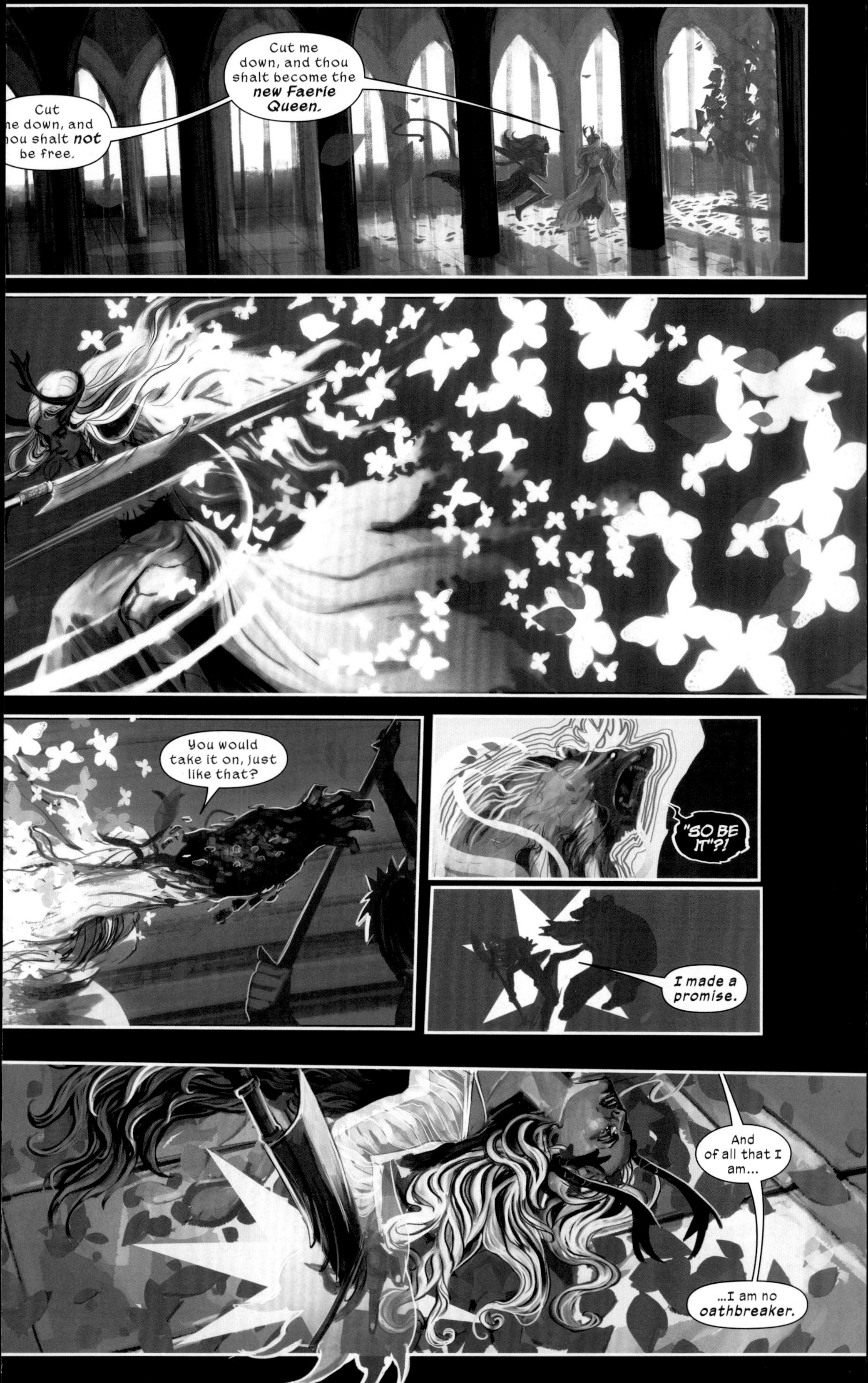

Cut me down, and thou shalt not be free.
Cut me down, and thou shalt become the new Faerie Queen.
You would take it on, just like that?
"SO BE IT"?!
I made a promise.
And of all that I am...
...I am no oathbreaker.

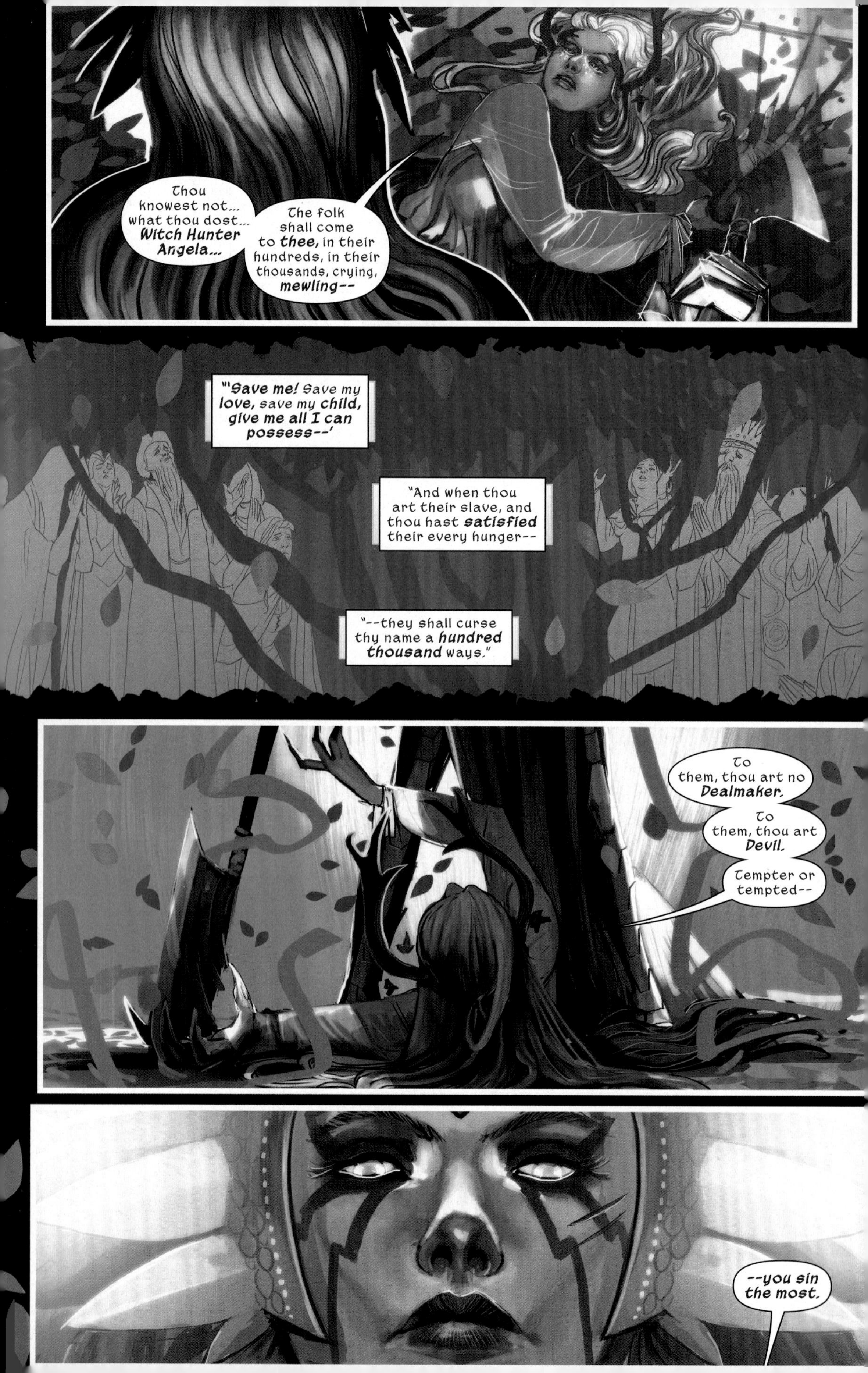
Thou knowest not... what thou dost... Witch Hunter Angela...
The folk shall come to thee, in their hundreds, in their thousands, crying, mewling--
"'Save me! Save my love, save my child, give me all I can possess--'
"And when thou art their slave, and thou hast satisfied their every hunger--
"--they shall curse thy name a hundred thousand ways."
To them, thou art no Dealmaker.
To them, thou art Devil.
Tempter or tempted--
--you sin the most.

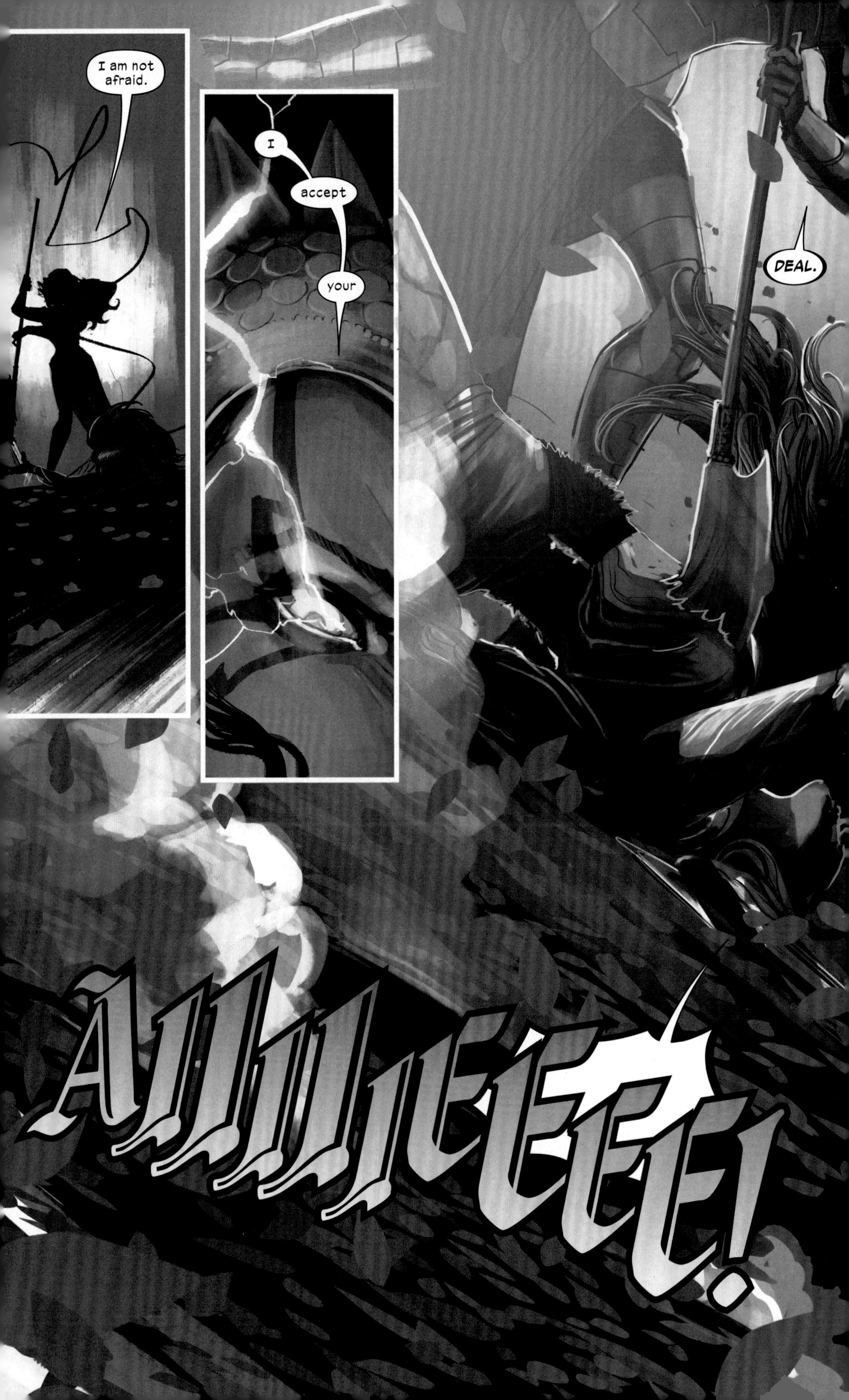
I am not afraid.
I
accept
your
DEAL.
Aiiiieeee!

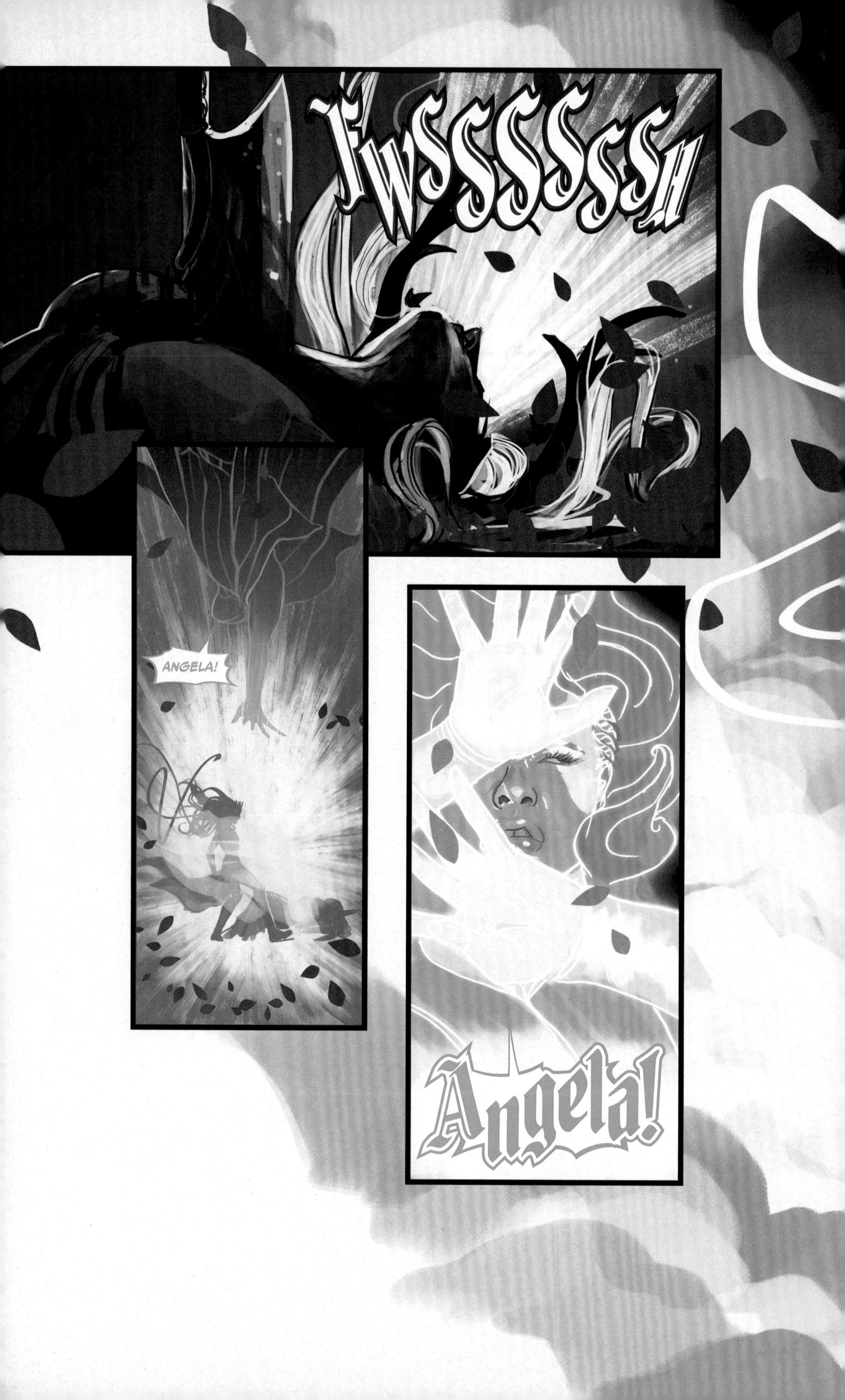
FWSSSSSSH
ANGELA!
Angela!

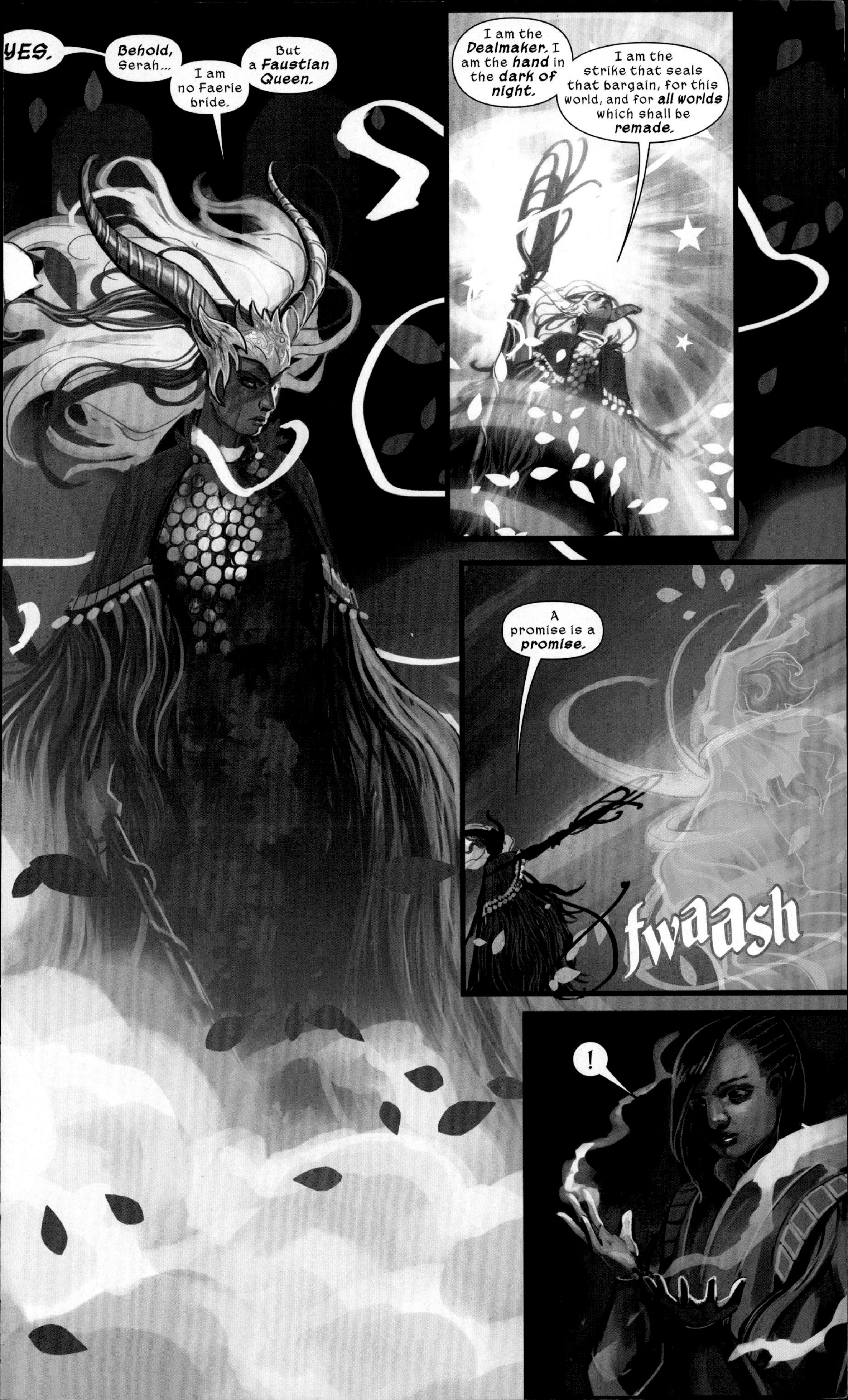

YES.
Behold, Serah...
I am no Faerie bride.
But a Faustian Queen.
I am the Dealmaker. I am the hand in the dark of night.
I am the strike that seals that bargain, for this world, and for all worlds which shall be remade.
A promise is a promise.
fwaash
!

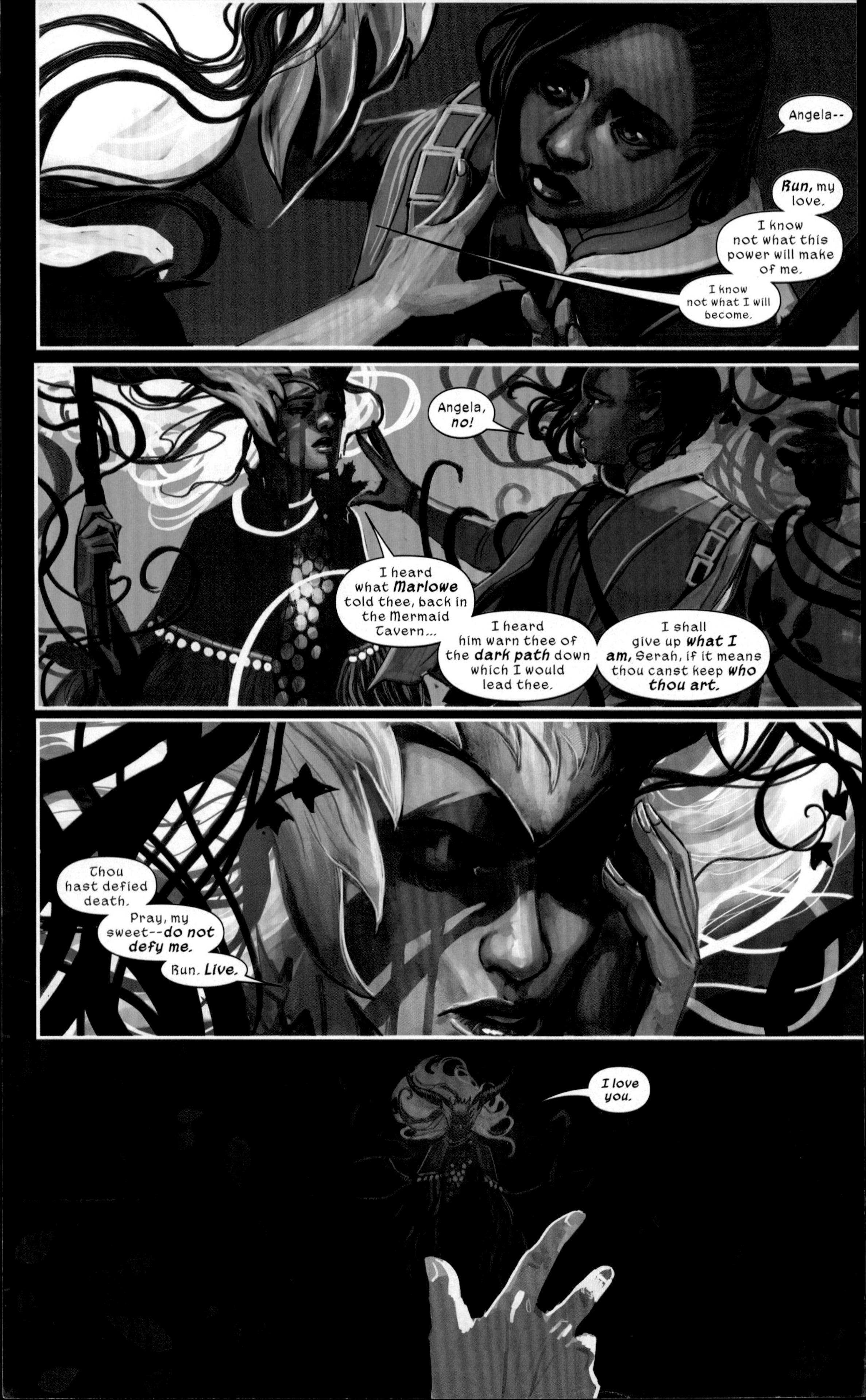

Angela--
Run, my love.
I know not what this power will make of me.
I know not what I will become.
Angela, no!
I heard what Marlowe told thee, back in the Mermaid Tavern...
I heard him warn thee of the dark path down which I would lead thee.
I shall give up what I am, Serah, if it means thou canst keep who thou art.
Thou hast defied death.
Pray, my sweet--do not defy me.
Run. Live.
I love you.

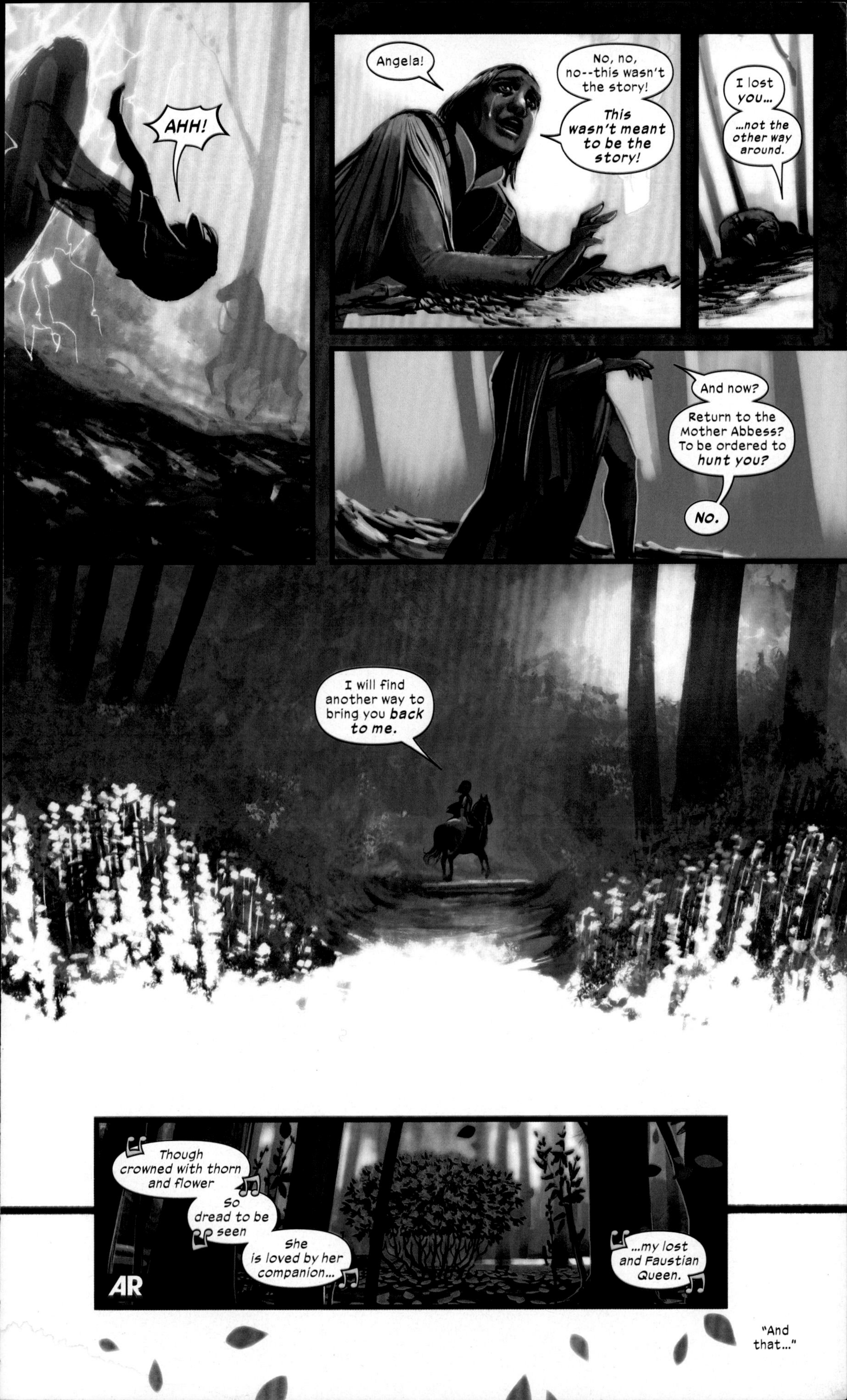
AHH!
Angela!
No, no, no--this wasn't the story!
This wasn't meant to be the story!
I lost you...
...not the other way around.
And now?
Return to the Mother Abbess? To be ordered to hunt you?
No.
I will find another way to bring you back to me.
Though crowned with thorn and flower
So dread to be seen
She is loved by her companion...
...my lost and Faustian Queen.
"And that..."

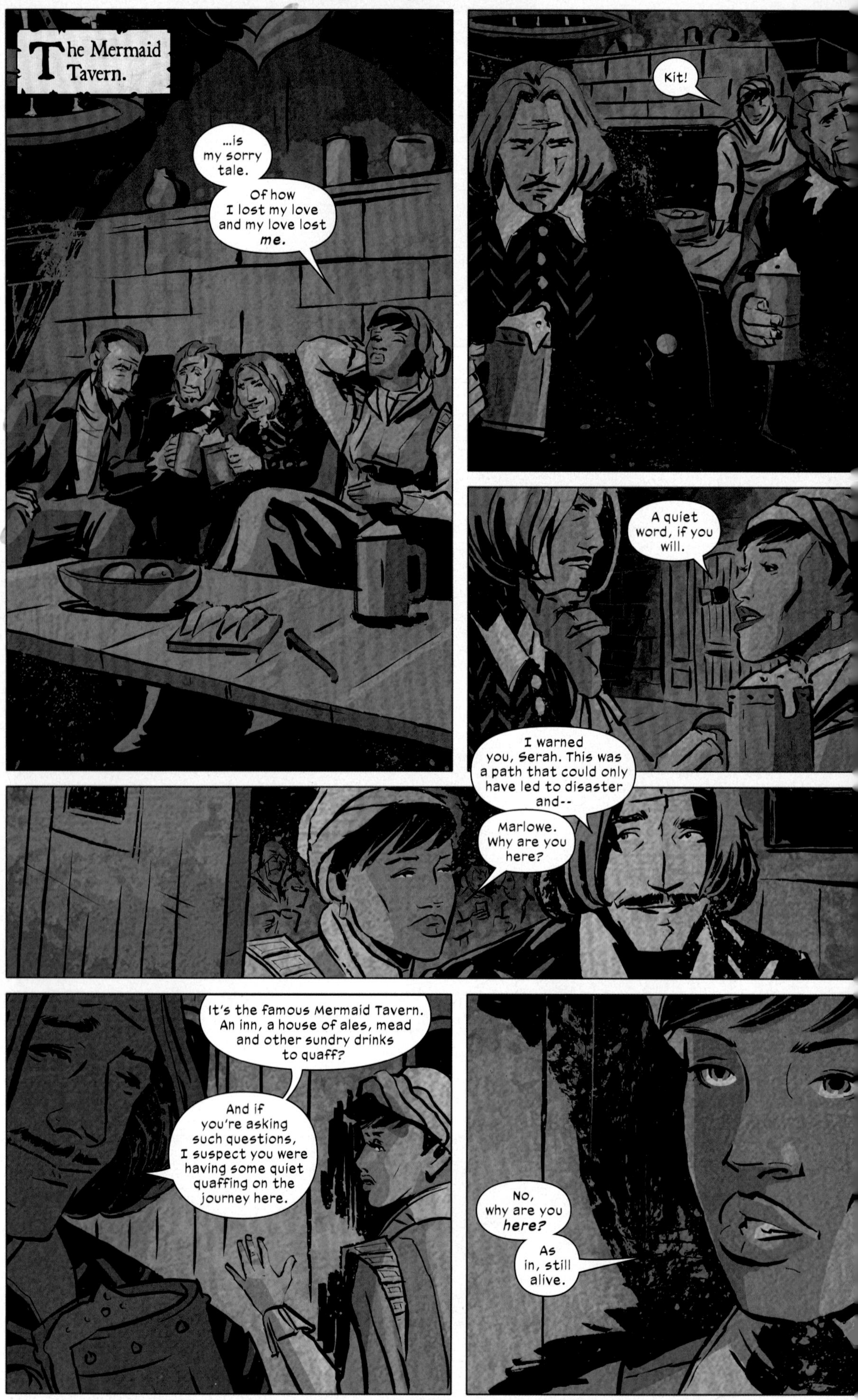
The Mermaid Tavern.
...is my sorry tale.
Of how I lost my love and my love lost *me.*
Kit!
A quiet word, if you will.
I warned you, Serah. This was a path that could only have led to disaster and--
Marlowe. Why are you here?
It's the famous Mermaid Tavern. An inn, a house of ales, mead and other sundry drinks to quaff?
And if you're asking such questions, I suspect you were having some quiet quaffing on the journey here.
No, why are you *here?*
As in, still alive.

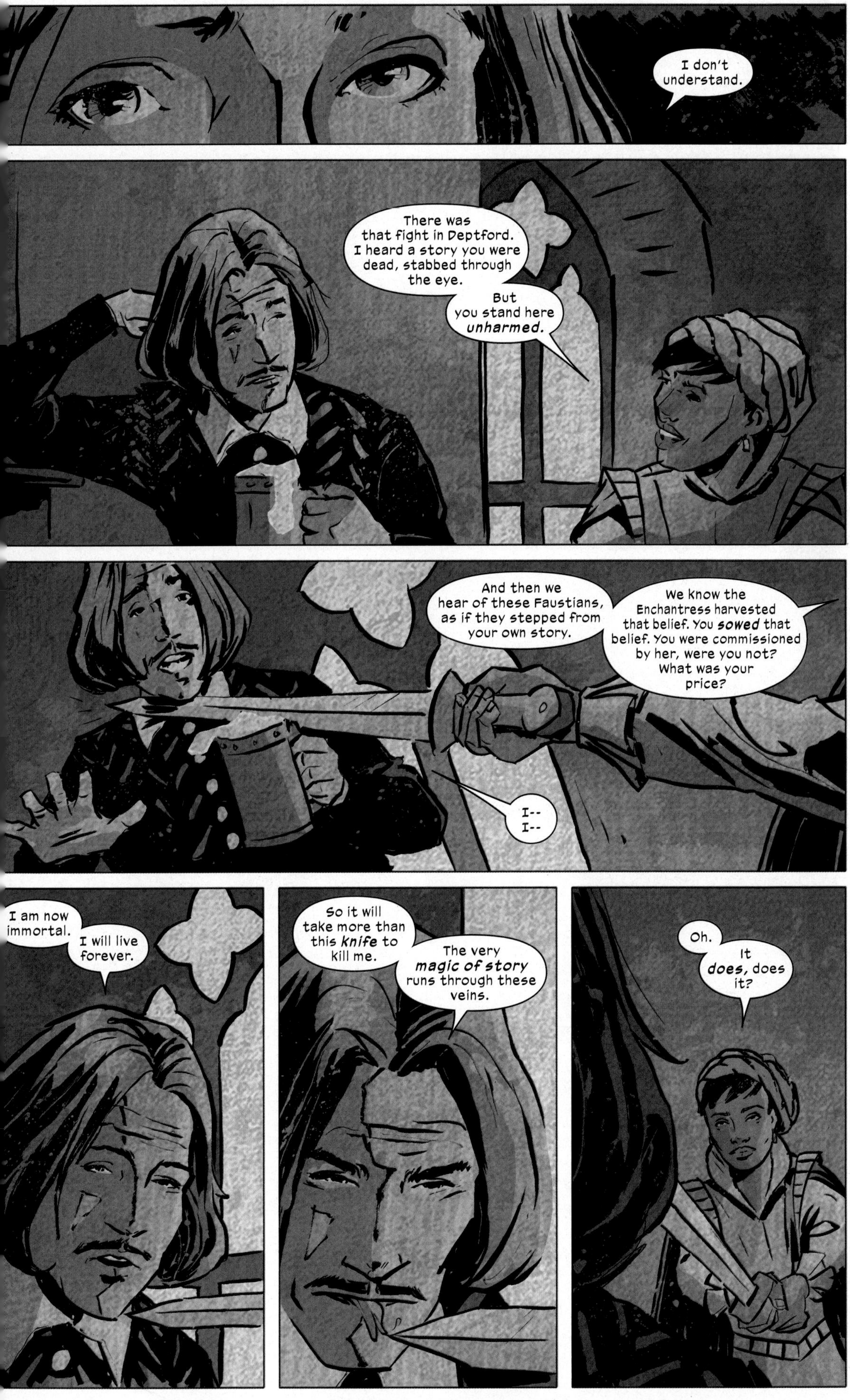
I don't understand.
There was that fight in Deptford. I heard a story you were dead, stabbed through the eye.
But you stand here *unharmed.*
And then we hear of these Faustians, as if they stepped from your own story.
We know the Enchantress harvested that belief. You *sowed* that belief. You were commissioned by her, were you not? What was your price?
I-- I--
I am now immortal.
I will live forever.
So it will take more than this *knife* to kill me.
The very *magic of story* runs through these veins.
Oh.
It *does,* does it?

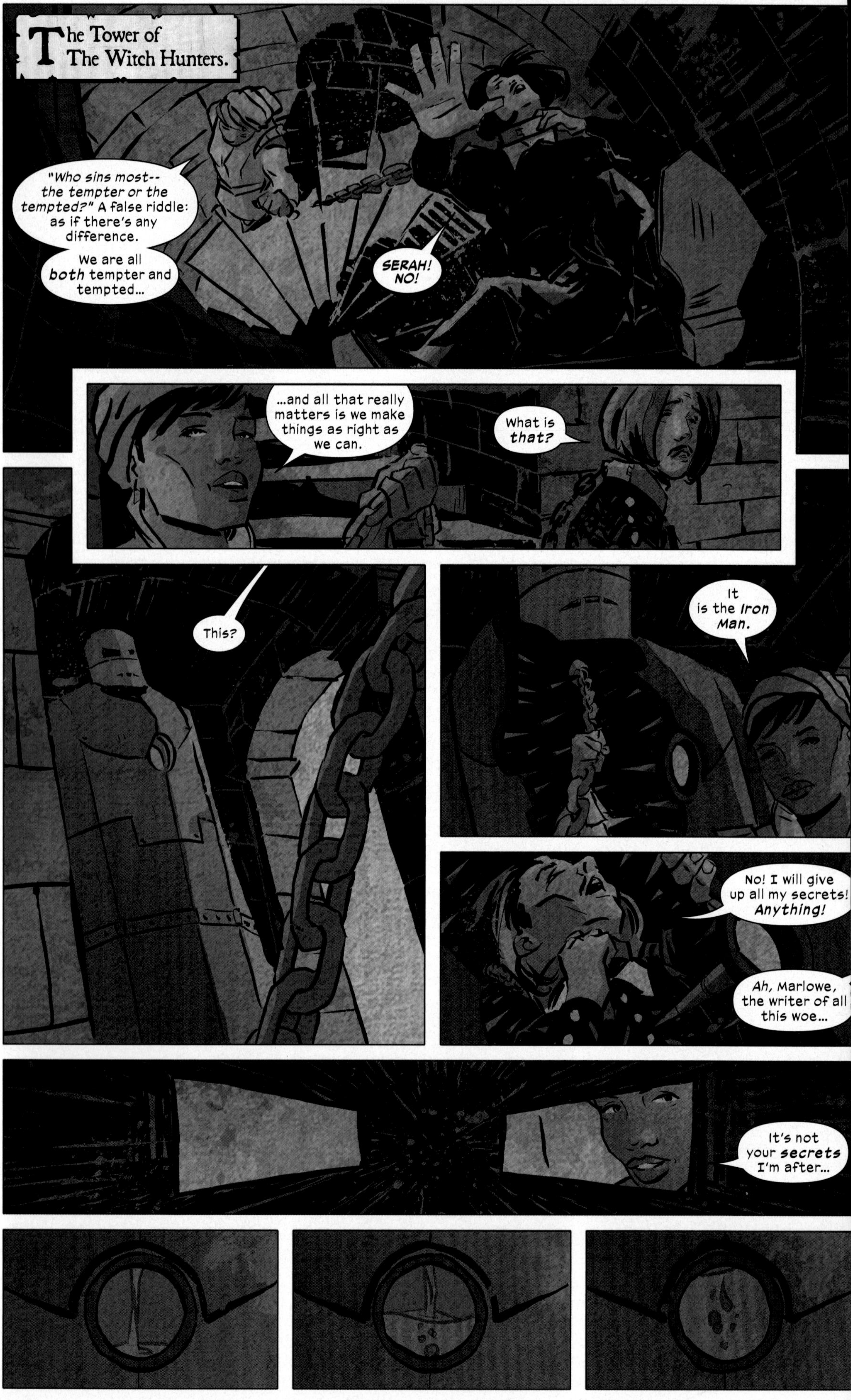
The Tower of The Witch Hunters.
"Who sins most-- the tempter or the tempted?" A false riddle: as if there's any difference.
We are all both tempter and tempted...
SERAH! NO!
...and all that really matters is we make things as right as we can.
What is that?
This?
It is the Iron Man.
No! I will give up all my secrets! Anything!
Ah, Marlowe, the writer of all this woe...
It's not your secrets I'm after...

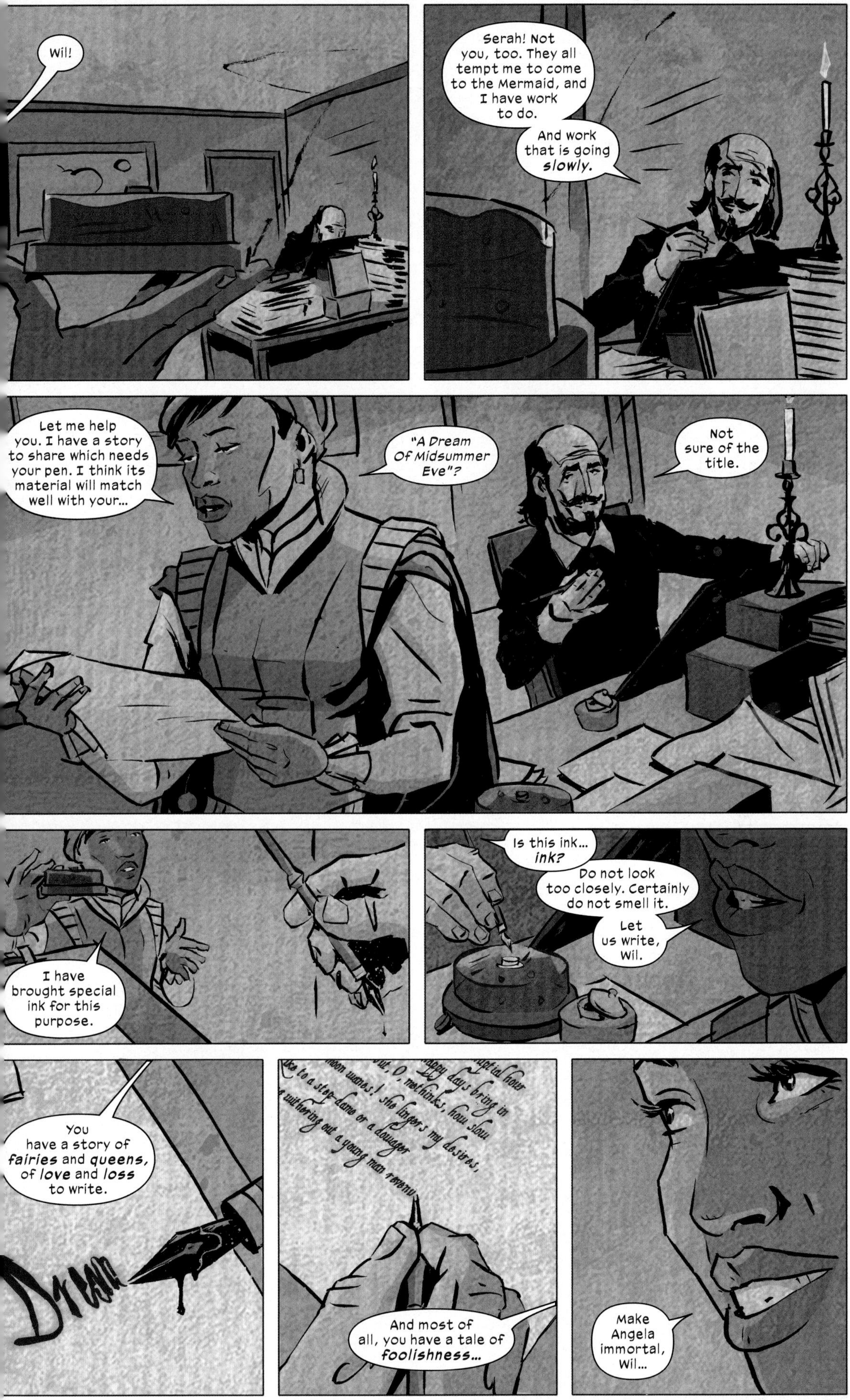
Wil!
Serah! Not you, too. They all tempt me to come to the Mermaid, and I have work to do.
And work that is going *slowly.*
Let me help you. I have a story to share which needs your pen. I think its material will match well with your...
"A Dream Of Midsummer Eve"?
Not sure of the title.
I have brought special ink for this purpose.
Is this ink... *ink?*
Do not look too closely. Certainly do not smell it.
Let us write, Wil.
You have a story of *fairies* and *queens,* of *love* and *loss* to write.
And most of all, you have a tale of *foolishness...*
Make Angela immortal, Wil...

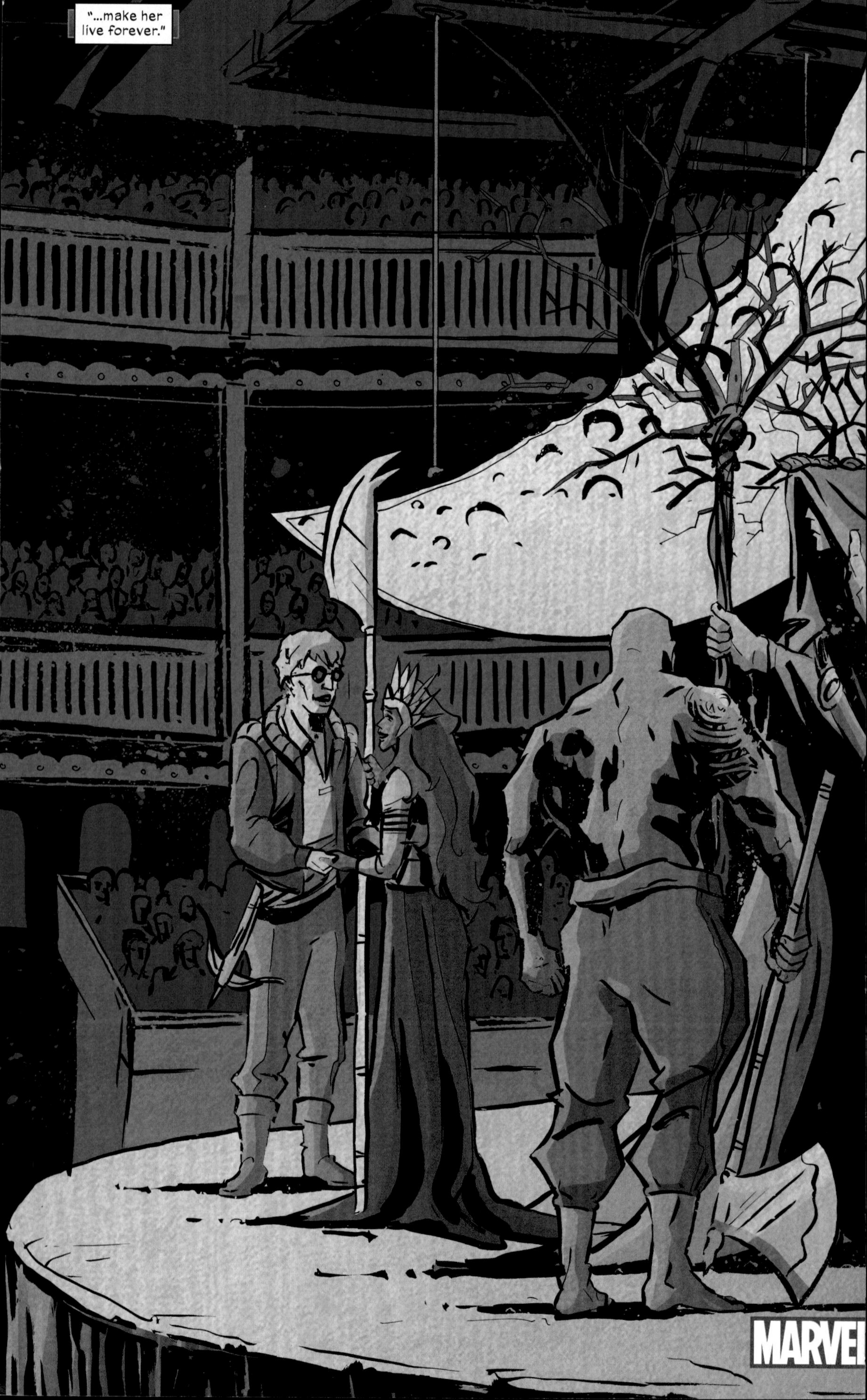
"...make her live forever."

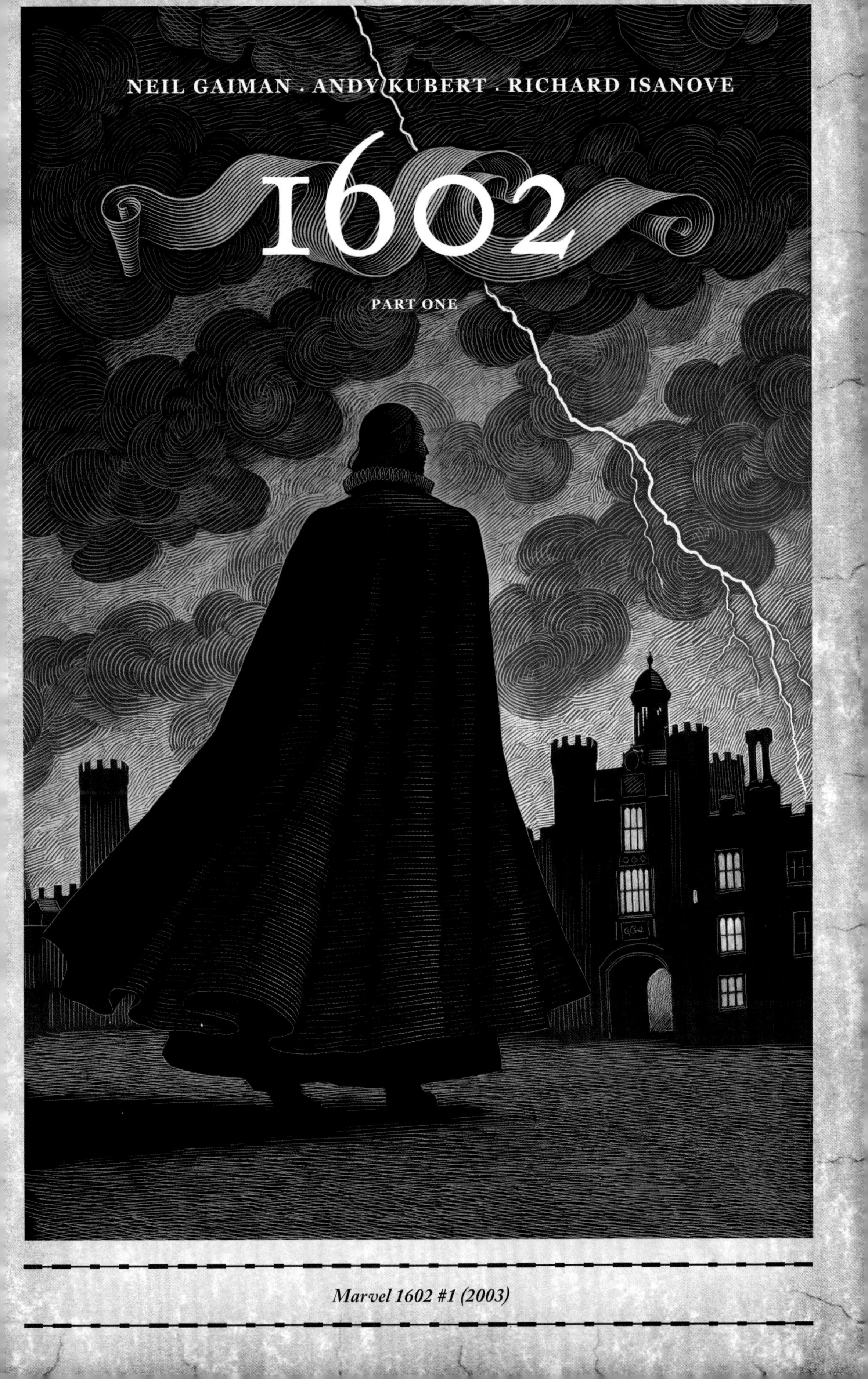
NEIL GAIMAN · ANDY KUBERT · RICHARD ISANOVE
1602
PART ONE

Marvel 1602 #1 (2003)

1602 *Part One*

In which we are Introduced to some of our Featured Players

Neil Gaiman
Writer

Andy Kubert
Illustrator

Richard Isanove
Digital Painting

Todd Klein
Lettering

Scott McKowen
Cover Artist

Joe Quesada
Editor

Nick Lowe
Assistant Editor

Nanci Dakesian
Managing Editor

Kelly Lamy
Asst. Managing Editor

Joe Quesada
Editor in Chief

Bill Jemas
President

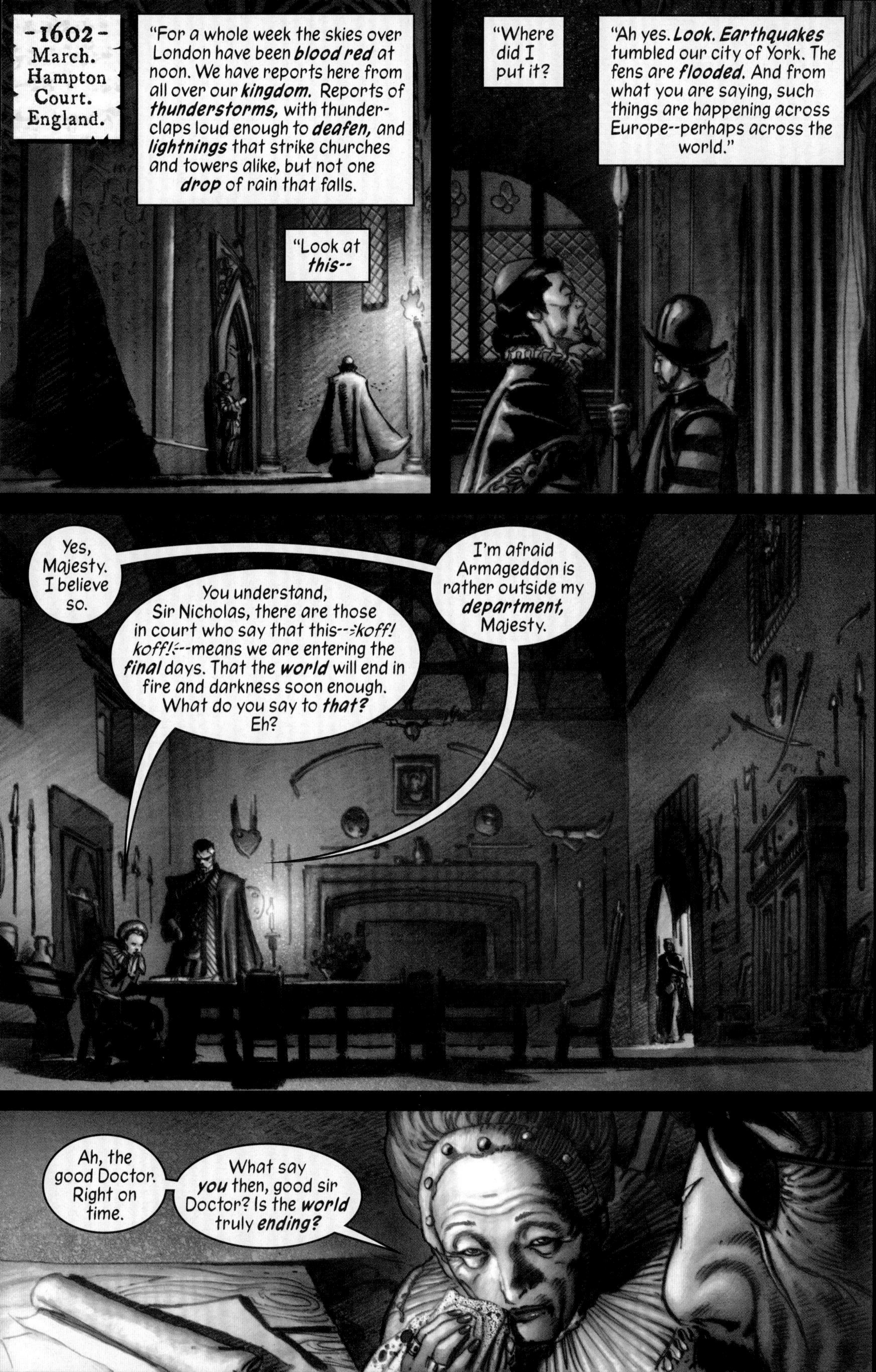
-1602-
March.
Hampton
Court.
England.
"For a whole week the skies over London have been ***blood red*** at noon. We have reports here from all over our ***kingdom.*** Reports of ***thunderstorms,*** with thunderclaps loud enough to ***deafen,*** and ***lightnings*** that strike churches and towers alike, but not one ***drop*** of rain that falls.
"Look at ***this--***
"Where did I put it?
"Ah yes. ***Look. Earthquakes*** tumbled our city of York. The fens are ***flooded.*** And from what you are saying, such things are happening across Europe--perhaps across the world."
You understand, Sir Nicholas, there are those in court who say that this--›*koff! koff!*‹--means we are entering the ***final*** days. That the ***world*** will end in fire and darkness soon enough. What do you say to ***that?*** Eh?
I'm afraid Armageddon is rather outside my ***department,*** Majesty.
Yes, Majesty. I believe so.
Ah, the good Doctor. Right on time.
What say ***you*** then, good sir Doctor? Is the ***world*** truly ***ending?***

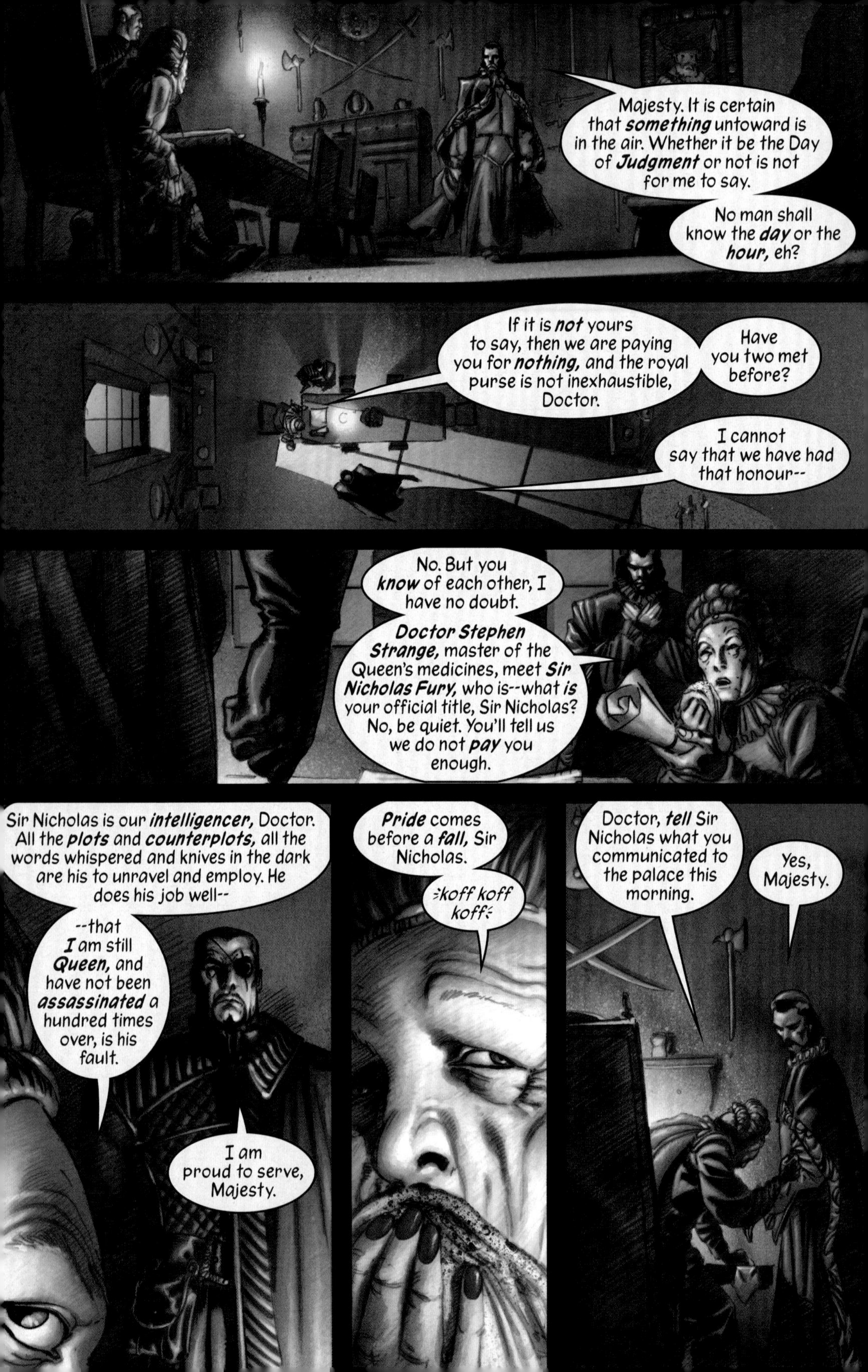
Majesty. It is certain that *something* untoward is in the air. Whether it be the Day of *Judgment* or not is not for me to say.
No man shall know the *day* or the *hour,* eh?
If it is *not* yours to say, then we are paying you for *nothing,* and the royal purse is not inexhaustible, Doctor.
Have you two met before?
I cannot say that we have had that honour--
No. But you *know* of each other, I have no doubt.
Doctor Stephen Strange, master of the Queen's medicines, meet *Sir Nicholas Fury,* who is--what *is* your official title, Sir Nicholas? No, be quiet. You'll tell us we do not *pay* you enough.
Sir Nicholas is our *intelligencer,* Doctor. All the *plots* and *counterplots,* all the words whispered and knives in the dark are his to unravel and employ. He does his job well--
--that *I* am still *Queen,* and have not been *assassinated* a hundred times over, is his fault.
I am proud to serve, Majesty.
Pride comes before a *fall,* Sir Nicholas.
koff koff koff
Doctor, *tell* Sir Nicholas what you communicated to the palace this morning.
Yes, Majesty.

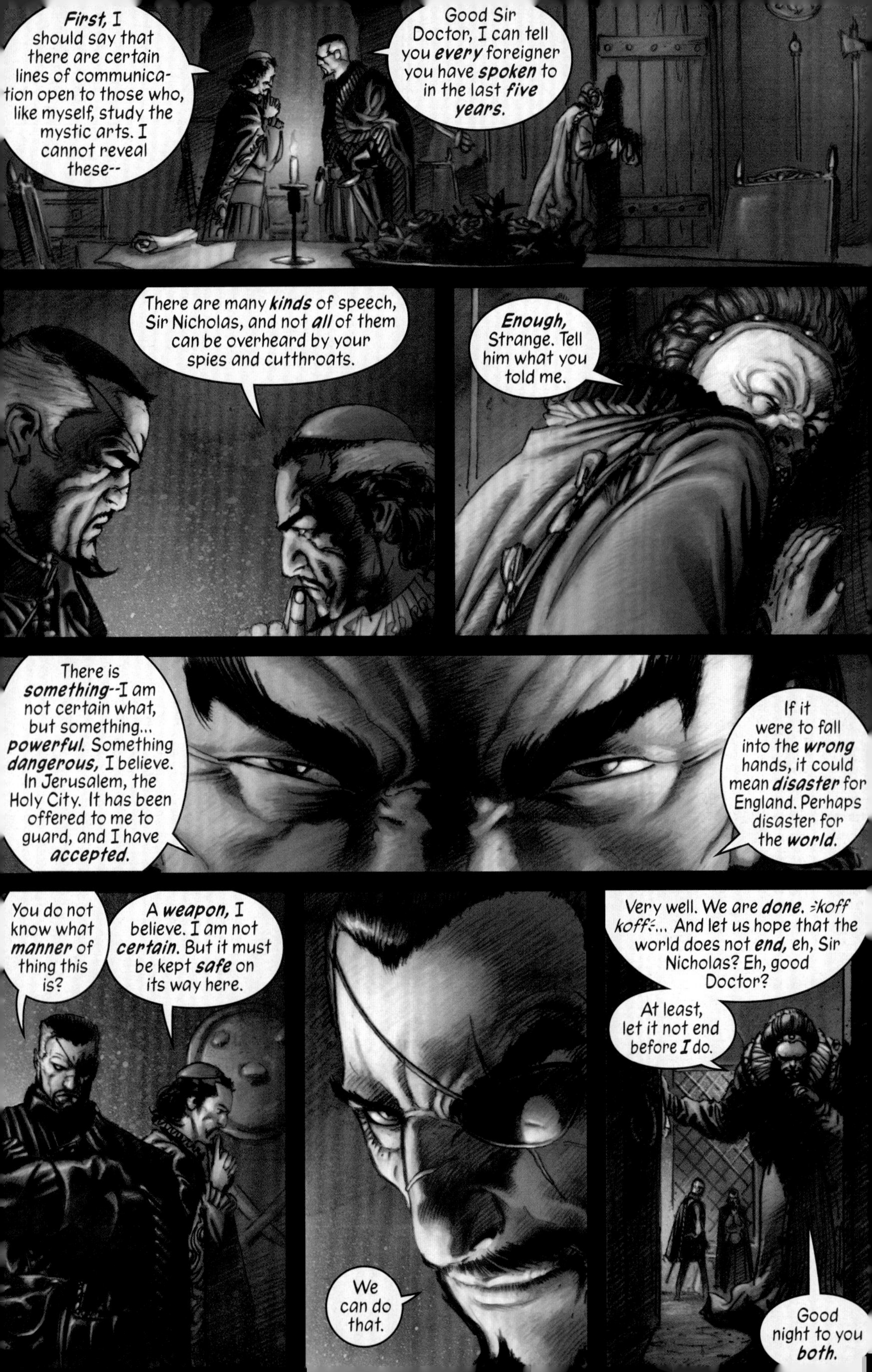
First, I should say that there are certain lines of communication open to those who, like myself, study the mystic arts. I cannot reveal these--
Good Sir Doctor, I can tell you every foreigner you have spoken to in the last five years.
There are many kinds of speech, Sir Nicholas, and not all of them can be overheard by your spies and cutthroats.
Enough, Strange. Tell him what you told me.
There is something--I am not certain what, but something... powerful. Something dangerous, I believe. In Jerusalem, the Holy City. It has been offered to me to guard, and I have accepted.
If it were to fall into the wrong hands, it could mean disaster for England. Perhaps disaster for the world.
You do not know what manner of thing this is?
A weapon, I believe. I am not certain. But it must be kept safe on its way here.
We can do that.
Very well. We are done. *koff koff*... And let us hope that the world does not end, eh, Sir Nicholas? Eh, good Doctor?
At least, let it not end before I do.
Good night to you both.

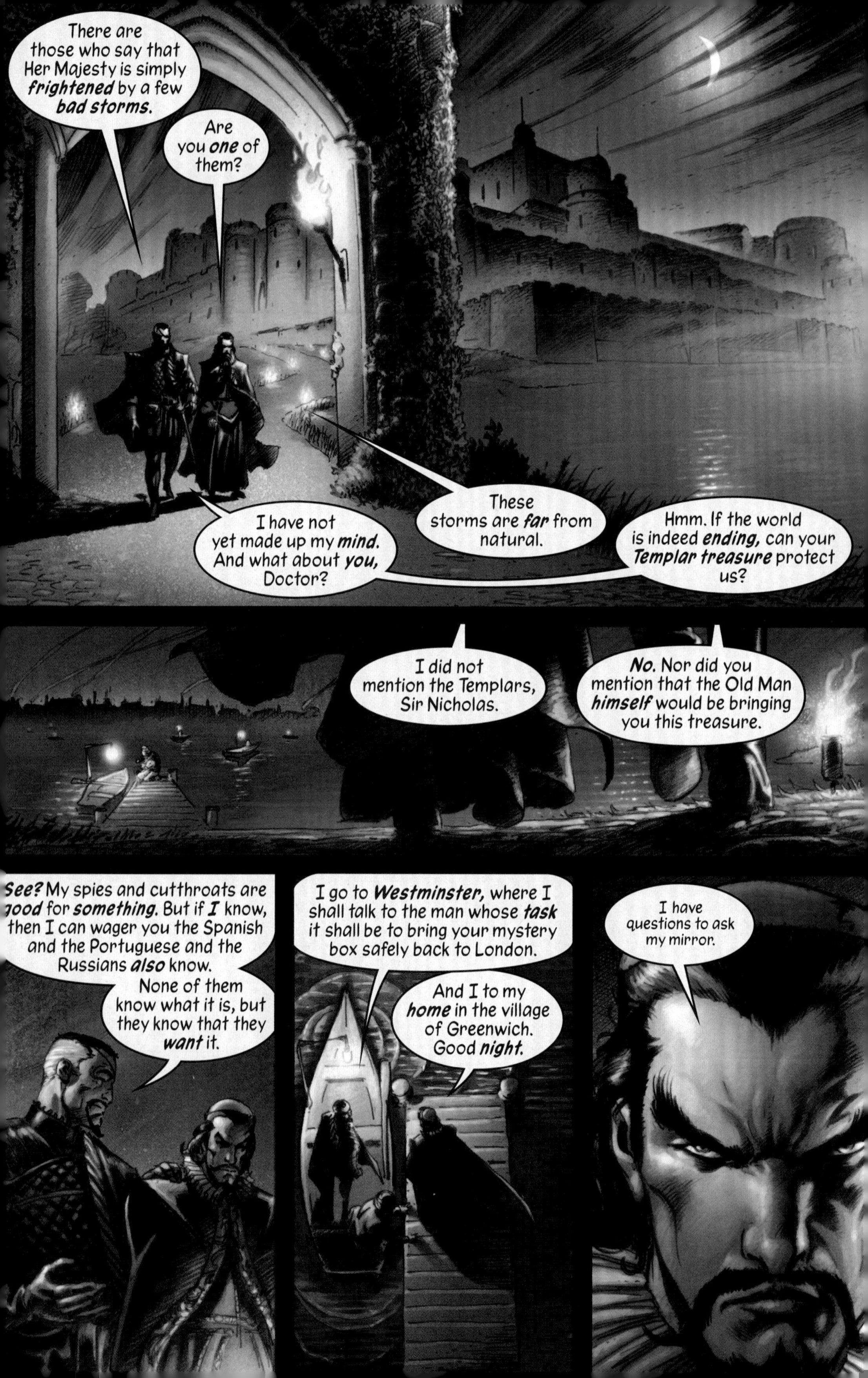
There are those who say that Her Majesty is simply *frightened* by a few *bad storms.*
Are you *one* of them?
I have not yet made up my *mind*. And what about *you,* Doctor?
These storms are *far* from natural.
Hmm. If the world is indeed *ending,* can your *Templar treasure* protect us?
I did not mention the Templars, Sir Nicholas.
No. Nor did you mention that the Old Man *himself* would be bringing you this treasure.
See? My spies and cutthroats are *good* for *something.* But if *I* know, then I can wager you the Spanish and the Portuguese and the Russians *also* know.
None of them know what it is, but they know that they *want* it.
I go to *Westminster,* where I shall talk to the man whose *task* it shall be to bring your mystery box safely back to London.
And I to my *home* in the village of Greenwich. Good *night.*
I have questions to ask my mirror.

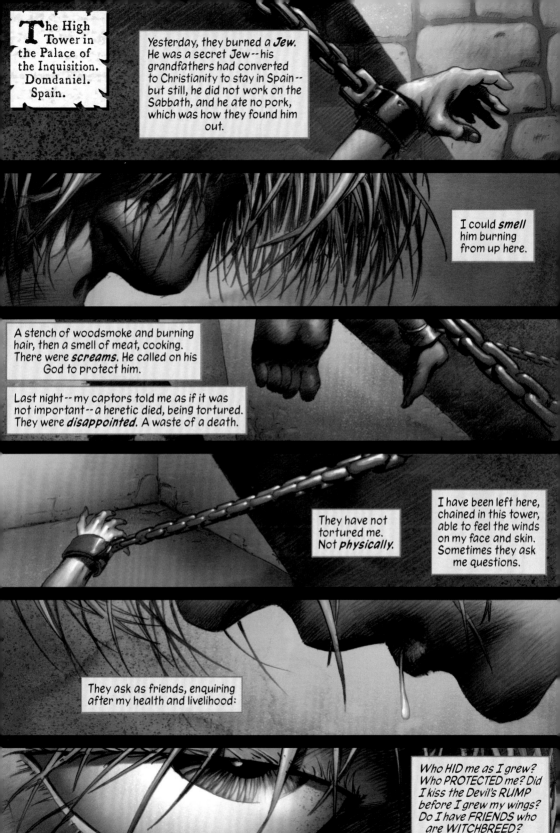

The High Tower in the Palace of the Inquisition. Domdaniel. Spain.

Yesterday, they burned a *Jew*. He was a secret Jew -- his grandfathers had converted to Christianity to stay in Spain -- but still, he did not work on the Sabbath, and he ate no pork, which was how they found him out.

I could *smell* him burning from up here.

A stench of woodsmoke and burning hair, then a smell of meat, cooking. There were *screams*. He called on his God to protect him.

Last night -- my captors told me as if it was not important -- a heretic died, being tortured. They were *disappointed*. A waste of a death.

They have not tortured me. Not *physically*.

I have been left here, chained in this tower, able to feel the winds on my face and skin. Sometimes they ask me questions.

They ask as friends, enquiring after my health and livelihood:

Who HID me as I grew? Who PROTECTED me? Did I kiss the Devil's RUMP before I grew my wings? Do I have FRIENDS who are WITCHBREED?

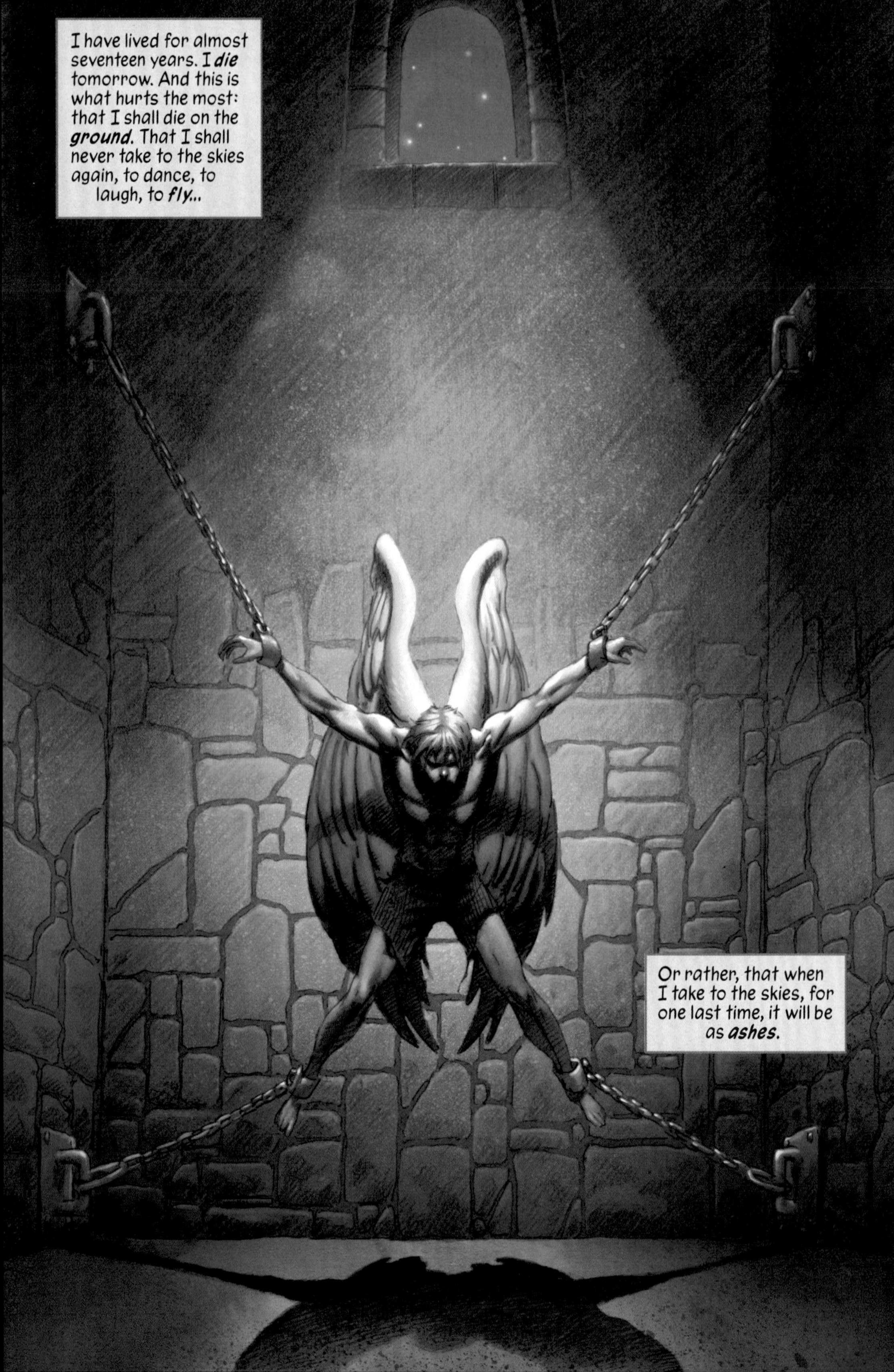
I have lived for almost seventeen years. I *die* tomorrow. And this is what hurts the most: that I shall die on the ***ground***. That I shall never take to the skies again, to dance, to laugh, to *fly*...
Or rather, that when I take to the skies, for one last time, it will be as ***ashes***.

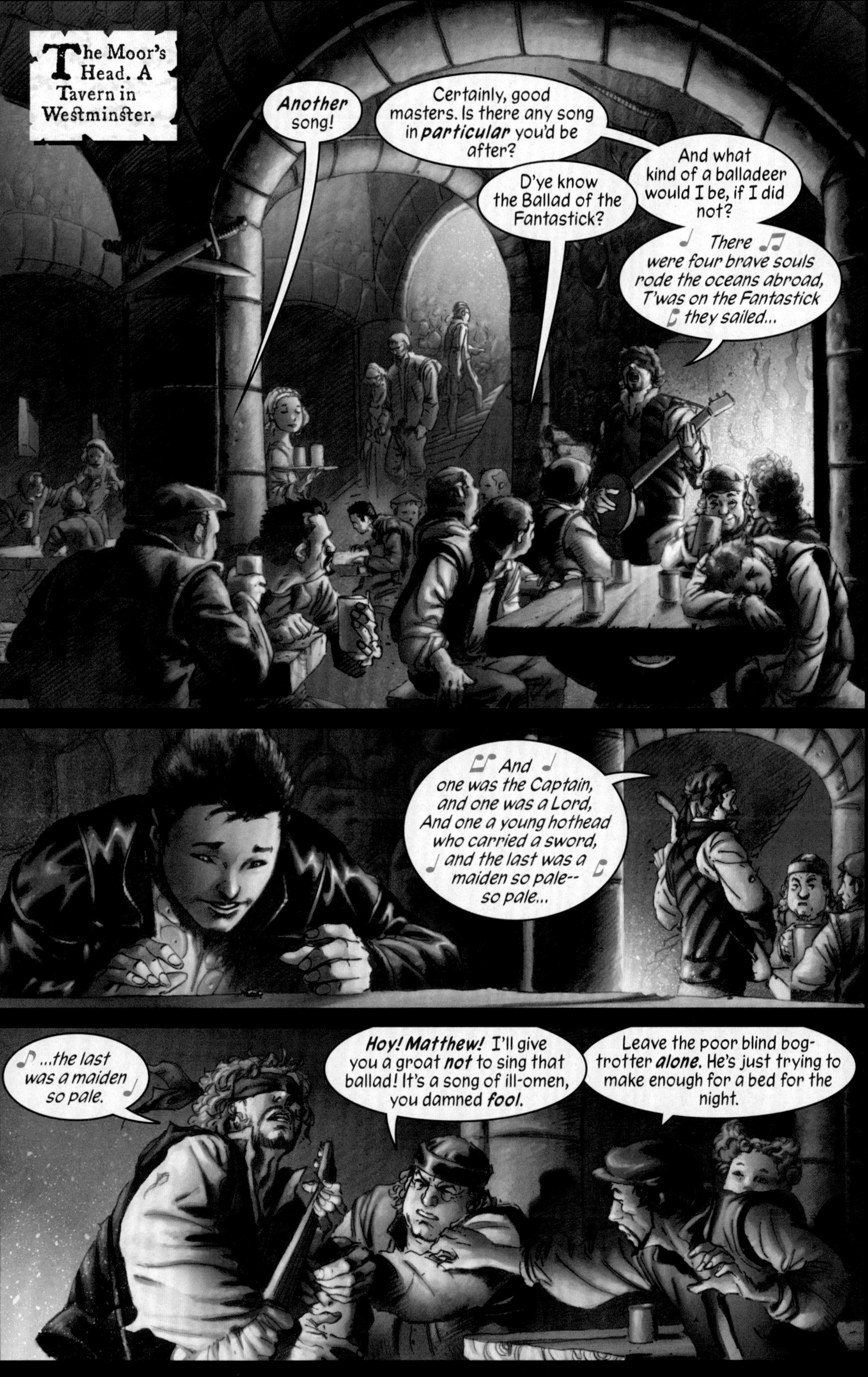
The Moor's Head. A Tavern in Westminster.
Another song!
Certainly, good masters. Is there any song in particular you'd be after?
D'ye know the Ballad of the Fantastick?
And what kind of a balladeer would I be, if I did not?
There were four brave souls rode the oceans abroad, T'was on the Fantastick they sailed...
And one was the Captain, and one was a Lord, And one a young hothead who carried a sword, and the last was a maiden so pale-- so pale...
...the last was a maiden so pale.
Hoy! Matthew! I'll give you a groat not to sing that ballad! It's a song of ill-omen, you damned fool.
Leave the poor blind bog-trotter alone. He's just trying to make enough for a bed for the night.

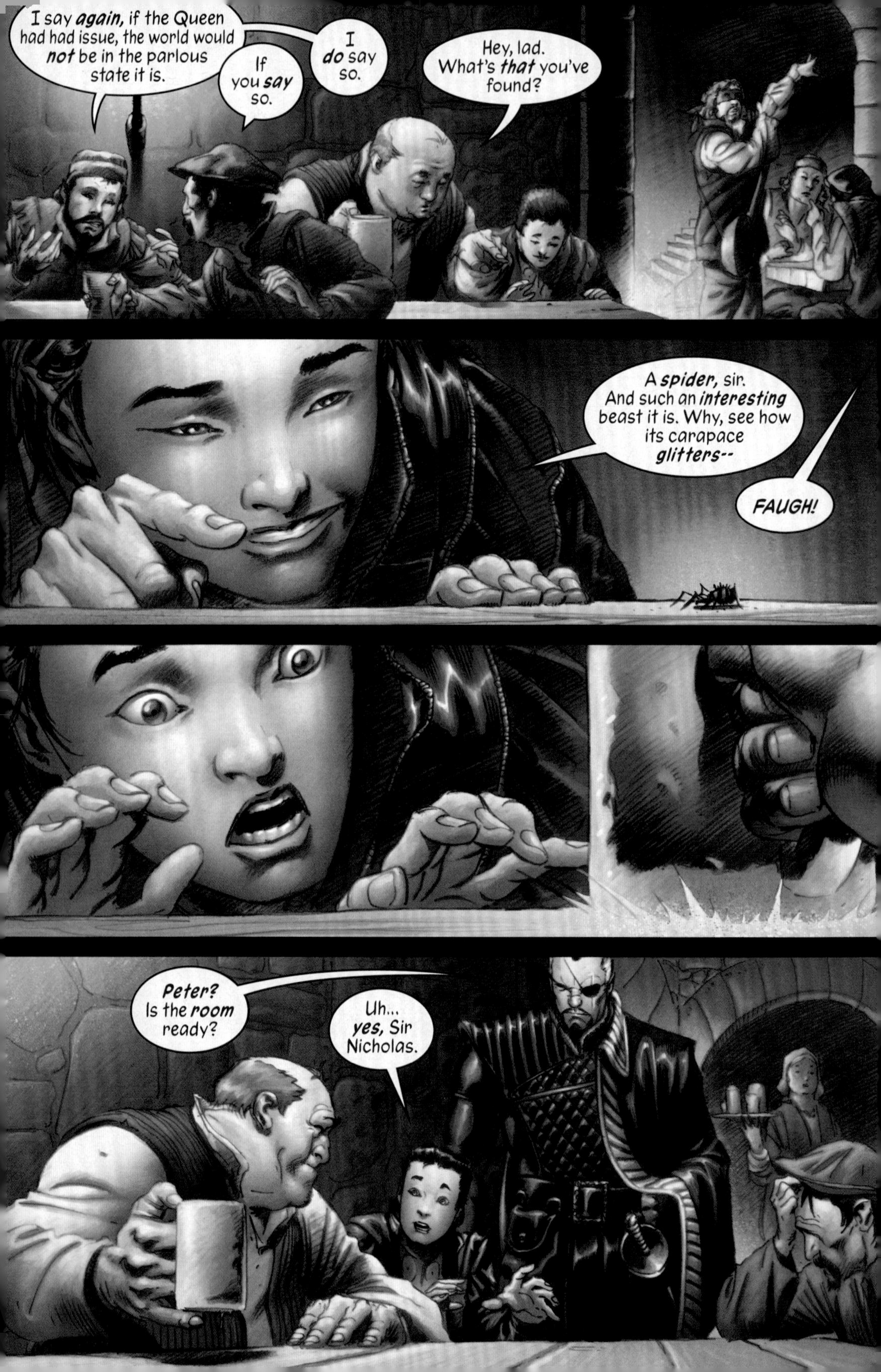
I say *again,* if the Queen had had issue, the world would *not* be in the parlous state it is.
If you *say* so.
I *do* say so.
Hey, lad. What's *that* you've found?
A *spider,* sir. And such an *interesting* beast it is. Why, see how its carapace *glitters--*
FAUGH!
Peter? Is the *room* ready?
Uh... *yes,* Sir Nicholas.

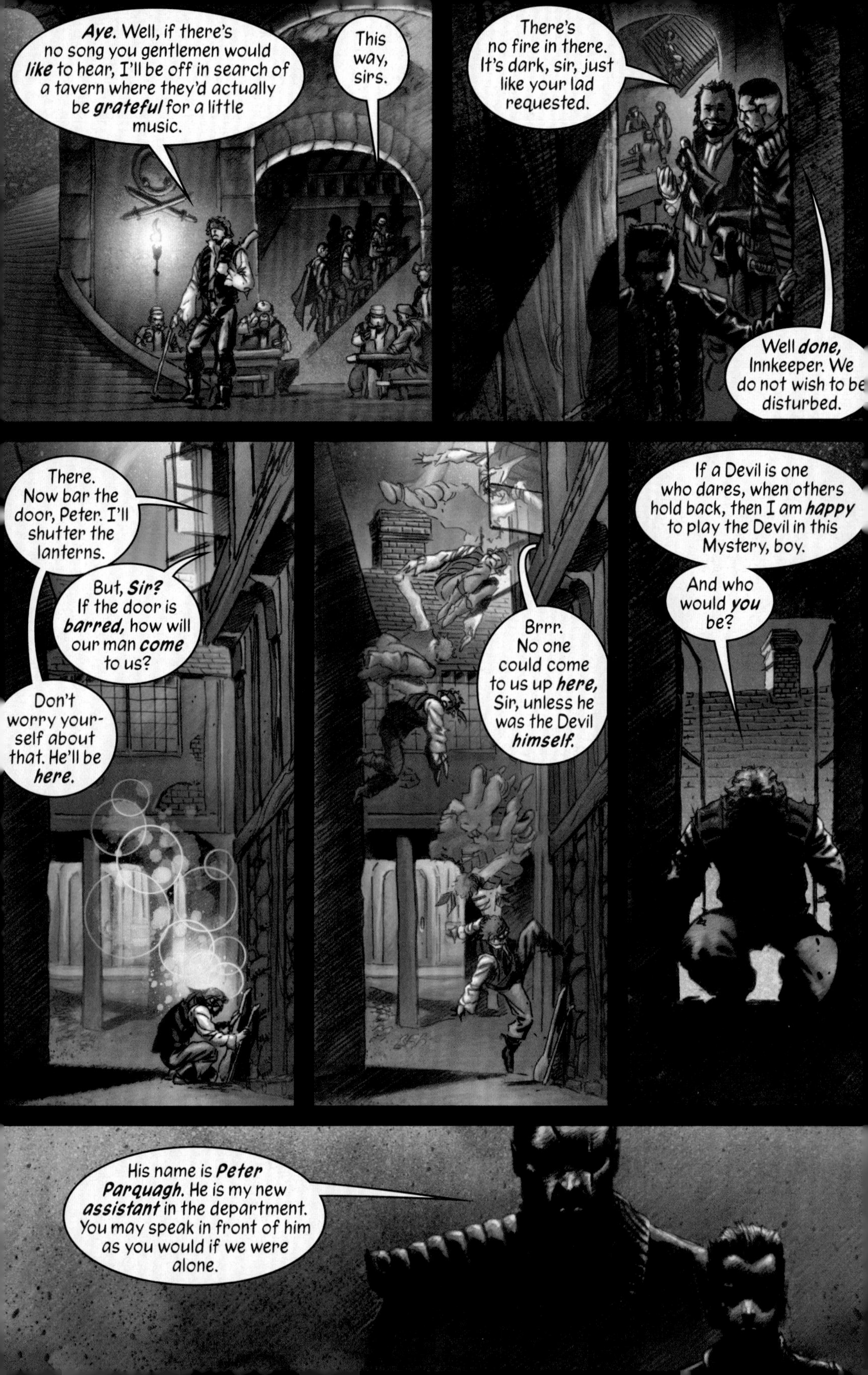
Aye. Well, if there's no song you gentlemen would like to hear, I'll be off in search of a tavern where they'd actually be grateful for a little music.
This way, sirs.
There's no fire in there. It's dark, sir, just like your lad requested.
Well done, Innkeeper. We do not wish to be disturbed.
There. Now bar the door, Peter. I'll shutter the lanterns.
But, Sir? If the door is barred, how will our man come to us?
Don't worry yourself about that. He'll be here.
Brrr. No one could come to us up here, Sir, unless he was the Devil himself.
If a Devil is one who dares, when others hold back, then I am happy to play the Devil in this Mystery, boy.
And who would you be?
His name is Peter Parquagh. He is my new assistant in the department. You may speak in front of him as you would if we were alone.

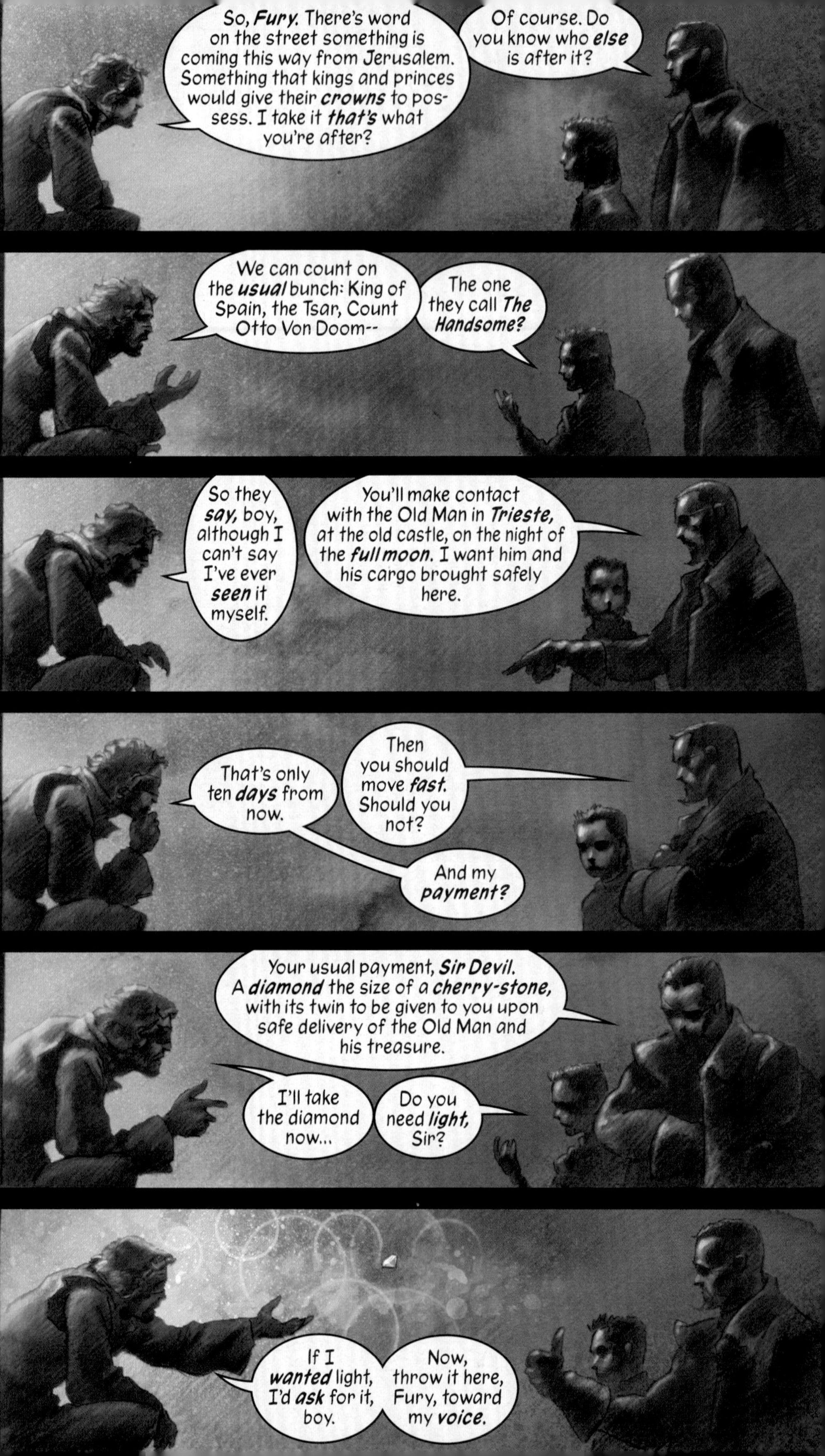
So, *Fury.* There's word on the street something is coming this way from Jerusalem. Something that kings and princes would give their *crowns* to possess. I take it *that's* what you're after?
Of course. Do you know who *else* is after it?
We can count on the *usual* bunch: King of Spain, the Tsar, Count Otto Von Doom--
The one they call *The Handsome?*
So they *say,* boy, although I can't say I've ever *seen* it myself.
You'll make contact with the Old Man in *Trieste,* at the old castle, on the night of the *full moon.* I want him and his cargo brought safely here.
That's only ten *days* from now.
Then you should move *fast.* Should you not?
And my *payment?*
Your usual payment, *Sir Devil.* A *diamond* the size of a *cherry-stone,* with its twin to be given to you upon safe delivery of the Old Man and his treasure.
I'll take the diamond now...
Do you need *light,* Sir?
If I *wanted* light, I'd *ask* for it, boy.
Now, throw it here, Fury, toward my *voice.*

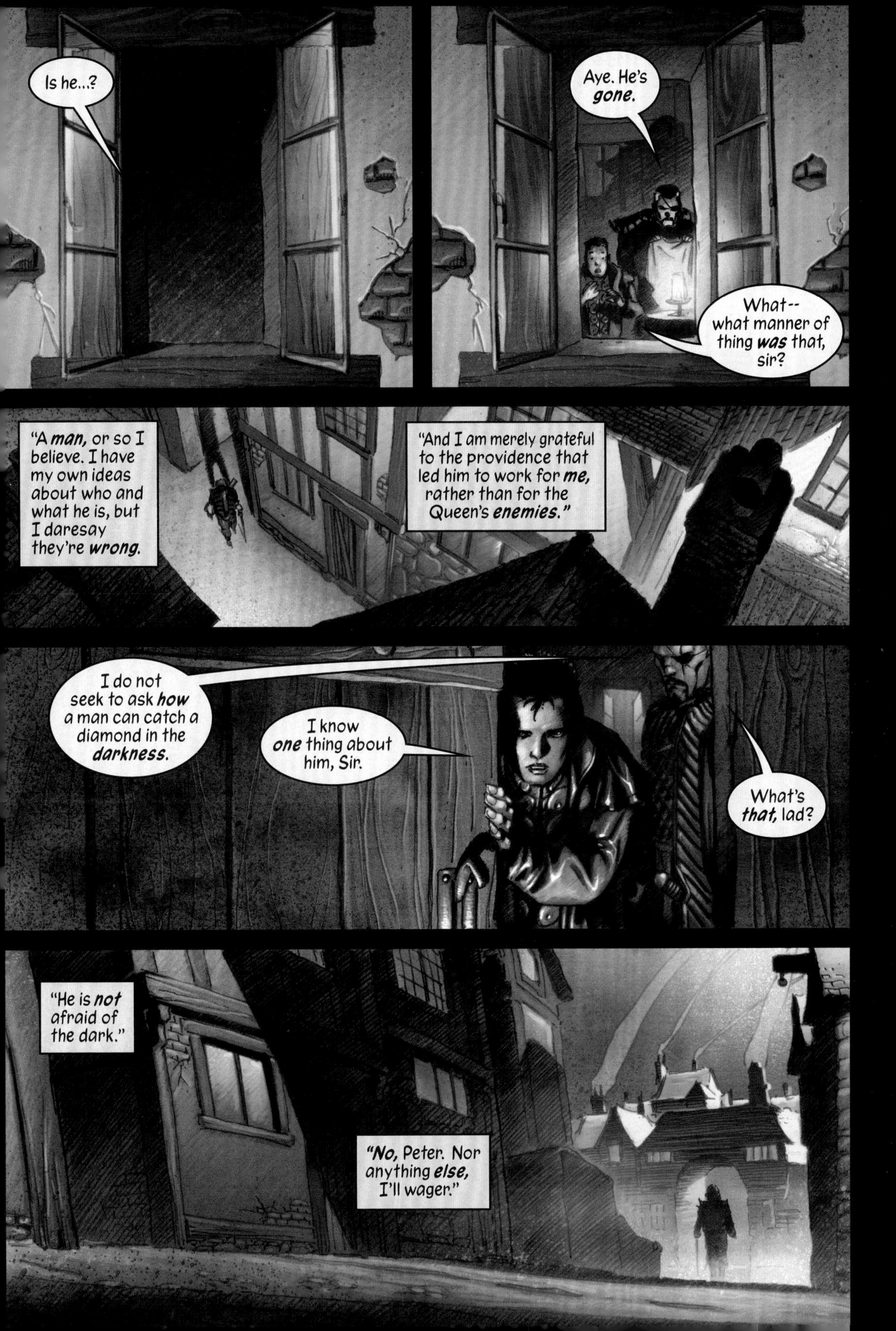
Is he...?
Aye. He's **gone.**
What-- what manner of thing **was** that, sir?
"A **man,** or so I believe. I have my own ideas about who and what he is, but I daresay they're **wrong.**
"And I am merely grateful to the providence that led him to work for **me,** rather than for the Queen's **enemies.**"
I do not seek to ask **how** a man can catch a diamond in the **darkness.**
I know **one** thing about him, Sir.
What's **that,** lad?
"He is **not** afraid of the dark."
"**No,** Peter. Nor anything **else,** I'll wager."

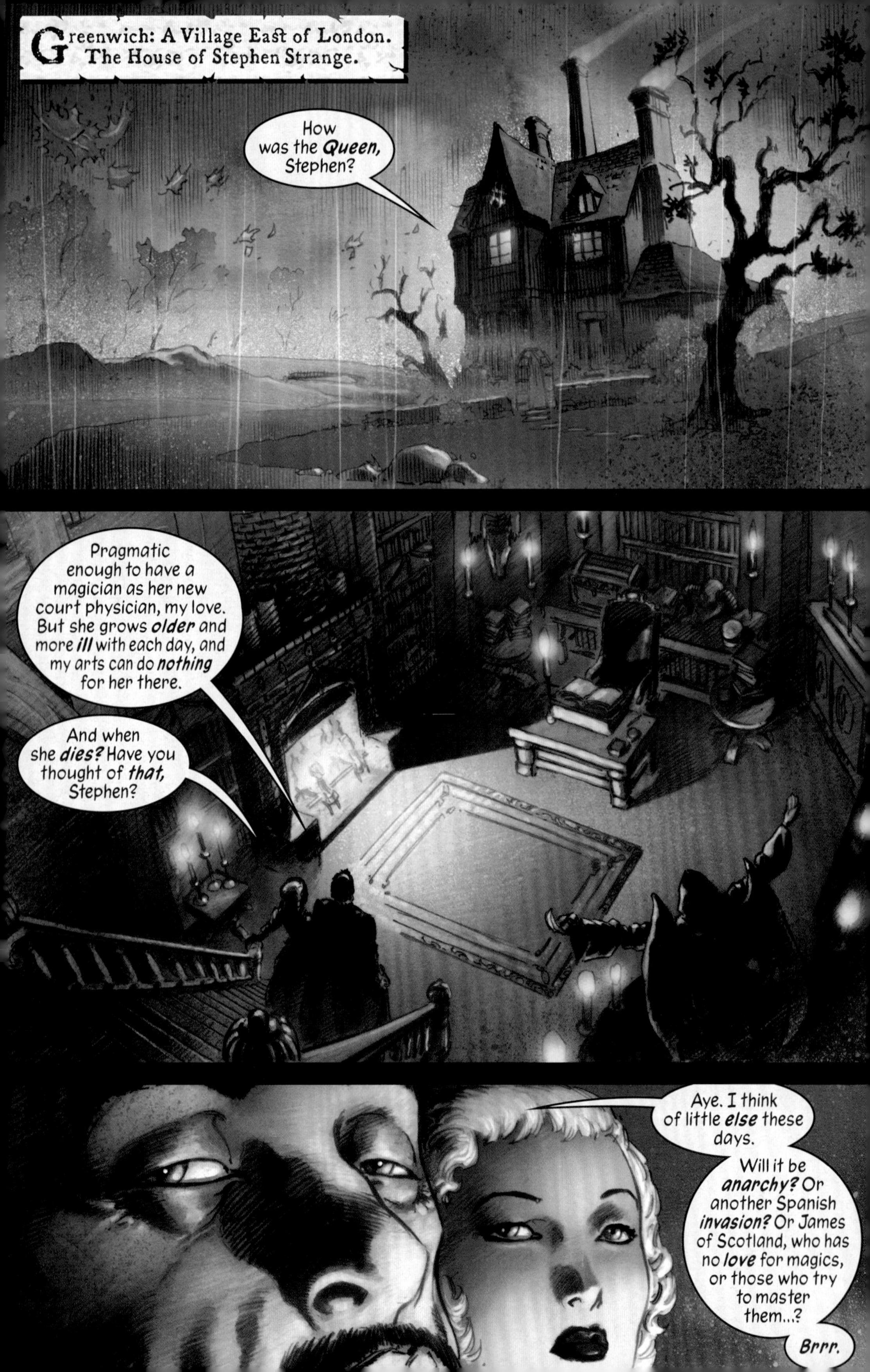
Greenwich: A Village East of London.
The House of Stephen Strange.
How was the Queen, Stephen?
Pragmatic enough to have a magician as her new court physician, my love. But she grows older and more ill with each day, and my arts can do nothing for her there.
And when she dies? Have you thought of that, Stephen?
Aye. I think of little else these days.
Will it be anarchy? Or another Spanish invasion? Or James of Scotland, who has no love for magics, or those who try to master them...?
Brrr.

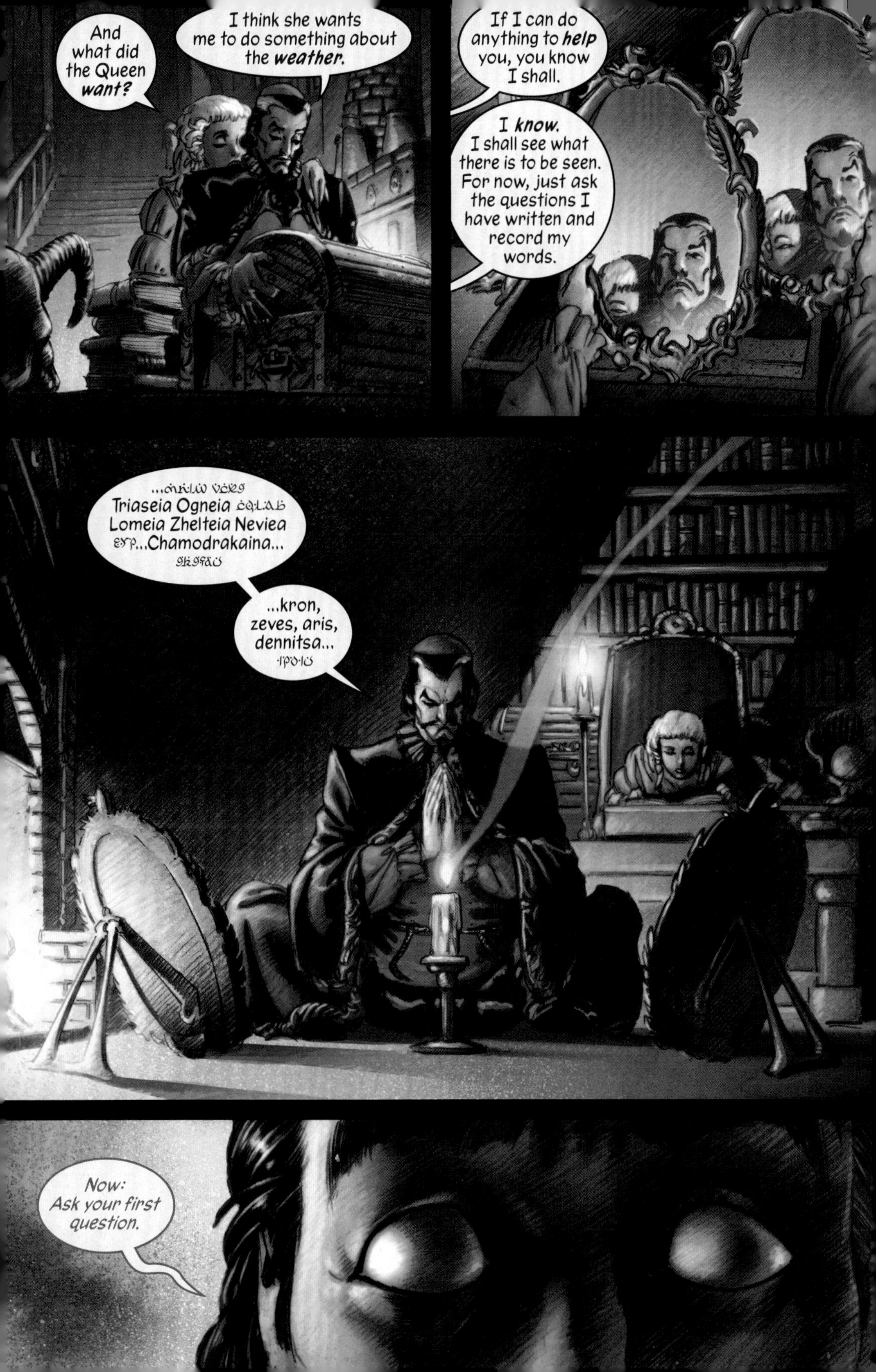

And what did the Queen *want?*
I think she wants me to do something about the *weather.*
If I can do anything to *help* you, you know I shall.
I *know.* I shall see what there is to be seen. For now, just ask the questions I have written and record my words.
Triaseia Ogneia Lomeia Zhelteia Neviea ...Chamodrakaina...
...kron, zeves, aris, dennitsa...
Now: Ask your first question.

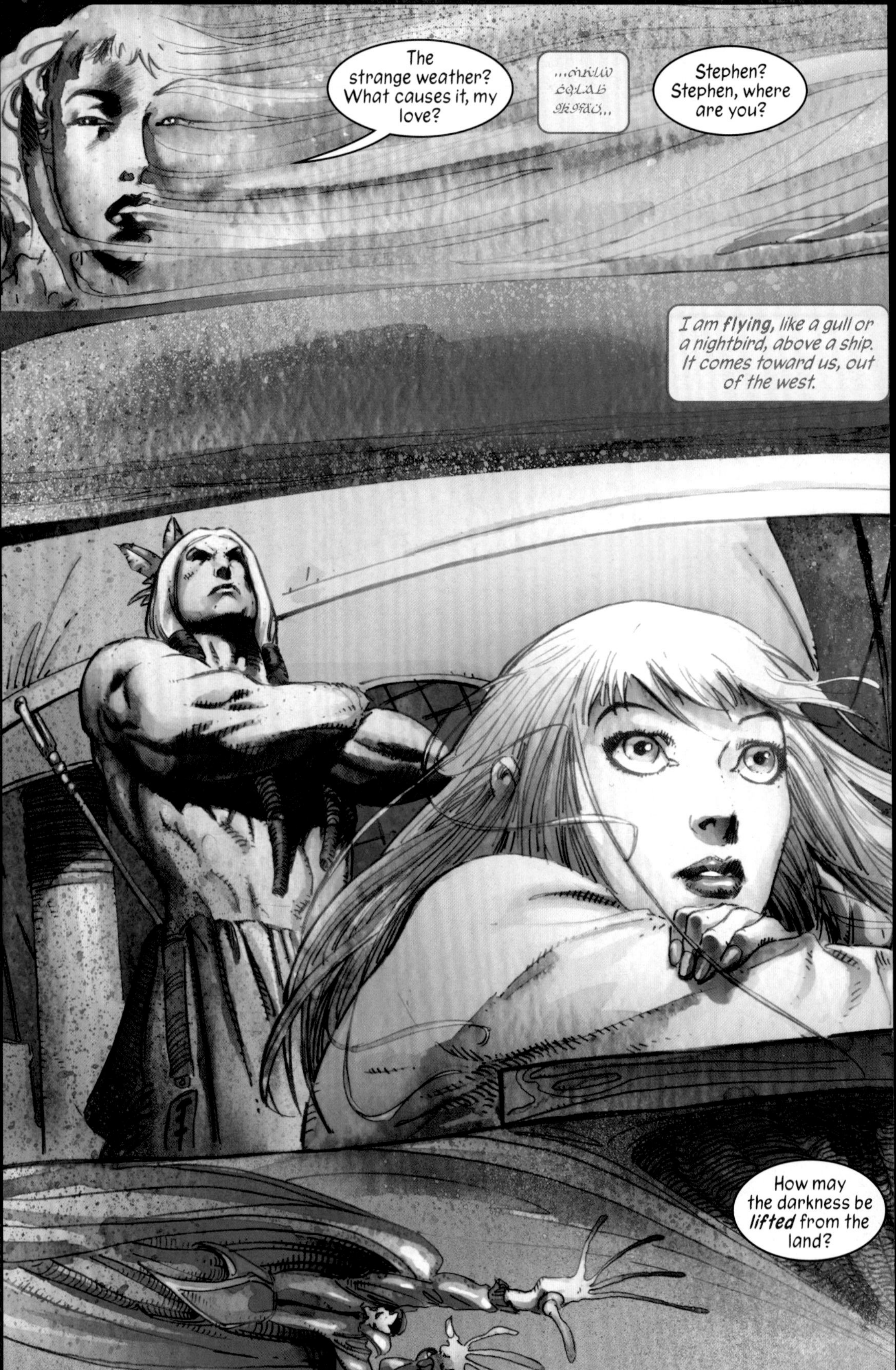
The strange weather? What causes it, my love?
Stephen? Stephen, where are you?
I am *flying*, like a gull or a nightbird, above a ship. It comes toward us, out of the west.
How may the darkness be *lifted* from the land?

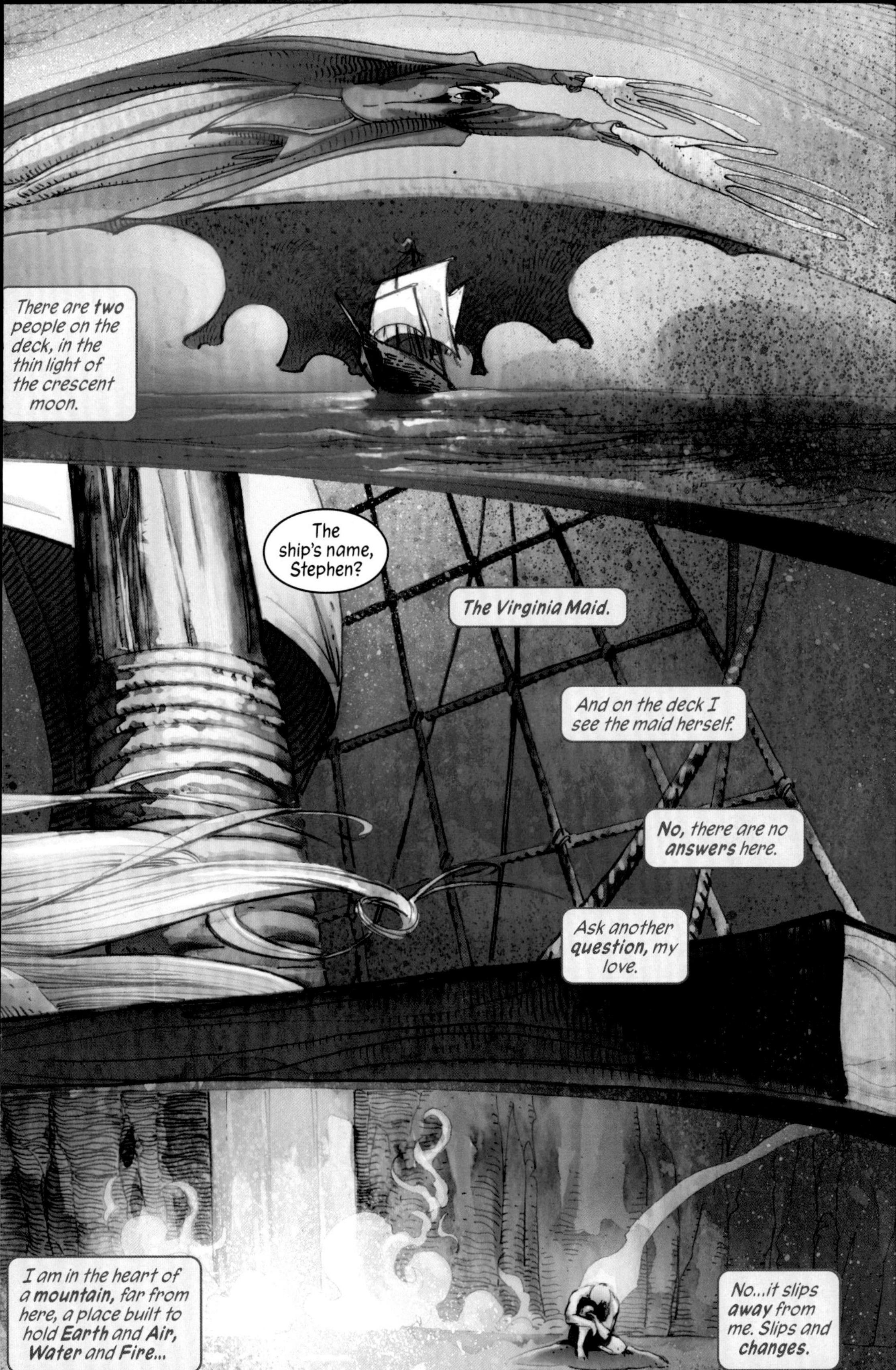
There are two people on the deck, in the thin light of the crescent moon.
The ship's name, Stephen?
The Virginia Maid.
And on the deck I see the maid herself.
No, there are no answers here.
Ask another question, my love.
I am in the heart of a mountain, far from here, a place built to hold Earth and Air, Water and Fire...
No...it slips away from me. Slips and changes.

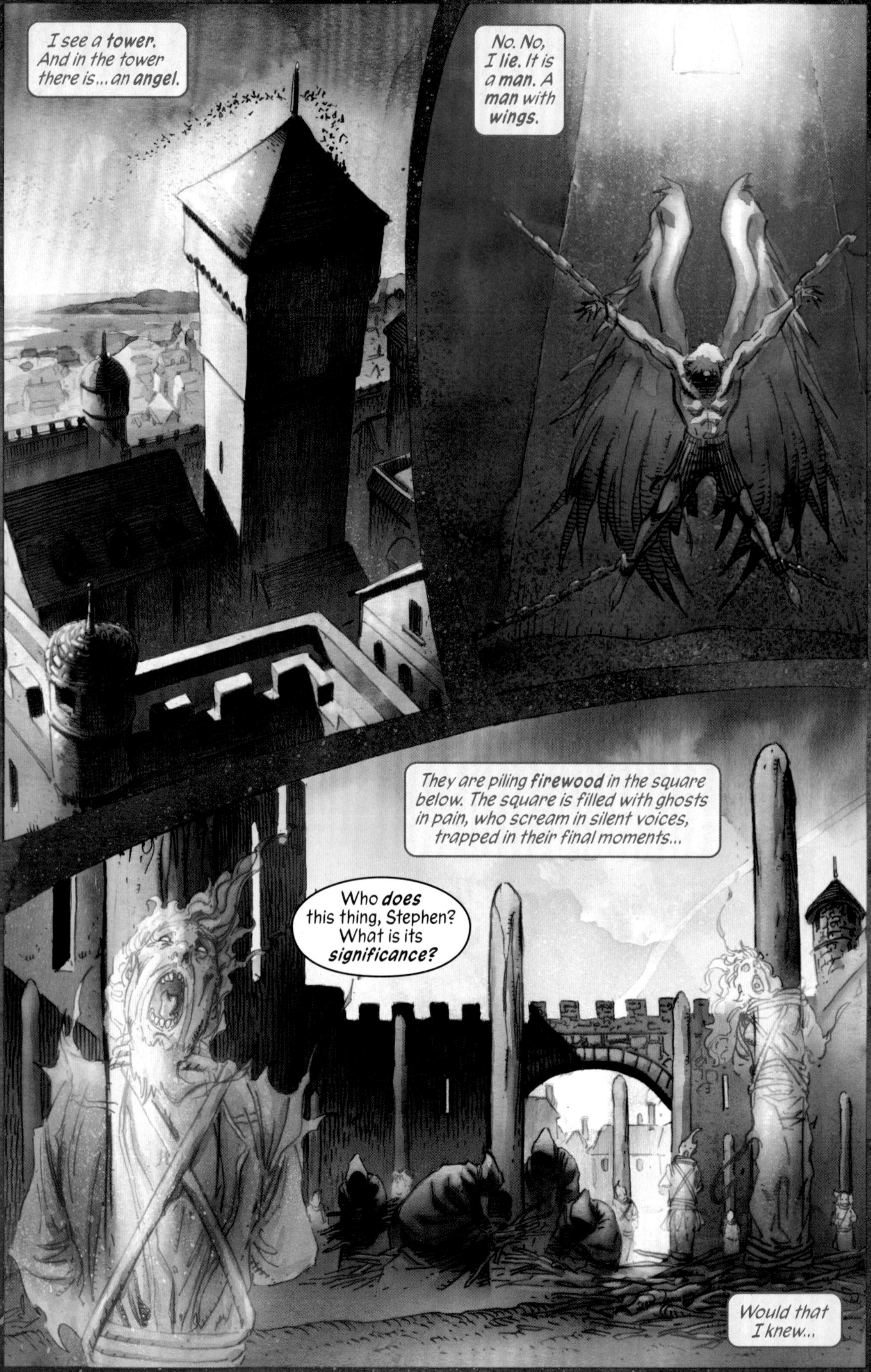
I see a tower. And in the tower there is... an angel.
No. No, I lie. It is a man. A man with wings.
They are piling firewood in the square below. The square is filled with ghosts in pain, who scream in silent voices, trapped in their final moments...
Who does this thing, Stephen? What is its significance?
Would that I knew...

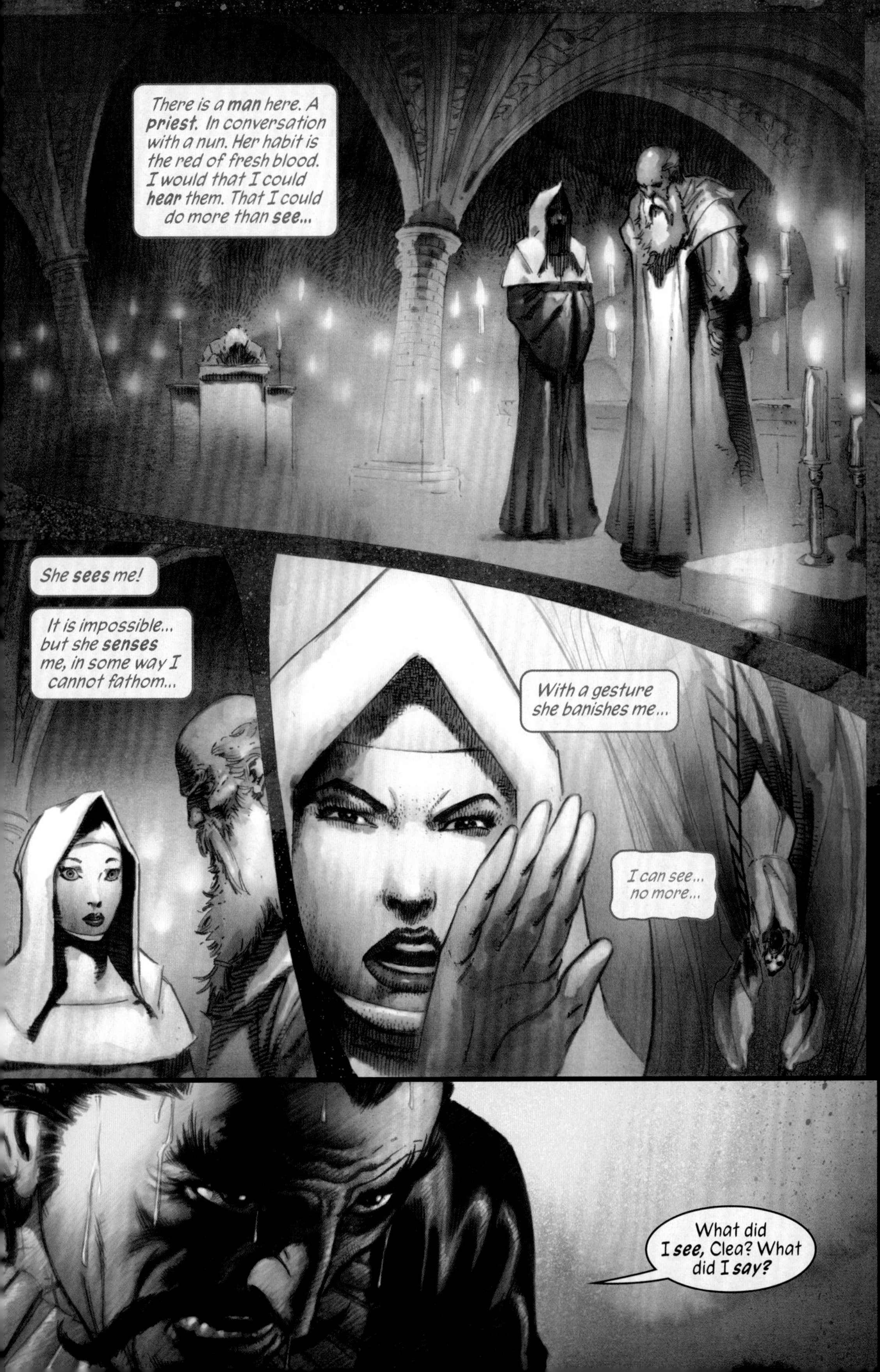
There is a man here. A priest. In conversation with a nun. Her habit is the red of fresh blood. I would that I could hear them. That I could do more than see...
She sees me!
It is impossible... but she senses me, in some way I cannot fathom...
With a gesture she banishes me...
I can see... no more...
What did I see, Clea? What did I say?

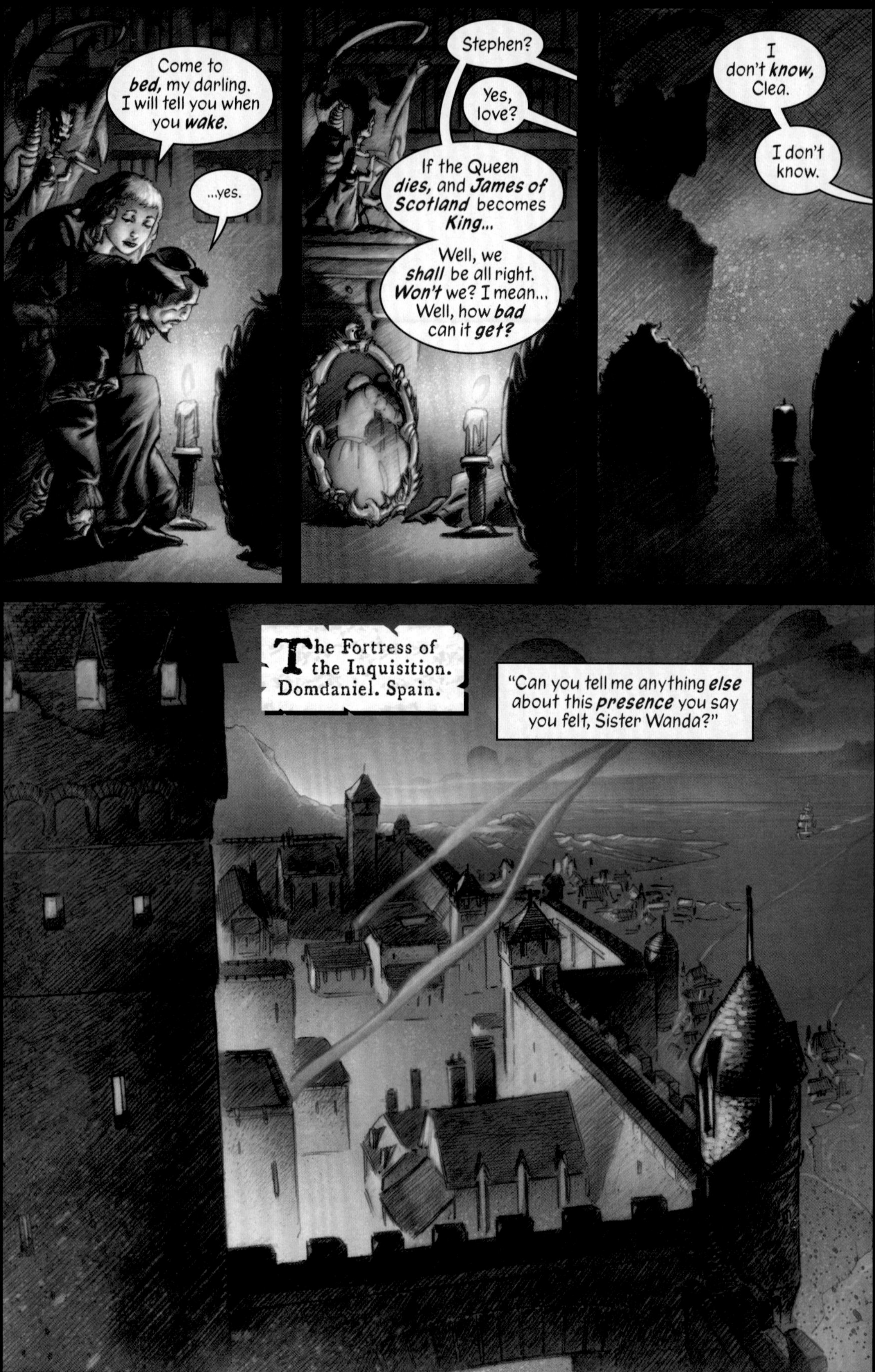
Come to bed, my darling. I will tell you when you wake.
...yes.
Stephen?
Yes, love?
If the Queen dies, and James of Scotland becomes King...
Well, we shall be all right. Won't we? I mean... Well, how bad can it get?
I don't know, Clea.
I don't know.
The Fortress of the Inquisition. Domdaniel. Spain.
"Can you tell me anything else about this presence you say you felt, Sister Wanda?"

Nothing, Grand Inquisitor. Perhaps...perhaps I simply *imagined* it.

I *doubt* it.

No, it was *Javier.* I have no doubt on *that* score.

Petros? Send a message to the guard: they must be *extra* vigilant at tomorrow's burning.

Yes sir.

You may *leave* us, Sister Wanda.

So *tell* me, Petros, *how* was the court of James of Scotland?

His Majesty sends you his *greetings,* Inquisitor.

And?

While James is of the *Protestant* faith, he feels that there is common cause against...

"...witches, magicians and the witchbreed, who infest England like lice crawling through a shepherd's crotch."

His words. Not mine.

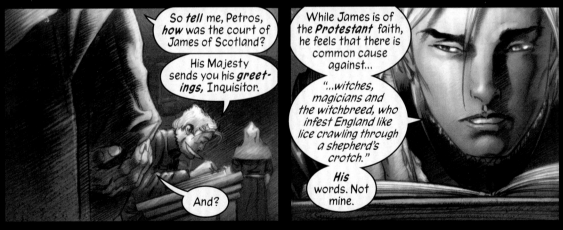

So is there room for an *alliance?*

He told me that the English have *long* memories. They have not yet forgotten Queen Mary--they call her Bloody Mary-- and her burnings.

He says that *any* work must be done *carefully* and *quietly*--and with public support and approval.

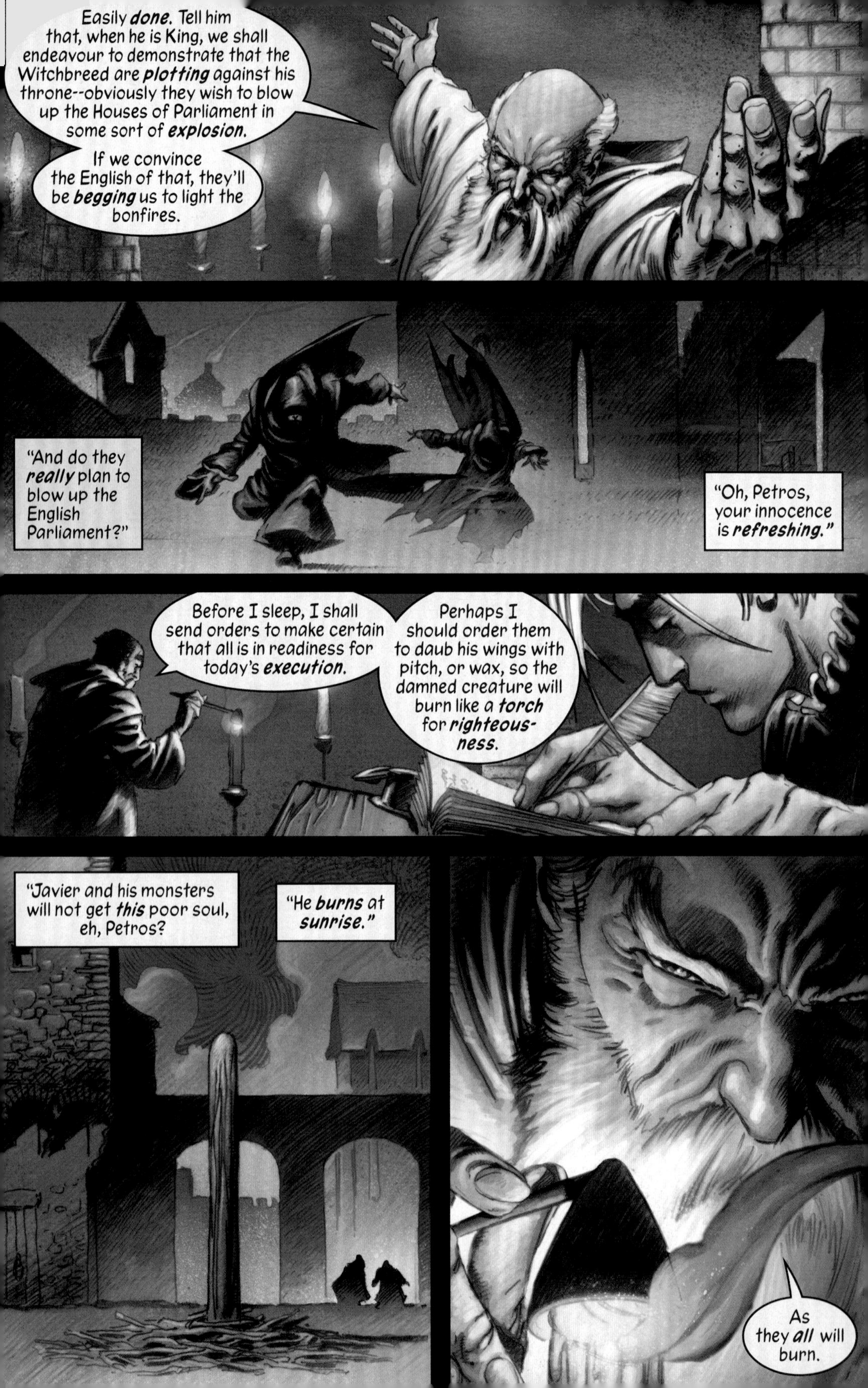
Easily *done.* Tell him that, when he is King, we shall endeavour to demonstrate that the Witchbreed are *plotting* against his throne--obviously they wish to blow up the Houses of Parliament in some sort of *explosion.*
If we convince the English of that, they'll be *begging* us to light the bonfires.
"And do they *really* plan to blow up the English Parliament?"
"Oh, Petros, your innocence is *refreshing.*"
Before I sleep, I shall send orders to make certain that all is in readiness for today's *execution.*
Perhaps I should order them to daub his wings with pitch, or wax, so the damned creature will burn like a *torch* for *righteous-ness.*
"Javier and his monsters will not get *this* poor soul, eh, Petros?
"He *burns* at *sunrise.*"
As they *all* will burn.

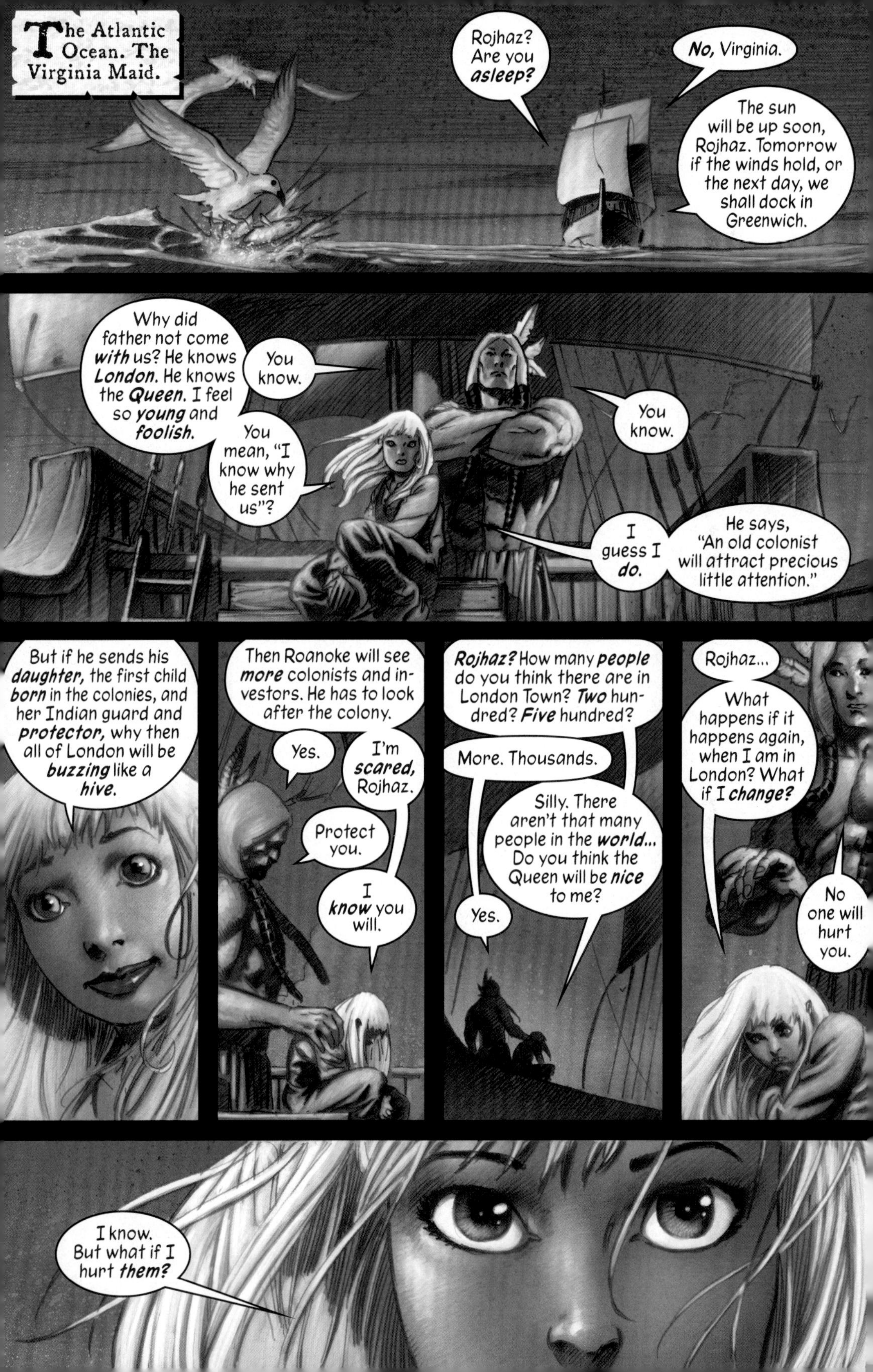
The Atlantic Ocean. The Virginia Maid.
Rojhaz? Are you *asleep?*
No, Virginia.
The sun will be up soon, Rojhaz. Tomorrow if the winds hold, or the next day, we shall dock in Greenwich.
Why did father not come *with* us? He knows *London.* He knows the *Queen.* I feel so *young* and *foolish.*
You know.
You mean, "I know why he sent us"?
You know.
I guess I *do.*
He says, "An old colonist will attract precious little attention."
But if he sends his *daughter,* the first child *born* in the colonies, and her Indian guard and *protector,* why then all of London will be *buzzing* like a *hive.*
Then Roanoke will see *more* colonists and investors. He has to look after the colony.
Yes.
I'm *scared,* Rojhaz.
Protect you.
I *know* you will.
Rojhaz? How many *people* do you think there are in London Town? *Two* hundred? *Five* hundred?
More. Thousands.
Silly. There aren't that many people in the *world...* Do you think the Queen will be *nice* to me?
Yes.
Rojhaz...
What happens if it happens again, when I am in London? What if I *change?*
No one will hurt you.
I know. But what if I hurt *them?*

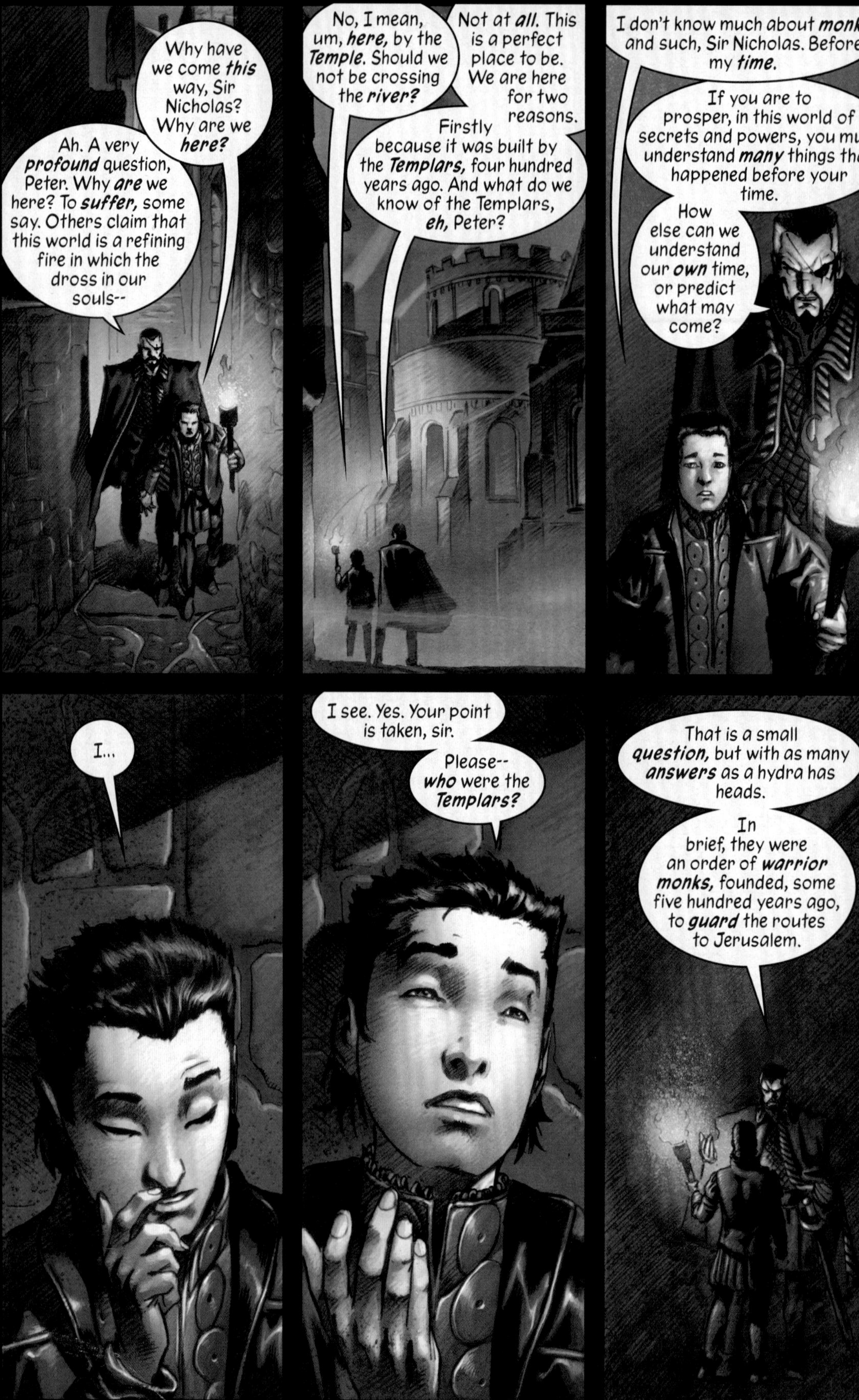

Why have we come this way, Sir Nicholas? Why are we here?
Ah. A very profound question, Peter. Why are we here? To suffer, some say. Others claim that this world is a refining fire in which the dross in our souls--
No, I mean, um, here, by the Temple. Should we not be crossing the river?
Not at all. This is a perfect place to be. We are here for two reasons.
Firstly because it was built by the Templars, four hundred years ago. And what do we know of the Templars, eh, Peter?
I don't know much about monks and such, Sir Nicholas. Before my time.
If you are to prosper, in this world of secrets and powers, you must understand many things that happened before your time.
How else can we understand our own time, or predict what may come?
I...
I see. Yes. Your point is taken, sir.
Please-- who were the Templars?
That is a small question, but with as many answers as a hydra has heads.
In brief, they were an order of warrior monks, founded, some five hundred years ago, to guard the routes to Jerusalem.

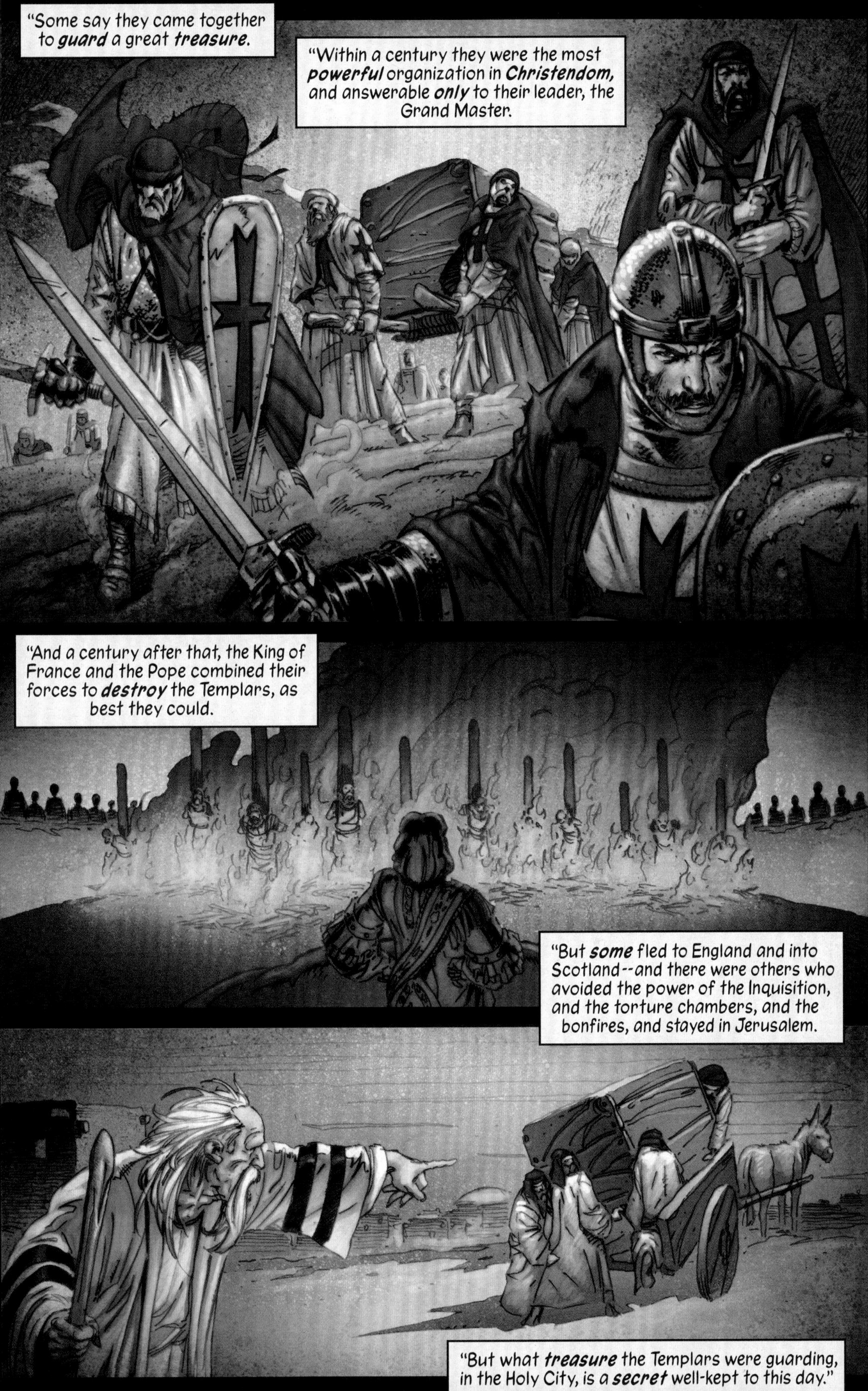
"Some say they came together to guard a great treasure.
"Within a century they were the most powerful organization in Christendom, and answerable only to their leader, the Grand Master.
"And a century after that, the King of France and the Pope combined their forces to destroy the Templars, as best they could.
"But some fled to England and into Scotland--and there were others who avoided the power of the Inquisition, and the torture chambers, and the bonfires, and stayed in Jerusalem.
"But what treasure the Templars were guarding, in the Holy City, is a secret well-kept to this day."

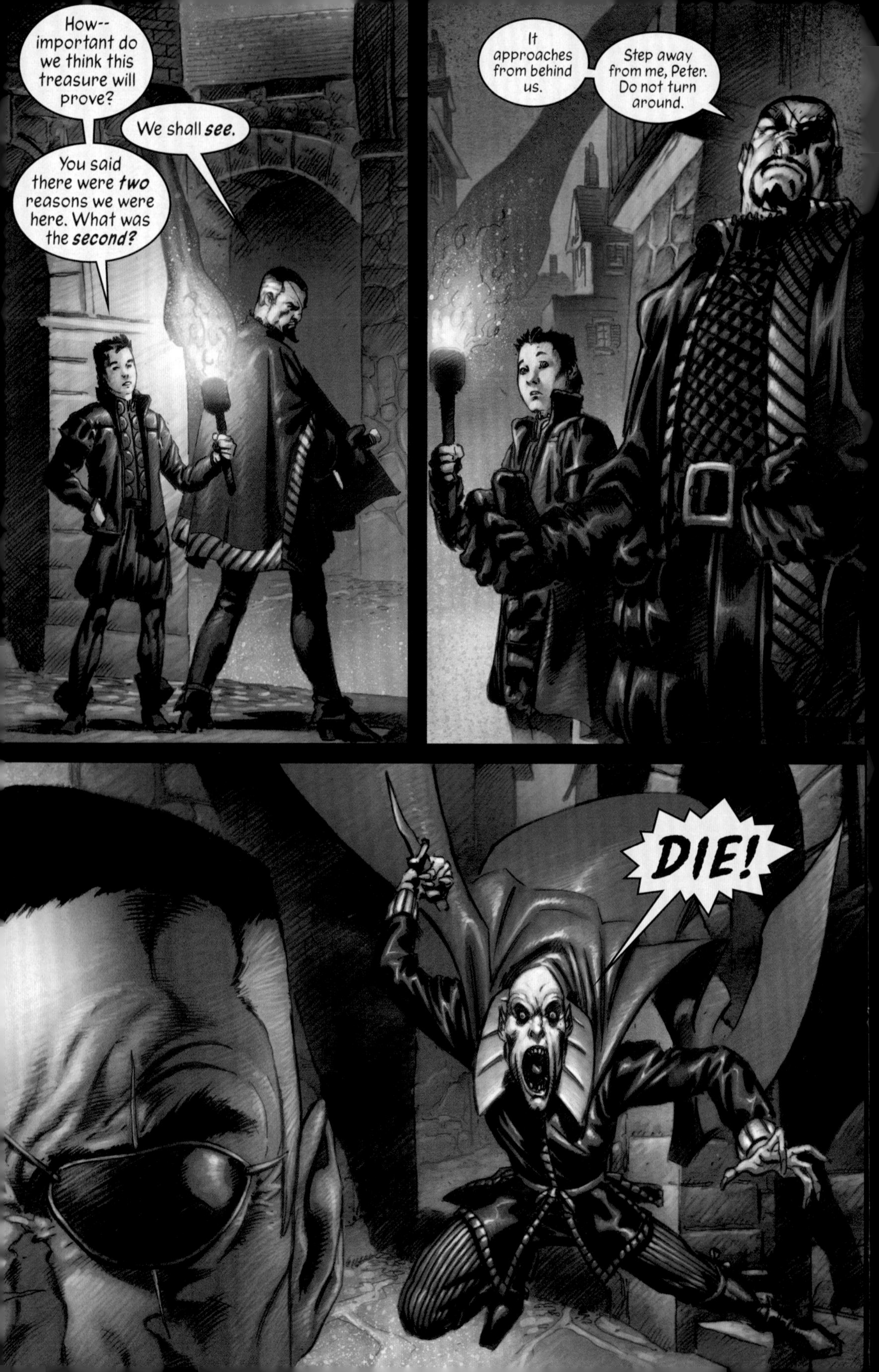
How-- important do we think this treasure will prove?
We shall *see.*
You said there were *two* reasons we were here. What was the *second?*
It approaches from behind us.
Step away from me, Peter. Do not turn around.
DIE!

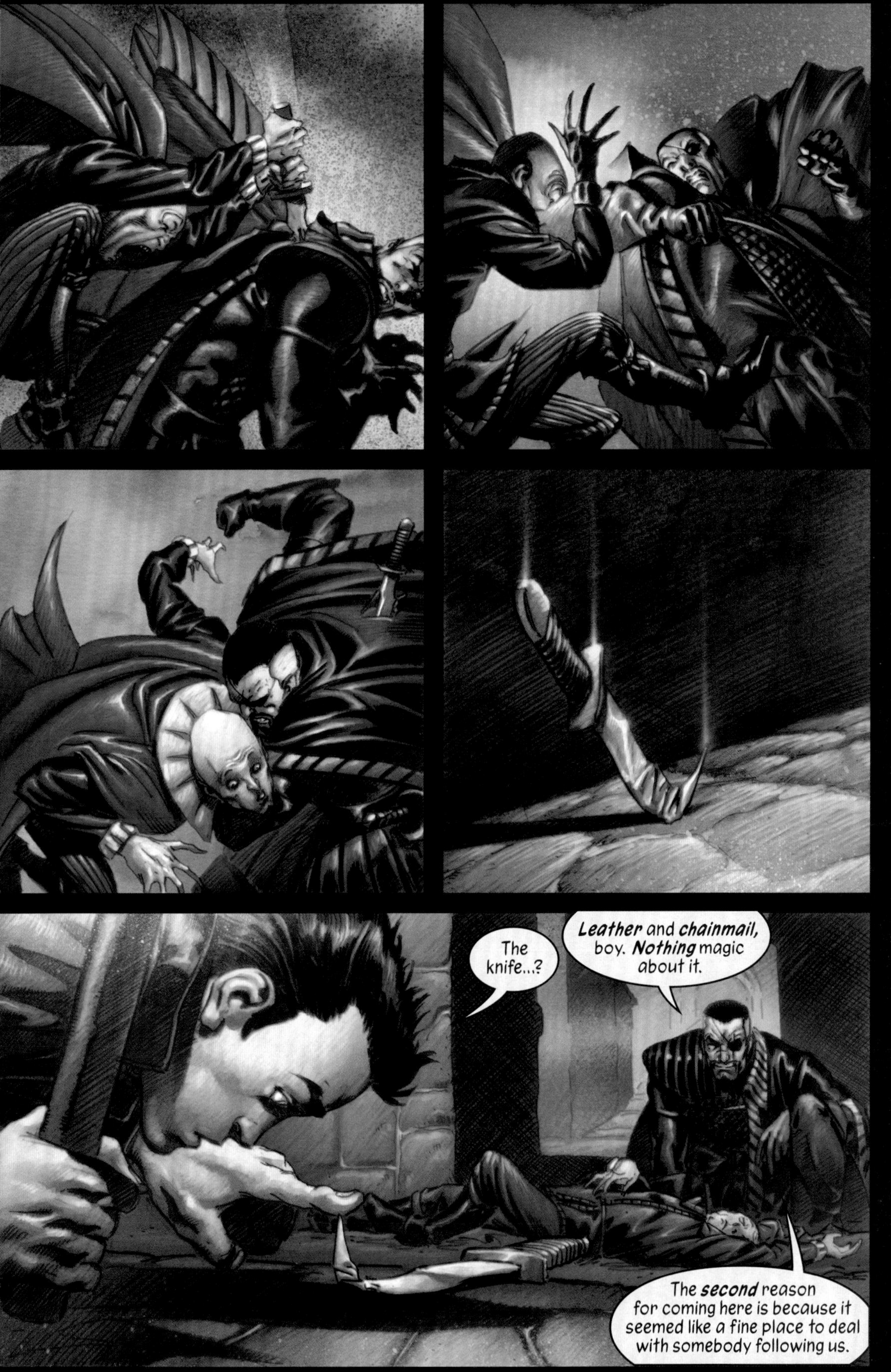
The knife...?
Leather and chainmail, boy. Nothing magic about it.
The second reason for coming here is because it seemed like a fine place to deal with somebody following us.

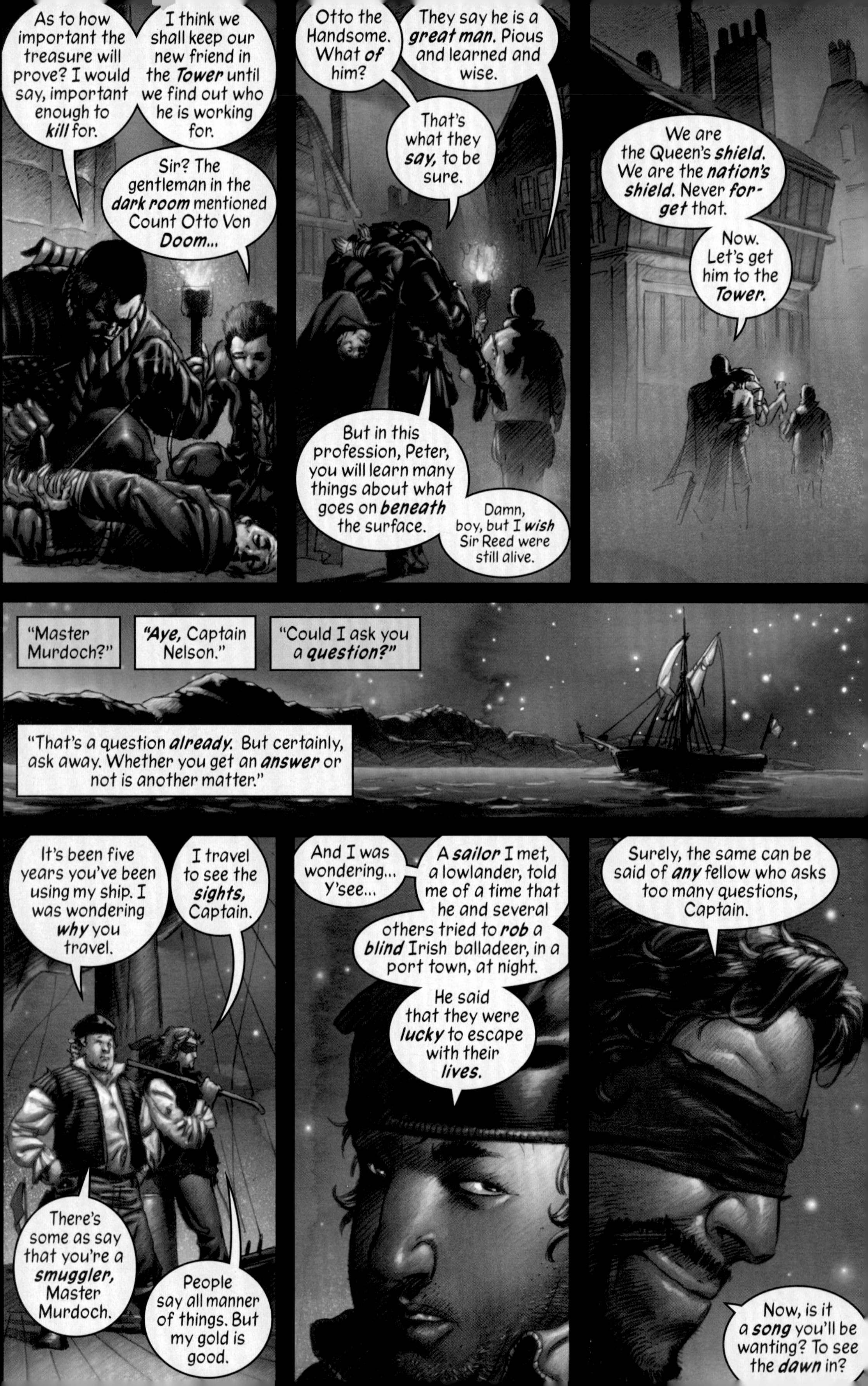
As to how important the treasure will prove? I would say, important enough to *kill* for.
I think we shall keep our new friend in the *Tower* until we find out who he is working for.
Sir? The gentleman in the *dark room* mentioned Count Otto Von *Doom*...
Otto the Handsome. What *of* him?
They say he is a *great man.* Pious and learned and wise.
That's what they *say,* to be sure.
But in this profession, Peter, you will learn many things about what goes on *beneath* the surface.
Damn, boy, but I *wish* Sir Reed were still alive.
We are the Queen's *shield.* We are the *nation's shield.* Never *forget* that.
Now. Let's get him to the *Tower.*
"Master Murdoch?"
"Aye, Captain Nelson."
"Could I ask you a *question?"*
"That's a question *already.* But certainly, ask away. Whether you get an *answer* or not is another matter."
It's been five years you've been using my ship. I was wondering *why* you travel.
I travel to see the *sights,* Captain.
There's some as say that you're a *smuggler,* Master Murdoch.
People say all manner of things. But my gold is good.
And I was wondering... Y'see...
A *sailor* I met, a lowlander, told me of a time that he and several others tried to *rob* a *blind* Irish balladeer, in a port town, at night.
He said that they were *lucky* to escape with their *lives.*
Surely, the same can be said of *any* fellow who asks too many questions, Captain.
Now, is it a *song* you'll be wanting? To see the *dawn* in?

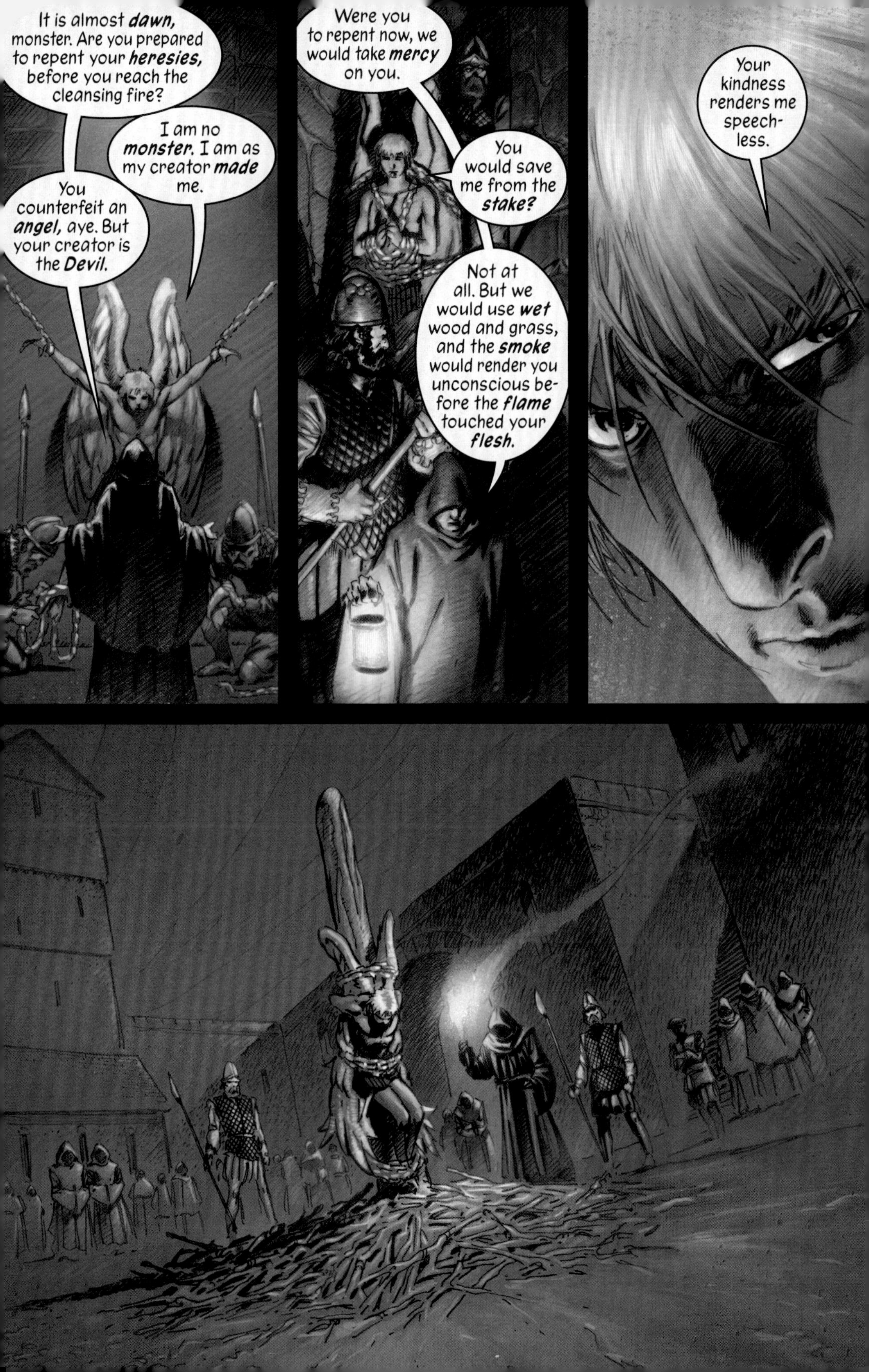
It is almost dawn, monster. Are you prepared to repent your heresies, before you reach the cleansing fire?
I am no monster. I am as my creator made me.
You counterfeit an angel, aye. But your creator is the Devil.
Were you to repent now, we would take mercy on you.
You would save me from the stake?
Not at all. But we would use wet wood and grass, and the smoke would render you unconscious before the flame touched your flesh.
Your kindness renders me speechless.

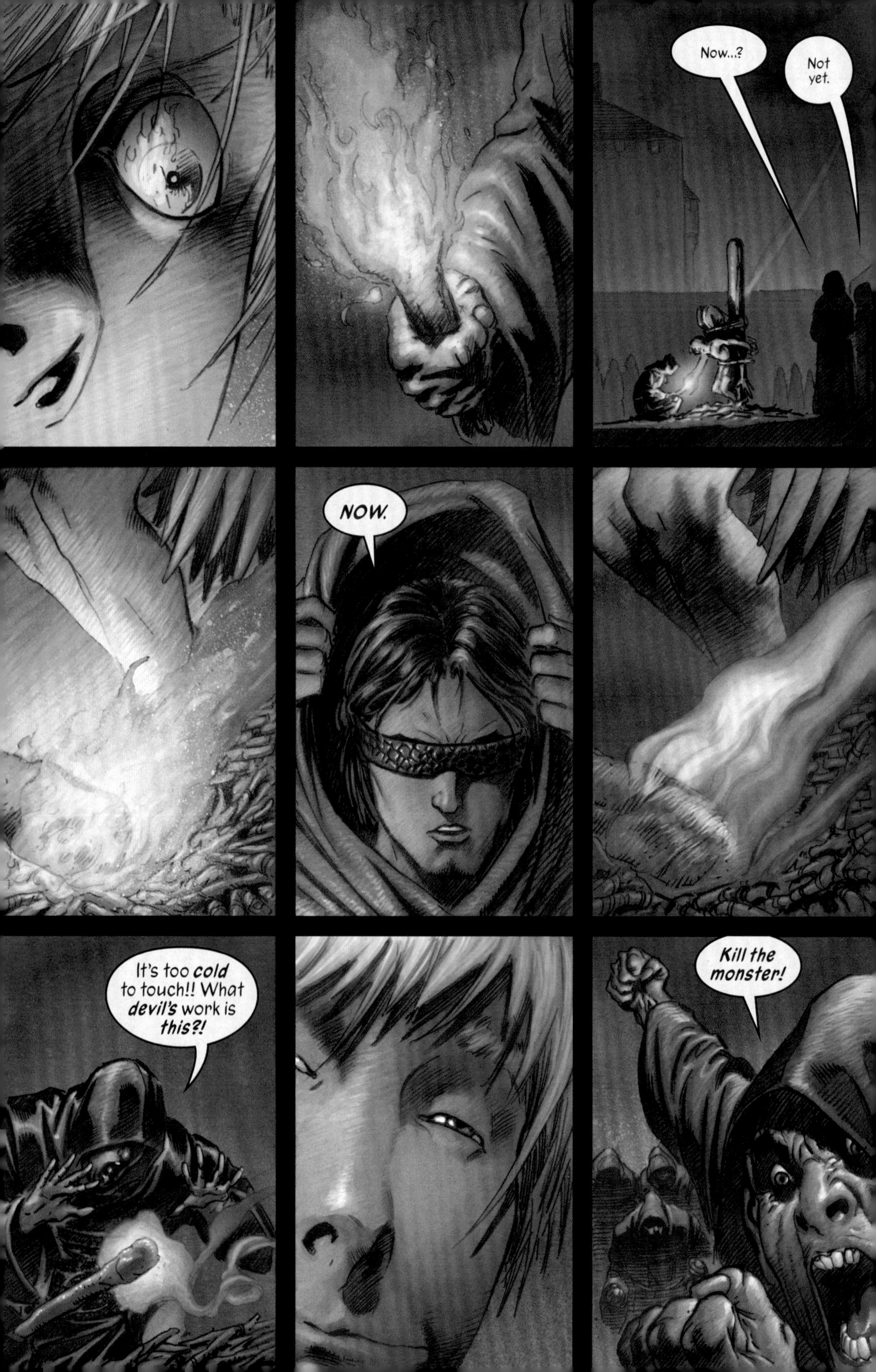
Now...?
Not yet.
NOW.
It's too *cold* to touch!! What *devil's* work is *this?!*
Kill the monster!

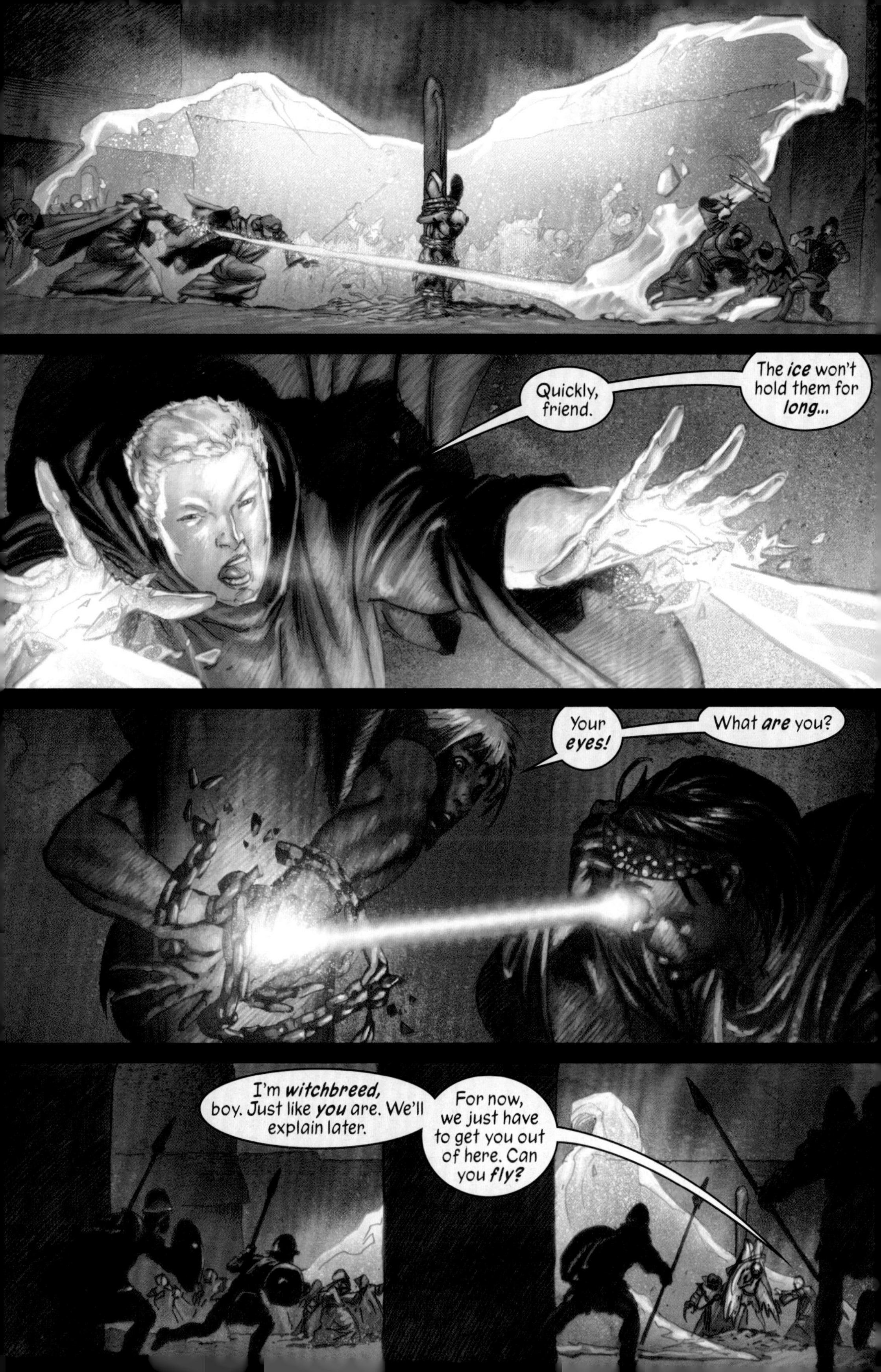
Quickly, friend.
The *ice* won't hold them for *long*...
Your *eyes!*
What *are* you?
I'm *witchbreed,* boy. Just like *you* are. We'll explain later.
For now, we just have to get you out of here. Can you *fly?*

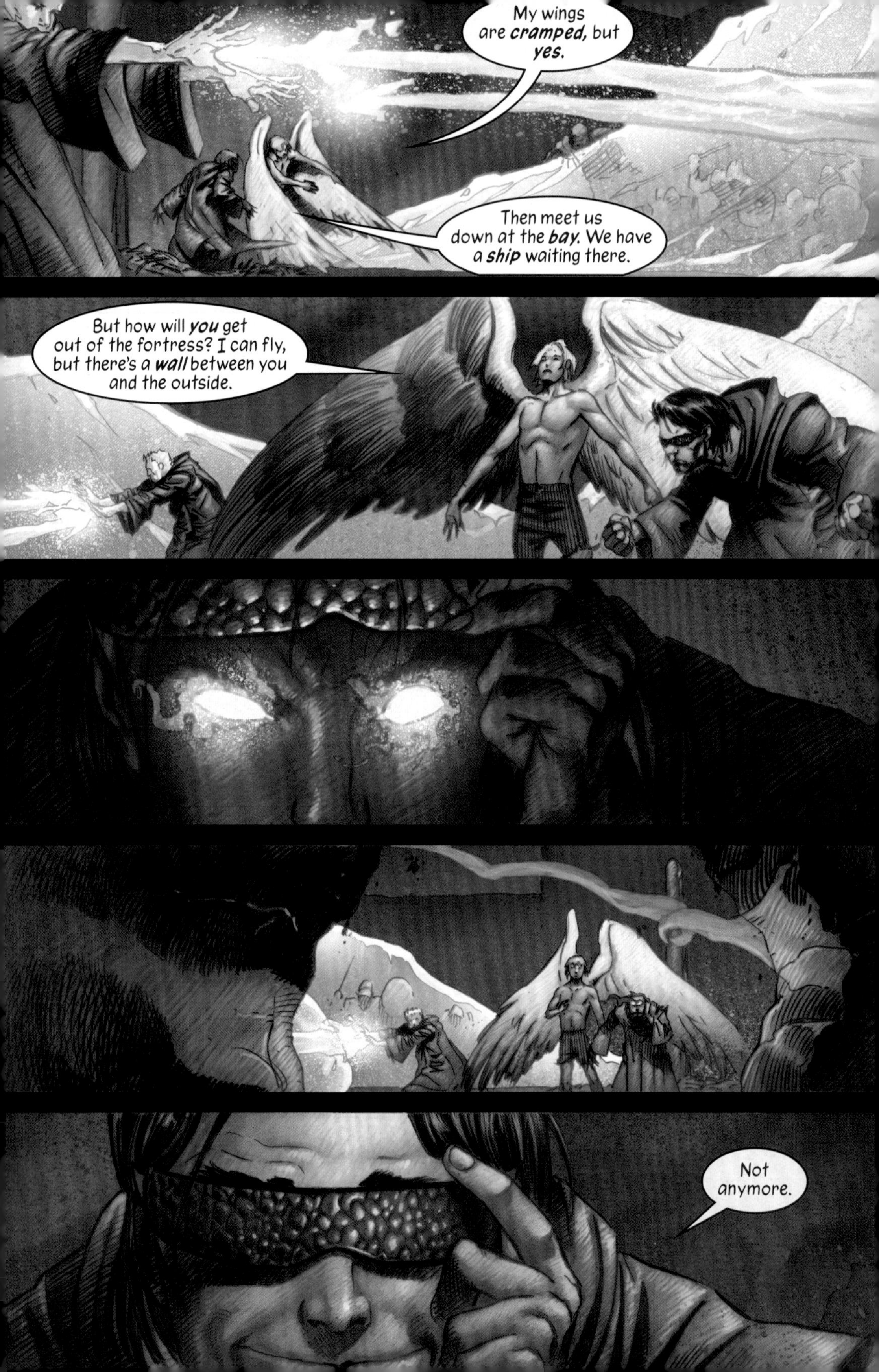
My wings are cramped, but yes.
Then meet us down at the bay. We have a ship waiting there.
But how will you get out of the fortress? I can fly, but there's a wall between you and the outside.
Not anymore.

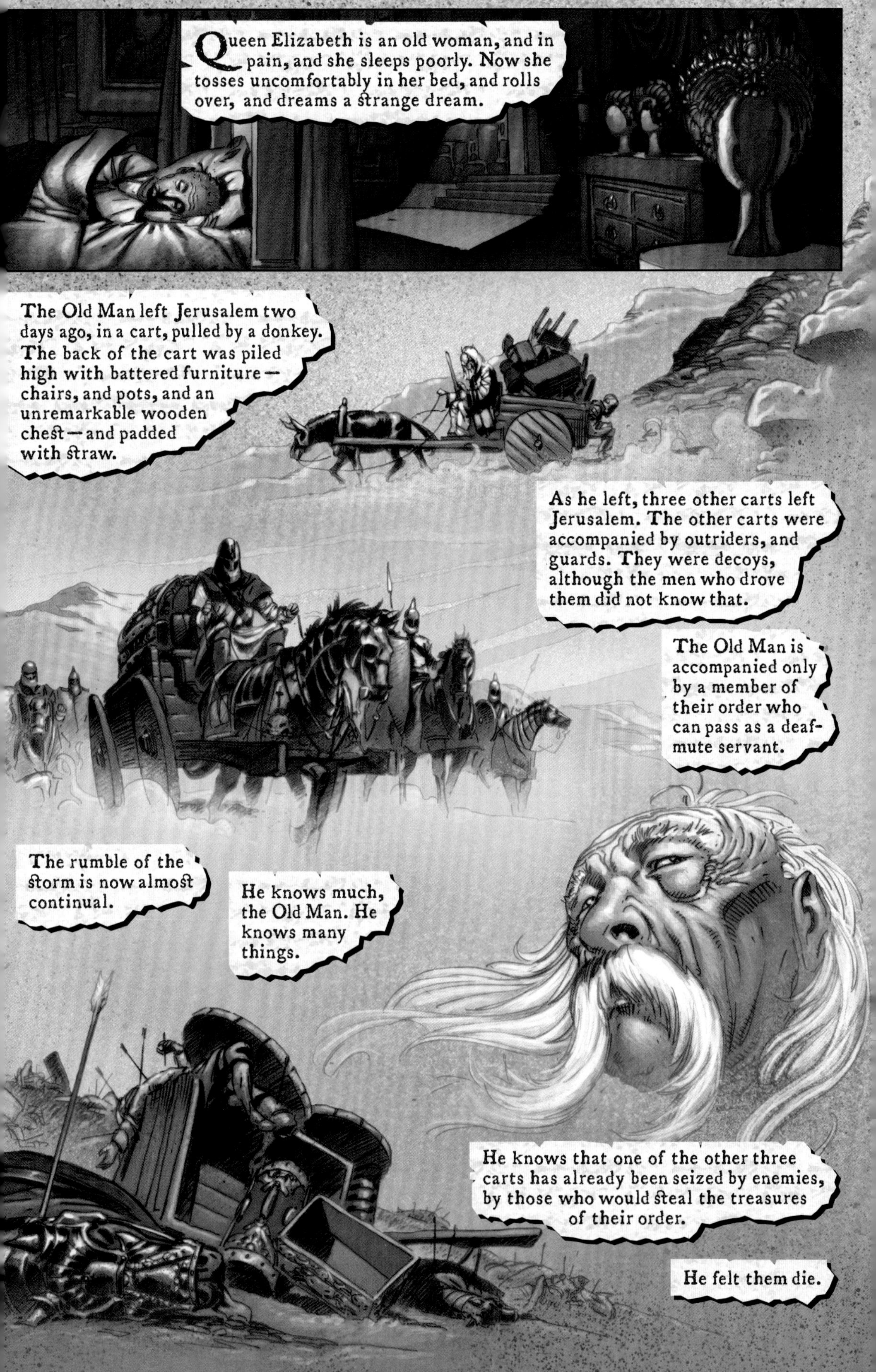
Queen Elizabeth is an old woman, and in pain, and she sleeps poorly. Now she tosses uncomfortably in her bed, and rolls over, and dreams a strange dream.
The Old Man left Jerusalem two days ago, in a cart, pulled by a donkey. The back of the cart was piled high with battered furniture — chairs, and pots, and an unremarkable wooden chest — and padded with straw.
As he left, three other carts left Jerusalem. The other carts were accompanied by outriders, and guards. They were decoys, although the men who drove them did not know that.
The Old Man is accompanied only by a member of their order who can pass as a deaf-mute servant.
The rumble of the storm is now almost continual.
He knows much, the Old Man. He knows many things.
He knows that one of the other three carts has already been seized by enemies, by those who would steal the treasures of their order.
He felt them die.

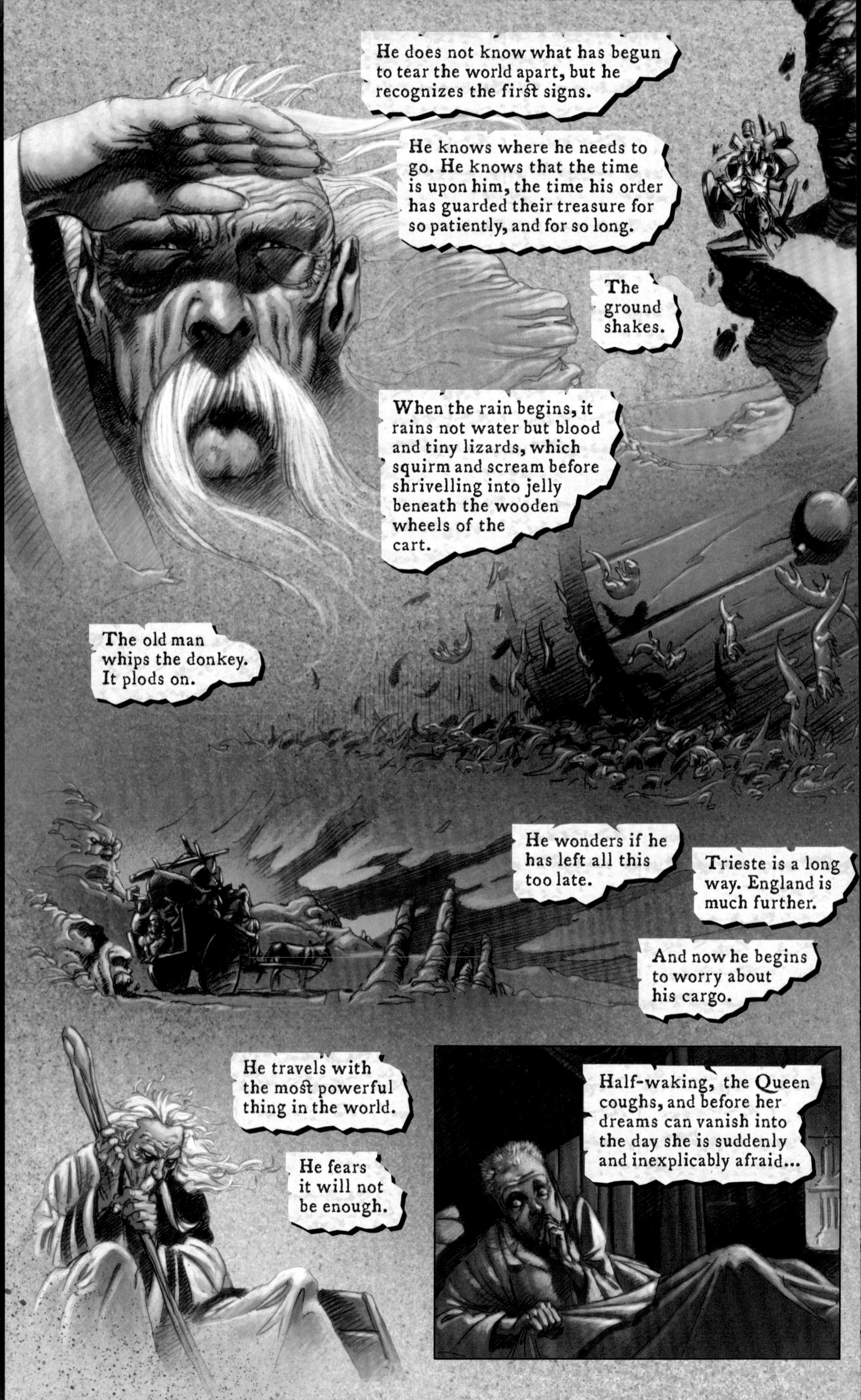
He does not know what has begun to tear the world apart, but he recognizes the first signs.
He knows where he needs to go. He knows that the time is upon him, the time his order has guarded their treasure for so patiently, and for so long.
The ground shakes.
When the rain begins, it rains not water but blood and tiny lizards, which squirm and scream before shrivelling into jelly beneath the wooden wheels of the cart.
The old man whips the donkey. It plods on.
He wonders if he has left all this too late.
Trieste is a long way. England is much further.
And now he begins to worry about his cargo.
He travels with the most powerful thing in the world.
He fears it will not be enough.
Half-waking, the Queen coughs, and before her dreams can vanish into the day she is suddenly and inexplicably afraid...

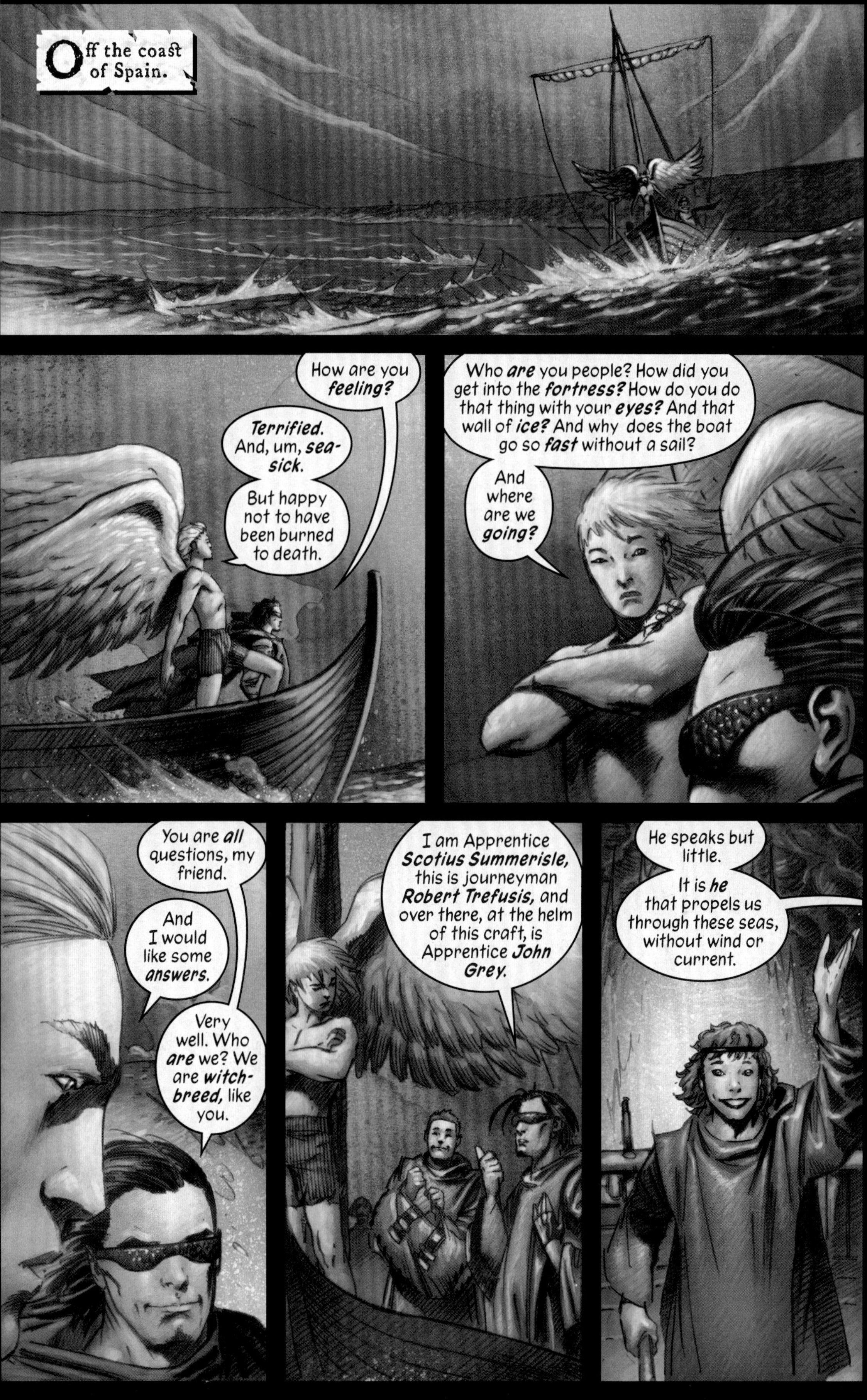

Off the coast of Spain.
How are you feeling?
Terrified. And, um, sea-sick.
But happy not to have been burned to death.
Who are you people? How did you get into the fortress? How do you do that thing with your eyes? And that wall of ice? And why does the boat go so fast without a sail?
And where are we going?
You are all questions, my friend.
And I would like some answers.
Very well. Who are we? We are witch-breed, like you.
I am Apprentice Scotius Summerisle, this is journeyman Robert Trefusis, and over there, at the helm of this craft, is Apprentice John Grey.
He speaks but little.
It is he that propels us through these seas, without wind or current.

We are almost in English waters. It is time to remove our robes. Monks are not welcome in England. *Fishermen*, on the other hand, will attract no attention.

Your *chest...?*

They *brand* monsters, where I come from, before they *drown* them.

Can you hide your *wings?*

I can *fold* them, to hide beneath my garb. And my mother made me clothes with room for them--she sewed them so cunningly that no man could tell.

They *killed* her, you know, when they *caught* me.

They said, *come back*, or *we kill her*, so I came back. But they killed her anyway.

I'm sorry.

We have garb for you, and cords to bind your wings.

Our master thinks of everything. We shall dock by noon, and a horse-cart will be waiting to take us the rest of the way.

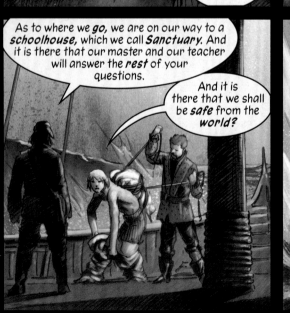

As to where we *go*, we are on our way to a *schoolhouse*, which we call *Sanctuary*. And it is there that our master and our teacher will answer the *rest* of your questions.

And it is there that we shall be *safe* from the *world?*

Aye. *Perhaps.*

For a *little* while.

To be Continued...

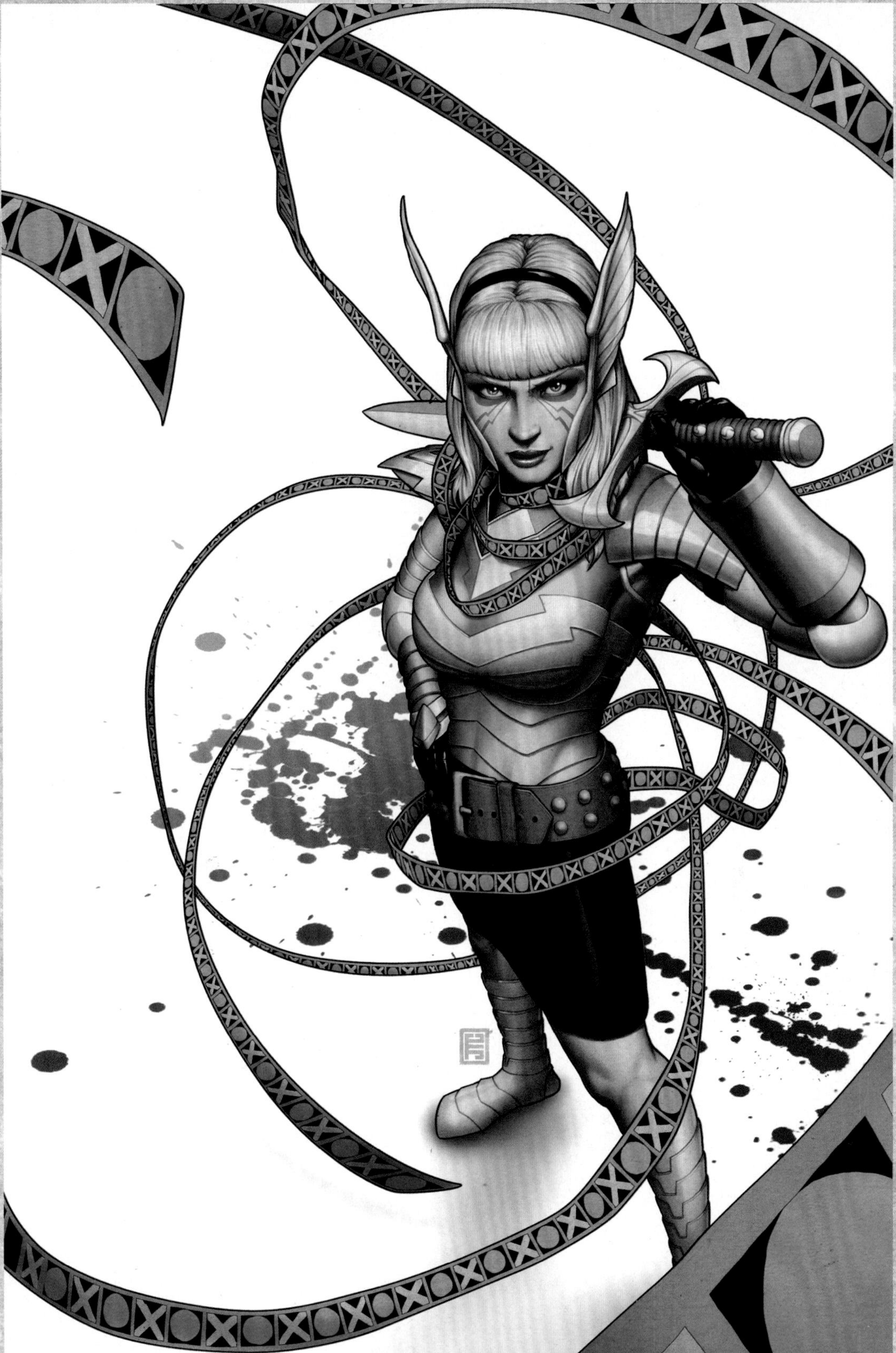

#1 Gwengela variant cover by John Tyler Christopher

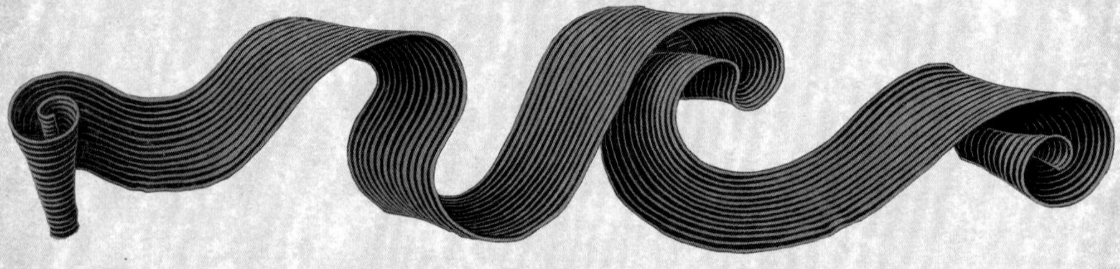